PRAISE FOR JEN LANCASTER

"If laughter is a great tonic for the spirit, then Jen Lancaster . . . is a double dose."

—USA Today

"Falling somewhere between David Sedaris and Laurie Notaro, Lancaster's goofy charm will no doubt continue to win fans, as well as influence the next generation of sardonic, winning, self-effacing memoirists."

—Publishers Weekly

"[Jen Lancaster is] like that friend who always says what you're thinking—just 1,000 times funnier."

—People

"[With] a wicked sense of humor, [Lancaster] adds just the right amount of sweetness to counteract the bitter."

—New York Post

"You'll revel in the lessons she gleans from her travails."

—Redbook

"Scathingly witty."

—Boston Herald

Welcome to
THE UNITED
STATES *of*
ANXIETY

OTHER TITLES BY JEN LANCASTER

NONFICTION

FICTION

Welcome to
THE UNITED
STATES *of*
ANXIETY

OBSERVATIONS
FROM A REFORMING NEUROTIC

JEN LANCASTER

Little
a

Published by Little A, New York

www.apub.com

Amazon, the Amazon logo, and Little A are trademarks of Amazon.com, Inc., or its
affiliates.

ISBN-13: 9781542007948 (hardcover)
ISBN-10: 1542007941 (hardcover)

ISBN-13: 9781542007924 (paperback)
ISBN-10: 1542007925 (paperback)

Cover design and interior illustrations by Philip Pascuzzo

Printed in the United States of America

First edition

For Paige McDaniel, Joanna Clarke, and Community Partners of Dallas, for your tireless work . . . and the greatest day of my life!

The short-term, dopamine-driven feedback loops
that we have created are destroying how society
works—no civil discourse, no cooperation,
misinformation, mistruth.

—Chamath Palihapitiya,
former Facebook VP of user growth

Don't worry, be happy.

—Bobby McFerrin

CONTENTS

LETTER FROM THE AUTHOR

March 21, 2020

As I was finishing the final edits on this book, everything in our country changed.

I'm polishing this work under a statewide lockdown because of COVID-19. I haven't left my home in more than a week, and the only person I've seen is my husband—unless you count the handful of delivery drivers I've spied from the window as they drop off our orders and scatter. During this crisis, I've discovered that I would thrive under house arrest. So there's that.

My hope is that when this book comes out in October, we're a nation of healthy and happy hand-washers. In a perfect future world, we'll have become rule-followers, blessed with limitless compassion and serious immunity. This best-case scenario in my mind allows us to gain appreciation for what we briefly lost during this uncertain time— and mourn the people who have passed. I imagine a highlight reel of Americans coming together and helping our communities; I envision us with full employment and a whole new batch of Bravo Housewives. I prefer to not envision the worst-case scenario.

Outside of staying inside, washing my hands, and waving heartfelt thanks to the delivery people and postal workers who are keeping us fed, sane, and functioning, I can't assist much with the pandemic panic this country is feeling. It's so early on in this moment, and the advice is evolving every day. However, I can invite you to join me as I uncover all that we don't need to fret about . . . from a socially appropriate distance, of course.

PART I

ONE NATION, UNDER STRESS

Maslow's Hierarchy:
psychology's gold standard of categorizing and ranking our
human needs.

ANXIETIES UNBOUND

My greatest takeaway from my college years on the ivy-covered grounds of Purdue University, the divine truth that revealed itself as I pored over volumes written by the world's most profound minds, was that I hated waitressing.

The portmanteau "hangry" didn't randomly become part of our lexicon; it speaks to our most primal, basic urge. Peckish diners' lizard brains perceived the feckless waitress as standing between themselves and imminent starvation/death, so it often got ugly when I forgot the extra salad dressing.

My burning desire to exit apron-based employment propelled me to get my shit together and graduate after eleven years of study. I ended up with a bachelor's degree in political science, but that's beside the point. *Any* degree was a ticket out of the service economy back in the 1990s. That ticket's not exactly still valid; it's not lost on me that every barista at my local coffee shop has a master's degree in classics and, unlike me, knows the difference between "further" and "farther." But back in the '90s, the assurance of that piece of paper was solid.

Though I've not taken anyone's drink order in a quarter of a century, in my stress dreams I'm always sweating through my oxford shirt and poorly tied tie, deep in the weeds, having been triple seated with eight tops, thanks to a clueless seventeen-year-old hostess. The bartender's taking forever to mix a single Rusty Nail because Sergey Brin hasn't yet invented Google. Empty plates are stacked tall as skyscrapers on the tables, which is confusing. Why would a party of four dirty up twenty-three plates apiece, even if I were serving tapas? There's no busboy in sight.

When I finally wake myself up, my heart's pounding and my stomach's knotted. I have so much adrenaline coursing through my system that ~~further farther~~ further sleep is impossible.

I've experienced much higher stakes in the past few decades, but none have felt as anxiety provoking as waiting tables.

I came to understand that I couldn't hold a job catering to people's most basic needs; the stress of it would eventually destroy me.

So it behooved me to understand the landscape of human needs, if only to avoid the terrifying responsibility. The "basic needs" concept comes from psychologist Abraham Maslow. In 1943, Maslow theorized that people are motivated by an escalating series of needs. In 1954, he organized those needs into categories and called the whole shebang Maslow's Hierarchy, leading me to believe that one of *Maslow's* needs was to slap his name on things. Admittedly, I can't find a source that says he intentionally named it after himself, but who could blame him if he did? He created a clear picture of what drives the human race, and presented it in a clever format that would go on to look terrific on generations of slide decks, so he deserves the credit.

I can't state this clearly enough: basic needs are a bitch and a huge anxiety trigger. In my adult professional life, I've done everything from negotiating multimillion-dollar contracts with humorless hospital administrators to being interviewed by Charlie Rose on national television, yet what still wakes me up in a panic is that damn forgotten side of ranch dressing.

Over the past few years, my anxiety levels have skyrocketed. My waitressing dreams have become so frequent that my concealer can barely keep up, and I'm already using the industrial stuff that can cover tattoos. This is it; I've reached the end of cosmeceutical science.

Here's the thing—I'm not alone when it comes to stress. So many of us feel like we're living in trying times. I'd give anything to go back to the innocence and ease of my 1970s childhood, despite growing up in the golden age of serial killers. With Gacy, Bundy, and Dahmer out there, none of us were safe, yet no one seemed bothered. I lived in New Jersey, just over the bridge, during the Summer of Sam, and my family's chief takeaway was that Berkowitz couldn't have been so bad if he liked dogs.

I'm desperate for that less panicked approach, for an uninterrupted night of sleep, to uncover the root of my growing anxiety.

How did I get from there to here? Something has changed in terms of my relationship to my basic human needs, and if I can pinpoint some of those changes, I hope that I can start to relax, to disengage. So I'll work my way up the hierarchy. I'll look at each brick in Maslow's pyramid and examine it in the light of our anxiety-riddled world. How else can I find self-actualization, especially if I'm too preoccupied by spackling the trenches under my eyes?

If Maslow and his pyramid could help me figure my way out of an eleven-year tenure at Purdue and into my adult life, I'd wager he's skilled enough to be my guide to work through it again at the crossroads of middle age.

THE STATE OF OUR STRESSED-OUT UNION

The plane was going down.

My father was midflight on his way home from Atlanta when the 747 hit a pocket of turbulence so severe that the plane shuddered and plunged. The abrupt altitude change caused luggage to burst violently from the overhead compartments. The beverage cart rocketed down the aisle, spewing cans of Canada Dry Ginger Ale and tiny bottles of Dewar's, before it slammed into the cockpit door. The cabin depressurized and passengers scrambled to secure their oxygen masks as the emergency Klaxon reverberated through the cabin.

Then, an engine failed.

It was a total nightmare scenario.

The pilots struggled to right the aircraft, to win a losing battle against gravity as the ground loomed ever closer. I imagine the passengers around my dad panicking and praying, their lives flashing before their eyes. Mothers clinging to their children. Strangers grasping hands. Religion suddenly rediscovered.

Faced with his own mortality, my father focused on what was most important to him—finishing the sports page. He figured if he was about to die, he'd better read faster. The tragedy of departing this mortal coil before checking box scores was more than he could bear.

Fortunately, the pilots prevailed and brought the plane down safely. My father disembarked on unweakened knees. He whistled on his way to the baggage claim to retrieve his vinyl Samsonite suitcase, packed with his favorite goldenrod-colored short-sleeved oxfords and tasteful plaid polyester ties. Then, he located his Ford Maverick in the airport parking garage, plugged in an eight-track of Scott Joplin, and drove home rocking out to ragtime.

My father was entirely unaffected by the events as they unfolded. He'd forgotten about the whole thing by the time he reached our home on South Prospect Avenue. The incident was barely a blip on his radar.

I didn't even know about his near-death experience, as he didn't find it germane to mention it, until decades later. How is that possible? A child vomited on my last flight, and I gave my forty-two thousand Twitter followers a real-time update. And boosted that to another twenty-six thousand on Instagram.

My dad's clinical detachment is a marvel. He kept his shit together on that faltering jet without distress, without trepidation, without the benefit of a vest-clad emotional support duck. He didn't spend my childhood dragging himself—or the family—down the what-if rabbit hole, obsessively imagining what *could have* happened.

We had my mother for that.

Perhaps you wonder, Did I inherit my father's ability to manage stress with grace, with panache, with nerves of steel? Did he pass down his preternatural calm, his dispassionate and unflinching disposition, along with his flat feet?

Spoiler alert? I am actively afraid of bread.

Carbs aren't the only thing that frightens me, not by a long shot. I *live* in the emotional rabbit hole. Lately, I fret about every damn thing, from the effects of fluoride in tap water to my Uber driver possibly down-rating me for being a chatty drunk. I'm a bundle of nerves, swaddled in a blanket of panic.

Anxiety is my constant partner, right there by my side like a bad college roommate, second-guessing my choices, disrupting my concentration, and causing low-level chaos on the reg. Sometimes my GAD (generalized anxiety disorder) manifests as a gradually tightening band of tension around my chest. Occasionally, it takes the form of an ice pick stabbing a sharp pain into my frontal lobe. Fun stuff.

When I'm able to slough it off, when it's not causing physical symptoms or putting me on edge, my anxiety still pops up out of nowhere to spoil nice moments. I fear good things happening because I believe something bad is sure to follow. Yin and yang, as comedy can't exist without tragedy. In my universe, pleasure and pain are opposite sides of the pendulum.

Frankly, I'm sick of it. Jane, get me off this crazy thing!

I've kept my rampant GAD on the down low; it's contrary to my nature to air my internal angst. Honestly, I'd rather livestream my mammogram than show vulnerability outside my immediate circle. I suspect this tendency is typical of my Generation X compatriots. We came up in an era that embraced privacy, that discouraged us from sharing our problems. I learned to stuff my fears deep down until they form a little ball, keeping the feelings buried under liberal handfuls of cheese and glasses of moderately priced Chardonnay.

For me, it's a strategy that works remarkably well . . . until the pressure builds up too much and I blow, losing my shit in front of a random stranger in the produce aisle, yelling, "Actually, yes. I *am* the grape police!" (In case you're reading this, hungry shopper, my apologies.)

What's sad is that I represent the majority of Americans; I'm not alone. So many of us suffer from anxiety. The cheap seats are packed with good people who've grown accustomed to denying that we're quaking with fear inside, racked with worry. Many of us compensate by raging on the outside.

When I was growing up, my family slept with our windows open. If we bothered to lock the front door, our spare key was ingeniously

11

placed right under the flower pot on our porch. Our house was robbed back in 1984, and the thieves didn't even need to unearth the spare key; the back door was already unlocked. Yet we were shocked when it happened.

A stranger prowled our house at will, a clear violation, but neither of my parents were too shaken up, largely because they considered insurance payouts akin to winning the lottery. I wasn't privy to the claim, but I suspect we lost a lot of Picassos and Fabergé eggs that day, and not just an ancient, broken Rolex and a carbon-flecked diamond ring.

Years later, my family started speculating that my high school boyfriend, who hadn't been in school that day, was involved. We didn't have proof, but there was the small clue that he'd been sentenced to prison for armed robbery shortly after we'd broken up.

The point is, our behavior didn't change. The key remained under the flower pot. We continued to ignore the lock on our back door. We weren't cautious, because we weren't afraid of anything, unlike now when I'm afraid of freaking everything.

The worst part is that *the world is safer than it's ever been*. Humanity's on an upswing, from long-term trends in health care to access to food. We've made tremendous strides in increasing literacy and vaccination rates. Child mortality? Incidences have plummeted.[1]

Global poverty is half what it was twenty years ago. Violent crimes have abated dramatically in the US, declining from 1993's high of 79.8 victims per thousand people to our current level of 23.2.[2] Per the *American Journal of Epidemiology*, DUIs are down, likely thanks to chatty drunks opting for rideshare services.[3]

Bottom line? The data supports that *these* are the best of times.

So . . . why the hell does it feel like the end of days?

Why does it seem like it's about to rain locusts? Why am I cuffing my pants for the coming rivers of blood? What happened to make us masses suddenly so afraid of everything? How did the USA become shorthand for the United States of Anxiety?

Despite all indicators pointing people toward happiness and contentment, so many of us are paralyzed by angst and weighted down with unnamed dread, largely because we've been conditioned to believe that danger lurks around every corner.

Since my blissful childhood, when my fear was encased in a calcified shell and nestled somewhere next to my pancreas, one of the biggest cultural shifts has been around mass communication. Thanks to technology, we're connecting quicker and cheaper than ever before.

Decades ago, my dad strictly forbade our family to make out-of-town calls before ten o'clock at night, when long distance hit the off-peak rates, and even then, only if one of us were bleeding or ablaze. Communication was a luxury. As my mother's whole family and social circle lived outside Jersey, this led to some epic arguments.

My father did not see the return on investment of twenty-five cents a minute for my mother to diss whichever sibling was on the outs. He may have had a point, considering an hour-long prime-time call ran fifteen dollars in 1970s money.[4] In today's dollars, that's equivalent to the cost of a new Tesla.

Conversations were so pricey that he resorted to unscrewing the phone's handset and hiding the receiver portion from my mother until nightfall. This continued through my young-adult life. If I wanted to contact college friends during summer vacation, I could either fork over most of my part-time sub-shop job's salary, or mail them a letter.

Today, unlimited thoughts are disseminated in a nanosecond at a fraction of the price. A handwritten letter is a treat for me now—quaint!—and you couldn't pay me to pick up your phone call. God help you if you leave a voice mail.

In theory, this easy and convenient communication should make people happier, more at ease. Our ability to live the old AT&T slogan of reaching out and touching someone is now practically unlimited. We're not faced with the choice between connection or groceries. We don't have to make collect calls with fake names to let our loved ones know we got home safely. Yet we've seen a 64 percent increase in antidepressant usage from 1999 to 2014.[5]

Something's changed. Bigly.

Gallup News just released their 2018 survey on the state of our anxious union. The data shows that not only do the majority of Americans report experiencing stress daily, but we are more likely to be stressed out than the residents of almost every other country in the world![6]

USA! USA! USA!

Oh. Wait. This is one of the competitions we *don't* want to win.

Gallup found that the collective American stress level trends 20 percent higher than most other countries. (Note: while the survey differentiates between stress, worry, and anger, I do not.)

According to the Gallup poll, as a nation, Americans feel like we're under more duress than the nation of Venezuela, where the lights are out, the inflation rate is 10 million percent, civil war's about to erupt, and citizens are eating cats and dogs to survive.[7]

I wonder if the Venezuelans are all, "Tell us again about how the cinematography is too dark on *Game of Thrones*, Susan."

The Gallup article goes on to explain, "The disconnect between a strong economy and Americans' increasing negative emotions illustrates how GDP and other hard economic data only tell part of [our mental health] story. In fact, the levels of negative emotions in the past several years are even higher than during the U.S. recession years. Given the ties that researchers are starting to find between negative [e]ffects like these and physical health and longevity, leaders need the whole story."

In other words, if it's not the economy, stupid, *why* are we so stressed and worried and angry?

Of all my own fears—and, oh, there are plenty—social media tops the list. *Admitting* that it is my chief worry causes me more distress, knowing people in other nations face daily threats to their safety and well-being. I'm terrified that one offhand joke, one out-of-context remark, will set into motion a public shaming, because I see it happen every day.

One of my friends is a professional comedian. A few years back, she tweeted something controversial that I thought was hysterical, knowing her and understanding the context. The rest of the country? Far less amused. She had the means to pay publicists and crisis managers to salvage her reputation, but it took a solid month, an apology tour that kicked off on the Howard Stern show, and a check with a lot of zeros on it. Most of us don't have that option.

What's so scary is that mob rule has displaced due process. The faceless masses are America's new arbiters of justice. I'm so fearful of the court of public opinion that I've stopped saying anything of value online, stopped unpacking what's important in my life, stopped trying to forge any kind of understanding over social media. I mostly post shots of my pets and complain about the weather. It's edgy stuff.

I read through my feed, taken in by others who are so angry, so frustrated at the state of things. Each tweet or Facebook post they author amounts to an enraged missive, the sheer number of which diminishes their impact. Shout long enough in capital letters and, eventually, people start to tune you out.

WE NEED TO CHANGE COURSE because cat memes and caps lock won't fix what's broken. And we are a broken nation; the data confirms it. For those who aren't unconscionably anxious, I guarantee their lives are impacted by a loved one who is. But I refuse to accept that we're beyond repair. Despite our problems, in the past fifty years, America has produced Google, MRIs, the Hubble Space telescope, and Lady Gaga.

We're on a winning streak!

The Gallup poll that gives so much backbone to my theory suggests that our leaders should consider the causes of the negative emotions that are flooding this country, in order to stem the flow of anxiety.

Pfft, good luck with that.

Taking a look at the last decades, it stands to reason that feeding our fears has made us easier to lead, saddling us with only black and white choices on issues nuanced by fifty shades of gray. Divide the people and conquer. Calming down the masses may not be on any leader's agenda, in any party.

I suspect no one is coming to save us; we can only save ourselves.

So I want to lend a hand in the good fight. I want to do the work, help those of us equally gripped by apprehension and trepidation by figuring out *why* we're so damned nervous and what we can do to finally chill the hell out.

Much as I'd like to blame my childhood for, you know, *everything*, I can't pin my skyrocketing stress level on my parents. They'd send me off on my bike without shin guards or a helmet in sight. They ~~forced~~ encouraged me to be free range, with their edict, "Don't you dare step inside this house until dinner." It's sad that kids today lack the privilege of being raised without the mantle of anxiety, of eating nut butter with abandon. Few pleasures compare to the way I once felt, finding Skippy and Marshmallow Fluff sandwiched between rare slices of Wonder Bread in my Super Friends lunch box.

Crusts removed, of course; I wasn't a monster.

So I want to identify the barriers that keep us living at the outer limits of fear and anxiety instead of reveling in those simple pleasures, celebrating all the wondrous things that make us diverse and unique. There is common ground between old and young, rich and poor, and black and white (privilege), I'm sure of it. I want to help shine a light on it. Or at least find a way for us all to get through Thanksgiving dinner without wanting to kick Uncle David in the junk.

Wouldn't that be nice?

Looking back on my dad's experience on the plane, I try to imagine how that same moment would look if it had occurred thirty years later. If he'd had the ability to share the event online back then, say, Facebook

Lived the thing, I bet he'd have viewed it quite differently in retrospect. What if he'd posted to Twitter in real time? Would the deluge of sympathetic responses have colored his memory? Would he have had his own hashtag? Would #LandSafeBigDaddy have trended? Would online venting have created a lifelong trauma?

But social media didn't exist for him. And even if it had, he probably wouldn't have touched it. My father always gave zero efs about anyone's opinion, an attitude that was made evident by his sartorial choices, favoring colors most often found in the condiment aisle, so I couldn't see him wanting to "share." He came from an era when martinis at lunch weren't an HR violation, they were just Tuesday. He resisted change and fads. Until the day he retired in the late '90s, he had Barbara, his secretary, print out his emails and leave them on his desk.

When I say "Barbara," I'm referring to a handful of Barbaras who performed tasks for him from the mid-1960s until retirement. Ever pragmatic, he only hired women named Barbara. He had no interest in learning a lot of new names. It's possible they weren't all actually named Barbara, but that's how we knew them and that's the name they answered to. My father refused to hire young, good-looking women; he believed they caused a distraction in the office. Also, their manicures slowed their words per minute. He must have figured that anyone named Barbara was born middle aged, so he gravitated toward them.

Assuming that my change-resistant, practical father could have avoided the siren song of social media, let's instead explore the whole "business travel" concept, as it existed in the mid-1970s. For that fateful trip, my dad would have had Barbara work out all the details with a travel agent. Between Barbara and the agent, they'd figure out the luxury hotels, rental cars, and best flights, charging it all to his corporate American Express card.

While Barbara greased the skids, my dad would enjoy unlimited corporate long distance as he chatted with his buddies in other offices who were headed to the same place. They'd debate about which four-star steak house they'd visit for supper and what professional ballgame they might attend.

My dad represented the management of a Fortune 500 logistics company, and he squared off against the head of the teamsters in all-day contract negotiations on his business trips. No one could begrudge him some after-hours fun and games. Still, business trips back then were pretty much grown-up spring breaks.

Once the logistics were set, Barbara would see to the dinner reservations and major-league sporting event tickets. Expense accounts weren't monitored—a phenomenon I credit with our thrice-weekly habit of going out to dinner over my entire childhood.

Barbara would then type up all the details on her IBM Selectric at the speed of light with her unadorned nails and tuck the travel documents into the proper pocket of his briefcase so he'd have them handy.

Packing for travel was a breeze for my dad. Barbara made sure his dry cleaning was managed. He also kept a second toiletry bag stocked with duplicates of every necessity, loaded and always ready, a trick I adopted years later to ease the stress of multi-city book tours.

On the day of departure, he'd drive himself to the airport. Our New Jersey home was approximately twenty miles from Newark, so he'd leave forty minutes before his flight departed, thirty if he didn't need to buy a newspaper. At the airport, he'd enter the terminal and walk directly to his gate after but a five-second delay at the brand-new metal detector. Handsy TSA agents would not exist for years.

Business travel was both elegant and expensive, especially in the '60s, long before the days of routine overbooking. The planes were beautifully appointed with wide aisles and huge restrooms. Air travel was a luxury for well-behaved men and women (but mostly men, specifically the white ones).

In those days, no one brought their own pillows from home, jamming up all the overhead compartment space with them. (Quick aside:

Why? Why do people do this? Please stop. Do you want bedbugs? Because this is how you get bedbugs.)

No one placed their bare, filthy feet on the bulkhead wall, either. No one completed the poor-behavior trifecta of carrying on an entire tray of sticky barbecue ribs, orally molesting them the entire flight from Memphis to Denver, and then tucking the bare bones in the seat pocket in front of him, all while seated *right next to me.*

Instead, passengers kicked back in their enormous thrones, with a roomy thirty-four-inch seat pitch—massive compared to today's airlines, where seat pitch has shrunk an average of six inches and seats can be as narrow as sixteen inches.[8]

Passengers contentedly sipped free, unlimited cocktails while cotton-gloved stewardesses prepared meals and then served them on white tablecloths. Some planes even had lounges large enough for pianos.[9] For my dad, a trip to Atlanta meant two peaceful hours completely removed from terrestrial worries, where a fella could sit with his thoughts as he read *Sporting News* and smoked, flicking ashes into the little trays that were built into the armrests.

It's possible my dad didn't fear dying on that flight because he was already in heaven.

Perhaps when times are different, people are different.

Because I equally enjoy worrying about the past as well as the present, I grilled my dad about his experience on that plane once he finally mentioned it to me. How had he not imploded from the panic? Hell, I needed a Xanax by proxy.

My dad claimed that he didn't worry because he was armed with facts. First, and regardless of how dire the situation might have *felt* to those around him, he understood he was safer in the air than in the Maverick. While statistical anomalies can occur—hence flipping to the box scores in the unlikely event of imminent death—facts are overwhelmingly reliable.

Also, so many of the men of my dad's generation had served in World War II or Korea. He was confident the plane was under the control of former fighter pilots, men who'd *been in the shit*. While a blown engine wasn't ideal, those military vets had performed the same lifesaving maneuvers before, after losing whole propellers to enemy fire. At least with corporate travel, they weren't dodging bullets fired by dirty (insert archaic racial slur here).

As Dad's own wartime experience entailed defusing Korean land mines, it feels almost inevitable that he's at the far end of the bell curve regarding managing stress and anxiety. But everyone has a breaking point. My father cannot stand anything gross. Had a child vomited on that flight, he'd still be recounting his trauma forty years later.

My point is, my dad trusted empirical data instead of drawing his conclusions from the reactions of everyone around him. That's why he was an ocean of calm, an island of serenity, topped in sideburns and wrapped in a terrible sport coat the color of a grainy German mustard.

I'm not saying that he landed safely because he placed his faith in facts, but I'm not saying he didn't. I'm also not saying that many of those stray bottles of Dewar's didn't end up in his carry-on luggage. In retrospect, that's an incredibly specific detail to recall, and he's a pragmatic man. Once at an unmanned Residence Inn breakfast buffet, he cleaned out the Quaker Chewy Granola Bars bin so thoroughly that we were still working our way through the chocolate chip variety six months later.

So I want to follow my father's example, looking to the facts for comfort when facing the things that cause anxiety, worry, and anger.

The information will buoy us amid a sea of worries. It's impossible to stop the worry completely; we aren't sociopaths. Instead, with more information, I hope that we simply won't have to worry about *everything*.

In so doing, maybe we'll all yell a little less. Maybe we'll use less caps lock. Maybe we'll foster a little common understanding.

Or, we could just crack open some tiny bottles of scotch while we hug our knees and wait for impact.

Either way, we'll feel better.

PART II

PHYSIOLOGICAL NEEDS: FOOD, SLEEP, CLOTHING, SHELTER, AND WI-FI

Maslow determined that the lowest level of human need is physiological in nature, so I'll start with the basic needs. He defined those basics as food, sleep, clothing, shelter, and high internet bandwidth for optimal streaming capacity.

I might have added in that last part, but I'm not wrong.

You Are What You Eat?

Remember when Kim Kardashian was just some random dark-haired chick who organized Paris Hilton's closet?

Cute but shy, Kardashian chilled out in the background of Paris Hilton's orbit as she filmed *The Simple Life*, seemingly content to refold stacks upon stacks of low-rise jeans. Little did we know she was just biding her time. After she made that sex tape with Ray J, she and her momager hired a publicist to spin her newfound notoriety and got her a makeover, and boom! Kardashian became a household name.

Well, the exact same thing happened with avocados, minus the sex tape.

Avocados, once known as "alligator pears," are a delineator between past and present, a line in the sand between "olden days" and current times. When I was growing up, avocado was an appliance color, not a food. The only place I ever interacted with that weird green fruit (nope, not a vegetable) was in Mexican restaurants, where it was exclusively used as a garnish. Back then, avocados were precisely as desirable as the kale lining the salad bar at the Sizzler. Times, they have a-changed. Now, kale's a religion and the avocado is America's sweetheart.

Avocados began gaining popularity in the early 1980s, despite the dietary warnings that had just come out about fats. Nutritionists had determined that the distinction between "healthy fats" and "problematic fats" was far too sciencey for an intellectually lazy American consumer to grasp, so they decided to label every fat verboten.

As a bulwark against the bad-fat press, the California Avocado Commission hired actress Angie Dickinson to promote their product. In the TV spot, Dickinson, clad in a white bodysuit, spike heels, and tennis bracelet, lounges on the ground, spooning avocado straight from the rind. As the camera pans up her enviable physique, she purrs, "Would this body lie to you?"[10]

Eventually, with diligent marketing and a Super Bowl tie-in, avocados arrived in America like an Escalade full of Jenners at the Met Ball.

In the early days of the 1900s, grocers had deemed avocados an indulgence, a curiosity that was earmarked for epicureans and the rich. If you've priced them recently, you'll note this philosophy hasn't changed much. However, today, 47 percent of avocados in America are purchased by consumers who are eighteen to forty-four years old, primarily in two-person households. The other half of the buyers make a minimum of $70,000 per year.[11] In many people's estimation, avocados aren't a luxury so much as they are a necessity, because a) nom nom nom, and b) no one's getting Instagram-famous by posting pics of naked wheat bread.

Avocados trigger the most pervasive driver in our country and our greatest dread—the fear of missing out. Really, if you didn't photograph your avocado toast, did you even brunch at all?

FYI, no one feels FOMO over Froot Loops.

Full disclosure? I like avocado toast. I was introduced to avocado toast in London's SoHo Dean Street Townhouse, back in 2014. As that is one of the fanciest sentences I've ever uttered, I regularly work it into conversation. It's possible my constant bragging is what finally brought avocado toast across the pond.

You're welcome, America.

The beauty of "AT" (not a *thing* yet, but I'm trying to make it happen) is its calming emphasis on the topping rather than the panic-inducing bread. I add a poached egg and smoked salmon to mine, in an attempt to ingest the exact amount of protein that makes it possible, nay, *necessary*, to drink mimosas all afternoon.

The way AT blew up, I fully assumed that it was the only thing millennials ate, until I made a few millennial friends in a stand-up class at the Second City theater in Chicago. While they were each tremendous avocado fans, they explained that they can't possibly consume them for every meal, what with their desire to pay rent. Yet, inevitably, every one of their sets included an avocado toast reference.

Cultural. Freaking. Touchstone.

It was clear to me that these millennials were caught in a sort of trap—the need to broadcast familiarity, affinity, and intimate interaction with the little green orbs, but also the paradox of lacking the responsibility and wealth that avocados require for full societal immersion. It's like their Tamagotchis had been reincarnated into a soft-fleshed fruit.

I mostly consume avocado-based dishes when I'm dining out. I hate buying them at the market. Bringing an avocado into my house feels like holding a live grenade—too much anxiety over when it might detonate. Plus, the whole pit-to-flesh ratio is unnecessarily stressful. There's precious little more troubling than a fruit that's all hat and no cattle.

Once I forgot to make guacamole for a party I'd planned, and consequently found myself with twelve avocados, each achieving peak ripeness at the same time. For a two-day period, I turned into the Bubba Blue of avocados because I didn't want to waste the approximate cost of my college tuition, circa 1985.

You know who loves avocados?

Vegans.

In fact, no one loves avocados more than they do. I should have invited a whole pack of them over, but I'm not sure I would have been able to make it through the night with my sanity intact.

Truthfully, if you are what you eat, if you identify yourself by that which you consume, if you tell me you're a vegan before you mention your first name, we're gonna have a problem. By "problem," I mean, "I shall quietly roll my eyes at you inside my own head," as I am a GD adult who's too polite to hurt your feelings over that which has zero impact on my life.

Eat whatever you like, because it's none of my organic beeswax. Anything entering or exiting any orifice on your body is *your* choice. I don't get a say; I don't want a say. It's that simple. (Unless you've been elected to Congress, apparently.)

My stand-up instructor was newly vegan. But, honestly, she wasn't a miserable pain in the ass about it. During our breaks, she'd snack directly from a bag of raw spinach, hand-to-mouthing those leaves like they were Cool Ranch Doritos. She encouraged our class to open sets with whatever obvious facts existed, to eliminate the potential for distraction. Like, if you hobbled onstage in a cast, you'd acknowledge it with a joke immediately, just to get people to stop obsessing about it. Otherwise, the audience would become uncomfortable. She practiced what she preached. Well aware of how weird her grazing looked, she quickly called herself on it, and we simply accepted her behavior as the norm.

If only we could all be less smug about our self-imposed dietary restrictions. No one is handing out medals for refusing a Diet Coke. I suspect the recently restricted are often self-righteous because they're trying to convince themselves that things like brie are no longer delicious.

Good luck with that.

So if dietary choices are nobody's business, why are our individual diets such a source of collective interest and anxiety? Why does it feel like it's everyone's duty to determine whether the vegetarian at the table takes in enough protein? My friend Quinn has been a vegetarian since long before we met. Ergo, Quinn's been nourishing herself her whole adult life. Yet, I still must stop myself from pointing out the pastas and salads on the menu whenever we're out together.

She knows; she can read.

This free-floating food anxiety I've noticed may be partly due to our newfound indulgence of defining ourselves by what we eat. Per *Bon Appétit*, there's a trend toward values-based food purchasing. Sophie Egan explained, "We have always been concerned about how food affects our health, but today we want to know how it affects the health of the planet, plus the well-being of the people who grew, harvested, and prepared it."[12]

To me, the dotted line is "I buy with virtue; thus, I am virtuous."

Suddenly, we're all living that *Portlandia* skit, enquiring about the life of Colin the chicken.

You know who never even saw an avocado? My father's WASPy parents, Nanny and Gaga, who'd been raised entirely on British fare. I can't confidently say the same for my mother's parents, though. As Italian immigrants, Noni and Grampa's diet consisted of whatever washed up on the beach in Sicily. Later, once they'd settled in Boston, their culinary repertoire expanded to include the weeds they picked in the yard and the small animals they trapped in the attic. (I wish this were a joke.) Avocados might well have worked their way into Noni and Grampa's freegan diet. Environmental conditions were favorable in the volcanic soil around Mount Etna.

Please note, I'm still stewing about having the only Italian *nonna* on earth who cooked badly. Noni, who deceptively looked like the kind of woman you'd see depicted on a jar of Prego,[13] passed down her disdain for meal prep to my own mother. I've repressed most of my memories of meals at Noni's house, largely due to PTSD, but I do recall her "cookies," sugar omitted, baked to the consistency of masonry with blackened bottoms. Her Sunday gravy, studded with indeterminate bone shards, was best described as "pointy." I didn't know Italian cuisine could be palatable until I got a job at the Olive Garden; I didn't know it could be transcendent until my first trip to Rome.

My *good* grandparents, on the other hand, approached every dinner like a culinary masterpiece, each dish made from scratch, served at precisely five thirty. Nanny's sour cream chocolate cake caused me to believe in a higher power, such was its divine inspiration. I recall steaming platters of roast beef, fork tender, the ideal proportions of brown and pink. Her vegetables, never too soft or too al dente, were the stuff of legend. Served upon her delicate Noritake china, the brilliant green of the string beans and the traffic-cone orange of the carrots epitomized freshness. Plus, Nanny used a spice so exotic, so delicious, that even at five years old, I demanded to know its name.

Salt. It was called salt.

Food, for my family, was never a source of anxiety—even when my mother decided to cook. My father had grown up in an environment where there was a predictability to it, a strict adherence to a schedule. Breakfast, lunch, and dinner were served at the same times every day, and that approach was pretty much universal across the country; that was the norm. Meals were square, and snacking was still a figment of our Cheetos-dust-covered imaginations.

Choices were limited in his childhood. Cooking habits had been dictated by food rationing during World War II. Due to shortages, Americans were encouraged to become more self-reliant by planting victory gardens. They were allotted ration coupons for items that have become the foundation of our (okay, *my*) diet now—coffee, sugar, bacon, butter, tea, eggs, cereal, cheese, and processed/canned food. If a person ran out of coupons, too freaking bad. They went without, yet they didn't complain, because they felt they were purposefully sacrificing for the greater good, in solidarity with the boys overseas. So families had to carefully plan their repasts; they had little choice but to eat fresh and avoid waste.

The uniformity and practicality led my father's family to have a much less stressful relationship to their kitchen table. The generations before mine didn't have the same issues with food allergies that we do in present day, largely because they were never exposed to much variety, per Joanna, my college roommate, who's been a dietitian for almost thirty years.[14] Spoiler alert? Everyone ate peanut butter back then. Now, everyone has a problem with something, and ordering a meal is like auditing a chemistry lecture.

Recently, a group of my friends met for a birthday dinner at a cool molecular gastronomy restaurant. There were ten adults at the table, and every one of us had something we couldn't—or wouldn't—eat. My husband, Fletch, said no to snails. Karyn drew the line at "cute" animals, like bunnies and lambs (screw you, ugly pigs), Gina wouldn't touch avocados, and Lee ate nothing but fruit, vegetables, and fish. Some avoided dairy due to lactose intolerance, others steered clear of nuts. As for me? I once had a bad experience with a beef heart, and now my motto sounds like an Ayn Rand philosophy—Offal Is Awful.

After we'd narrowly navigated dinner, our server gave us a tour of the kitchen, largely because we were a fun group, despite our dietary proclivities. He showed us their sophisticated order input system, designed to protect customers with allergies. Each diner was assigned an emoji depicting what they couldn't ingest. Those who eschewed beef got a cow with a slash through it; those who couldn't do peanuts got a squirrel with an X over it. People with multiple issues had the emoticon of an angry guy covering his ears and screaming. There were a lot of screaming-dude emojis at our table. I still feel sorry for that lovely waiter and kitchen staff, but our collective guilt resulted in a massive tip. I hope his stress dreams aren't about us.

Since 1990, British hospital admissions for food allergies have increased more than 500 percent, and one of the causes is that our diets have changed and expanded to include more processed foods.[15]

When I was a kid, my family once took my father's aunts out for Chinese food at the Hunan Palace outside Boston. Great-Aunts Arabella and Caroline were both in their eighties and had never tried Asian food before. They sang with delight as they sampled their way through meats and vegetables seasoned with chili peppers and garlic. Coming from England by way of Nova Scotia, they had palates shaped by the rationing of both world wars; they had no idea that Asian flavors existed. They weren't stressing themselves out over whether a menu was "keto" or "raw" or "vegan"—those classifications didn't yet exist. *Access* to diverse food was still a novelty.

In less than one hundred years, we've gone from the necessity of my Italian grandparents stuffing anything not still wriggling into their maws to specialized emoji systems and preachy Facebook entries on the ethics of line-caught tuna. While this is certainly our right, perhaps even our responsibility, I wonder how the undernourished of Burundi, 73.4 percent of its population,[16] would react to some of our social media shares. If they'd be clamoring to hear more about the audacity of not being served pasture-raised eggs.

In defining ourselves by our diets, we've replaced the stress of not having enough to eat with the need to demonstrate how much better we eat than our peers, while still harboring the deep-seated guilt over exactly how good we have it, what with all the eating. No wonder we get snappy when someone's sustenance credo differs from ours.

Social media plays a huge role in our food intake anxiety. There are far too many media out there begging us to share our repasts—built entirely upon the assumption that we will. And not in a Jesus-fishes-and-loaves, agape-love way, I mean featuring shots of our ramen like we're the paparazzi and it's Bennifer in their heyday.

At a sushi restaurant last winter, I watched a gorgeous young couple spend their entire evening photographing their meal. Were the plates stunning? Absolutely. I'm talking orchids tucked between the maki and sashimi, lying on a bed of banana leaves. (Everyone knows flowers = fancy.)

I'd chosen that restaurant because they had a reputation for quality sushi; the presentation was a bonus. At no point did the two seem to appreciate the freshness of the fish or the ideal consistency of the rice. There I was, savoring every bite of my dragon roll like a *sucker*.

I tell myself that I enjoyed the meal more, yet I have no proof that this is true. Those young Adonises could have derived far more satisfaction from their visual feast and (likely) public broadcast. The reality of social media is that I'm the saber-toothed tiger; I'm the one about to go extinct, not those with their cameras in hand. The masses insist that dinner must be ready for its close-up. Chef Ned Bell of the Four Seasons Hotel in Vancouver said, "It affects me when I see a bad review. But it affects me more when someone takes a bad photo of my food. I worry about what my food looks like on the social media world."[17]

Per Ehab Shouly, director of the Tea Terrace on Oxford Street in London, "Today's dining experience is no longer just about having great food and drink. It's all about creating unique experiences that our customers can document on Instagram and social media."[18]

Maybe the emphasis is on the experience because millennials spend 44 percent of their food dollars on eating out.[19] This trend makes me think about airlines before regulation. The cost of flights was the same across the board, so airlines differentiated themselves through customer experience—the finest amenities and dressing their stewardesses in hot pants. It stands to reason that, if diners can get their avocado toast fix anywhere at a similar price, chefs had best make their presentations stand out.

After my first stand-up class, my friend Gina, another Gen Xer, and I had a late supper with Sami, a tattooed millennial in combat boots and fishnet tights, and—wait. A word first? If you're looking to feel past your prime, if you're hoping to find a way to remain terminally unhip, if you want to revel in the joy of being a painfully suburban dinosaur, then definitely keep the stasis of your current life. But if you seek growth and change, join a group where almost everyone's twenty-five years your junior. And a smart-ass.

Enrolling in the class was not my idea, it was Gina's—a friend I suspect might be a vampire because a) I never see her in daylight, b) she doesn't age, and c) she's always drinking red "wine." Anyway, Gina and I had recently started a podcast together. She'd been through Second City's improv program years before—possibly decades because, vampire. She rationalized that we could improve our comic timing by learning to perform stand-up. We were well into our second bottle of "pinot noir" when she suggested it.

Taking a comedy class was something I'd always wanted to do in theory, but I'd never intended to follow through; talking about it was enough. We'd been friends for more than a decade, so Gina knew that I'd agree to anything, given enough vino. She wasn't wrong.

In our new class, I felt like Jane Goodall, observing the millennials in their natural habitat. Sure, I'd seen them at a distance, but I'd never interacted with one up close, save for one junior publicist who thought that sending me on a book tour to Michigan during an ice storm was a capital idea. Once, she'd emailed me twenty-six separate times about how to ship a box via UPS, perhaps concerned that I was recovering from a traumatic brain injury and not an Achilles rupture. Of course, misspelled press releases were her home-run swing. For a long time, I assumed that she was representative of her entire generation. Fortunately, she wasn't.

I couldn't believe how *open* my millennial classmates were, happy to share all the intimate details of their lives with a room of near strangers. Introductions were peppered with instructions on which pronouns they used and a frank discussion of sexuality, whereas I don't even pee with the door open and I've been with my husband for half my life. One woman neatly explained the duality of her identity as a fourth-wave feminist and a professional stripper. Another kept stepping out of class to use his vape pen. I was the only middle-aged, married, straight, white, suburban woman in the room. Dressed in head-to-toe Eileen Fisher, paired with reading glasses, I was a stegosaurus.

We each had to tell a funny story after the introductions. I recounted an experience I'd had with my college roommate Joanna. We had an (old) girls' night, attending the opera, then staying at the Peninsula hotel instead of heading back to our respective burbs. At three thirty in the morning, sober and wide awake, I realized my choices were to either drive home or stanch Joanna's snoring with a pillow. I chose the former.

What I've learned over years of early media calls on book tours is that regardless of how fancy the hotel is—no matter what, at three thirty in the morning, every person leaving the hotel is an escort. Fact. This truth culminated in the desk clerk thinking I was the oldest, fattest, most successful call girl she'd ever seen. The punch line involved my reading glasses. The class of U-neck-T-shirt-wearing whippersnappers laughed, and I discovered that comedy can bridge gaps.

I was hooked.

One kid performed a set about giving up animal products after watching a documentary on the dangers of cow farting. He spent three days informing everyone on social media why consuming meat and dairy was bad before he fully understood what telling everyone he was vegan would entail: actually *being* vegan. He eventually ended up a vegetarian, straddling the comedic fence by mocking both vegans and carnivores. The lesson I learned was, if you're going to be a jerk about something, make sure you're funny.

Anyway, that night, the three of us sat down at Corcoran's, across the street from Second City. Gina and I did our usual dining out dance—starter salads, wine, whatever entrées caught our fancy. Sami ordered fish tacos off the appetizer menu. Immediately, I spouted a line about "lesbians and their fish tacos," then winced. The '80s are over and I'm not the Diceman. Hell, even Andrew Dice Clay is no longer the Diceman; he's moved on to taking roles in Academy Award–nominated movies. My dining companion's sexual preferences should not be fodder for my punch lines.

I quickly sputtered, "I'm so sorry, I'm old and I'm an asshole."

Right before class ended, we had covered the Second City credo, which asserts that improv and comedy should be open to everyone, regardless of race, religion, gender identity, or sexual orientation. Considering that my generation had no issue with the movie *Soul Man*, in which a man applies blackface to secure admission to Harvard—let that sink in for a second—it occurred to me that I might not be the arbiter of contemporary humor. While I'd been up in the suburbs, dicking around in my rose garden, the world had totally changed.

Ha! No stress there.

Sami shrugged. "I just did a five-minute set on being gay. I'd be offended if you didn't make the callback."

It turns out, millennials aren't solely ruled by righteousness, like I'd assumed. When our meals were served, Sami didn't photograph *anything*. "Aren't you breaking protocol?" I asked, genuinely concerned that her phone hadn't made an appearance.

"Bad lighting," she explained.

That's when I realized I had much to learn, and not just about punch lines and performances. Sami landed her own shots about Gen X not being able to work phones . . . *after* showing me how to join a group text. She wasn't wrong.

When the waitress asked us about the check, Gina and I both replied, "Split three ways?" like we've done a hundred times over our twelve-year friendship, while Sami said, "Separate, please." It was our only cultural rift. Gina took her Gen X income and paid Sami's bill on the sly.

According to Victoria Pope in a *National Geographic* article, "Food is more than survival. With it we make friends, court lovers, and count our blessings. The sharing of food has always been part of the human story. From Qesem Cave near Tel Aviv comes evidence of ancient meals prepared at a 300,000-year-old hearth, the oldest ever found, where diners gathered to eat together. Retrieved from the ashes of Vesuvius: a circular loaf of bread with scoring marks, baked to be divided. 'To break bread together,' a phrase as old as the Bible, captures the power of a meal to forge relationships, bury anger, provoke laughter."[20]

Food is our most basic need. The abundance of and access to it, particularly when consumed in the company of others, should be what decreases our collective anxiety. That it hasn't and doesn't is our own failing, and entirely within our own control. We've bastardized the meaning of "sharing" food, to our society's detriment. But the three of us took the first step away from anxiety that night, as we formed a new friendship over the intergenerational breaking of bread. Metaphorically, I mean. No one touched the damn dinner rolls.

As for you, avocado? Don't get too complacent in your newfound popularity, lest you go out of style like so many stoves and refrigerators before you.

For the rest of you, remember, your long-suffering grandmothers made you a million meals and never once posted a single photograph of them for "likes."

Maybe they should have, so they'd finally have the recognition they all deserve. And would it kill you to pick up the phone to call them?

FEAR OF A FAT PLANET

I wrote the book on weight loss.

Okay, I wrote *a* book on weight loss. I spent a year trying to shed pounds by engaging in every possible diet, exercise fad, and nonsurgical intervention. At the end of 365 days of careful eating and plenty of physical activity . . . I was still obese. Recounting this failed experiment in *Such a Pretty Fat* became my first *New York Times* bestseller.

Imagine how well the book might have done had I succeeded.

It's safe to conclude that our relationship with food and our bodies is a national obsession. It had certainly become a personal one for me. During that year of diet immersion, I'd planned to call my memoir *Pretty Fat.* I spent nine months writing before it occurred to me to secure the URL PrettyFat.com. As this was 2007, claiming a URL wasn't a *thing* yet. When I finally got around to it, I found out that the site was already in use. If you take away nothing else from me, please let it be this: reduce your stress by always googling potential titles first, lest you name your weight loss memoir after a big-girl fetish site. Best to check Urban Dictionary, too! I'm sure *someone's* gourmet cookbook plans were waylaid by the new meaning of "truffle butter."

Actually, I'd advise you against googling that one.

Here's the thing—food is at the very bottom tier of Maslow's Hierarchy; we *must* eat to exist. It's simple physiology. At the brain-stem level, we're compelled to take in as much sustenance as possible because nourishment is imperative to continuing our species. We're preconditioned to pack away the caloric energy required to run from encroaching four-legged predators. We're hardwired to consume. In theory, we should celebrate every ounce gained because, #winning.

"Oh, you put on three pounds? High five, girl! Looks like someone's gonna survive the winter!"

In an era when we're embracing body positivity, when plus-size models are included in the *Sports Illustrated* swimsuit edition (I *see* you, Ashley Graham), when designers are finally acknowledging that half this nation's women are at least a size 14, when Chrissy Metz, Roxane Gay, and Lindy West are role models, how is it that body dysmorphia—the preoccupation with our real *and* perceived physical flaws and defects—is on the rise?

Why do we still obsess over what the scale says?

Why do we hate what we see in the mirror?

Why can't we cut ourselves a break?

These constant questions are harshing our collective mellow.

I've been fat, I've been thin, and I've been all sizes in between. Spoiler alert? I was rarely happy in any weight class. I couldn't stop worrying about the numbers, regardless of how I looked or felt. This need to conform to an ideal has been linked to anxiety for as long as I could trace our history. If people aren't stressed about just procuring enough food to survive, they fall off a cliff of anxiety directly into stressing about how the food they eat affects their outward appearance. To my weight-obsessed mind, it's practically an all-encompassing anxiety our society has faced for centuries, and women—go figure—have traditionally been the most heavily scrutinized and most universally tortured.

The first time I entered a plus-size store to shop for size 14/16 jeans, I was devastated, tormented over no longer being able to sausage myself into my old pants. At no point did it occur to me to think about the relative privilege of my situation.

When interviewed by Ira Glass, *Bad Feminist* and *Hunger* author Roxane Gay identified "different kinds of fatness. There's the person who's maybe 20 pounds overweight, who's fine as they are. But if they want to lose weight, they just need to go on Slim Fast for a couple weeks or something. And then you have people who are—I like to call them Lane Bryant fat, which means they can still buy clothes at Lane Bryant, which goes up to 28 in size."[21]

There I was, in a complete lather over needing 14/16s, despite still being able to shop in the department store for pants that would fit. I had choices, even if I didn't love all of them. Perspective came to me only years later when I was having trouble cramming myself into the largest pants in the Lane Bryant store. I'd have told size 14 me, "Slow your roll there, Kate Moss."

Just a few hundred years ago, the plus-size body type was the ideal. Artists fought to sketch bigger girls in the buff. Look at Auguste Renoir's *Nude from the Back*—the subject has zero muscle tone and, like, *handfuls* of back fat. She'd never be able to find a flattering bra today, yet she was the hotness in that era.

How about Peter Paul Rubens's painting of *The Three Graces*? These rotund gals were *goddesses*, literally. If I hosted skinny-dipping parties with my friend group, we'd look a lot like this—vaguely lumpy, but well accessorized with cute haircuts.

I'm telling you, I was born in the wrong time. I'd have crushed it back then. Sure, there were plagues and crusades and everyone had serious BO, but I'd have been fighting everyone off with a stick.

Curious how the notion of physical perfection has changed over the years, I started digging. Why is the quest for perfection so anxiety triggering?

I stumbled upon an enlightening article on Medical Daily about the ways in which the ideal female body has transformed. The first thing I noticed on this web page was a picture of Renoir's *The Large Bathers*, where a group of heavy women frolicked au naturel in the water. Again, it could have been my friend group on our past girls' trip to Turks and Caicos. The only things missing were our mobile phones and tumblers full of frozen mojitos.

The 1800s were, it seems, all about Rubenesque figures, sensuous and pale and fleshy, influenced by Rubens's baroque painting style. Presumably, he celebrated this female form because a larger woman had resources. It wasn't so easy to achieve that rounded physique in those days. That woman needed access to a surplus of calories, and there was a dearth of deep fat fryers back then, and Shake Shack wasn't an option yet on Seamless. Likely she had a whole staff to keep up with her caloric needs, so she was rich. She had leisure time. She could sustain a pregnancy and produce lots of heirs, and that's why she was the hotness back then.

At least, I assume those were the qualities he was celebrating. It's possible that in modern times, Rubens would simply be a PrettyFat. com enthusiast.

But really, I should have stopped looking there, because what I found after those beautiful, bountiful times was a lineup of insane ideals that swung wildly from one obsession to the next, and this was long before the magazine industry dictated the standards. What I found was that in times of plenty, society demanded twenty-six-inch waists, in times of scarcity, strapping shoulders; how messed up is that?

The dizzying list of contradictions is so insane that, to do it justice, to really understand why we've arrived in this era of peak body anxiety, we should start in the past and work our way forward.

The period from the 1890s to the 1910s gave us the Gibson Girl, a soft, supple, dainty woman with a frame defined by a tight-as-shit swan-bill corset.[22] Charles Dana Gibson published a series of pen-and-ink drawings in *Life* magazine that defined the Gibson Girl, and that, in turn, influenced how the country idealized women's bodies. His vision was every bit as important as Helen Gurley Brown's or Hugh Hefner's would be in their own iconic magazines decades later. Except those

Gibson Girls weren't afraid of mashed potatoes. They were just completely unrealistically proportioned. Frankly, I don't know how they kept their balance.

The Gibson Girls were proper ladies, typified by their nipped-in waists, sloped shoulders, and busts large enough to topple them over. Basically Christina Hendricks from *Mad Men* dressed like a barbershop-quartet groupie. Their long hair was artfully piled up on their heads, with stray tendrils framing their faces, similar to a fancy topknot that's come loose during a run.

Surprisingly, with those zeppelin-sized tatas, the Gibson Girls' "slender necks" received top billing. Thin, spindly necks were a *thing*. The small waist was an illusion, reined in by tons of whale bone and some sturdy cord that crushed many vital organs, but no one was spot training their necks. There's no sit-up equivalent. It became an iconic, inborn advantage that drove the masses wild.

My spinach-scarfing Second City instructor, Erin, would have despised this period. She'd been pushed into comedy when her high school's wrestling coach tried to recruit her, lauding her "thick neck." Exactly what every young lady wants to hear. She channeled her mortification into stand-up. By being funny, she took control of the situation. Eventually she lost weight and turned vegan, and now her neck is entirely unremarkable. While the Gibson Girls were maybe least likely to be recruited to a high school wrestling team, they were athletic. Gibson depicted them riding bikes or playing golf or engaging in water sports, as though they were starring in the turn-of-the-century version of Kotex commercials.

But, like all things, the era of the spaghetti-necked, sporty, dessert-loving Gibson gal had to come to an end. Everything changed with the advent of the flapper. See you in hell, long hair! Sayonara, corsets! In the 1920s, flappers flipped the bird at convention. They redefined what it meant to be a woman. They drank and smoked and drove cars—conceivably all at the same time. They listened to jazz; they banged Jay Gatsby. They were liberated, free.

I have to assume the only thing they did not do was eat, as evidenced by their long, lithe, and lean frames. Suddenly, being thin was a conscious choice, not just a byproduct of scarcity.

Judging by the lack of source material such as fashion ads and articles in my research, in the 1930s, most of the country was too busy with the Depression to have depression over body ideals. A brief respite. But also, they were legitimately hungry. The dearth of snacks would have made the entire generation Instagram-ready by today's standards. Their standing thigh gaps would have garnered them VIP access at Lollapalooza, not that they'd have had the energy to care about Childish Gambino headlining the show.

The only standout body fact about the era was that a woman's shoulder width was a standard of beauty. Enter the lasting legacy of shoulder pads. Ladies would tailor old men's suits to give the illusion of broad shoulders. The idea of this strikes me as hopeful and brave and heartbreaking all at once.

But the fickle tastemakers turned from the era of scarcity and masculine shoulders to the pinup-girl era. During 1940s wartime, women became empowered. With the men gone, it was up to them to fill all the necessary roles, not only managing their households and raising their children, but also taking factory jobs. Instead of faking shoulders, women began *shouldering* the burdens of balancing home and work. (See what I did there?)

Five million Rosies and their rivets and sassy bandanas entered the workforce between 1940 and 1945.[23] So the men were called away from the country and women's bodies were, for the first time in recent history, primarily appreciated for functionality, likely a temporary break from intense body scrutiny and shame.

We can do it!

No one ever mentions the other part of that declaration: "We can do it, at half the pay a man would earn, and only until the guys return and we find ourselves SOL." As difficult as it might have been for women to transition into those jobs, with the long hours and dangerous conditions, imagine how hard it must have been to be forced to walk away once they'd mastered them.

With the end of rationing and empowerment, curvy became the new black again. There was pressure in this era to beef up. I could almost get behind that if I ignored my strong suspicion that the ideal "bulk" would translate into about a size 6 in today's standard clothing sizes. Diet plans were meant to add curves, not eliminate them. People suddenly had disposable income again, and the print industry boomed, ushering in the heyday of pinup magazines.

(Can we just take a second to reminisce over the antiquated notion of *paying* for pornography? Say what you will about how screwed up and stressed out we are as a nation in modern society—at least "noods" are free.)

Thanks to the advent of pinup mags, women's bodies were on constant display. The girls' photos were then made into illustrations and their "trouble spots" were tweaked. Legs were lengthened, boobs made bigger, and waists winnowed down.

Basically, post-WWII, women went from being in charge to being unrealistic objects of scrutiny.

Who run the world? Not you, girl.

Everything went off the rails in the 1960s when the world embraced the Twiggy look. In her heyday, Twiggy weighed in at five foot six and ninety-one pounds.[24] At the same height in junior high, I was so trim that my jutting hipbones rubbed white patches on my jeans, and I weighed almost forty pounds more than she had. This unbelievable fact sent me on an image search to verify exactly how teeny Twiggy had been.

Good Lord, that woman was mesmerizing on camera. Her size didn't even register because I was captivated by her flawless, symmetrical face and the intensity in her enormous doe eyes in every shot. Only after *studying* the photos did I notice that her elbows were wider than her upper arms. There was no gradation of width above the kneecap. Her limbs were twigs, hence the nickname.

Like a butcher inspecting a side of beef, I scrutinized her photos until it occurred to me that assessing her with such impunity made *me* part of the problem. All that was missing was my posting *You. Sandwich. Now.* on her Instagram page. I closed my search.

Twiggy, a supermodel who spawned an entire aesthetic and made serious money for being so captivating, was ashamed about being so slight. She'd try to hide her bony clavicle and was publicly "blamed for anorexia back in the 60s," she said, "which was unfair because I ate like a horse . . . I probably eat a third of that now."[25] Given the thickness of her hair and her skin's radiance in those pre-Photoshop days, I believe her.

Regardless of the ways women achieved it, being androgynously thin was the next big (small) thing, and the prevailing message was that hourglass figures were passé, unless you were Sophia Loren or Brigitte Bardot. How frustrating must it have been for women to have finally achieved peak curve-itude, only to have the target moved again?

Weight loss centers and diet doctors came into vogue in the early 1960s. Jean Nidetch founded Weight Watchers after someone presumed she was pregnant, not fat.

Please never do this.

Unless you are suited in scrubs and latex gloves in the labor and delivery room, don't ever assume anyone is pregnant. Once I was out of town for a morning TV interview, feeling very good about myself, what with the morning TV interview and all. I was sporting a darling brand-new Marc Jacobs empire-waist dress. I felt super fancy in it.

In the green room, there was a woman who was nine months pregnant. She was on the show to discuss birthing options, *which is how I knew she was pregnant*. Then, an anchorman came in, flashed his big white teeth at both of us, pointed at our midsections, and exclaimed, "Babies!"

I wanted to die.

While I don't remember the interview, I do recall, with exceptional detail, stuffing the dress in the trash can back at my hotel. It's possible that everyone would be less stressed about weight and diets if stupid people kept their goddamned mouths shut. Myself included.

So I empathize with Nidetch, who went on to lose the weight with the help of a doctor. During the process, she noticed that the clinic discouraged participants from discussing their many thoughts and feels. That didn't sit right with her. Sure, she lost the weight, but she maintained her weight by inviting friends into her Queens, New York, home to discuss their own struggles and support one another.

Thoughts and feels for the win!

She began running a few local support groups. The rest is Oprah screaming, "I love bread!" history.

For those who didn't want to diet their way to Twiggy's figure, drugs offered an appealing alternative. Medical amphetamine use exploded during the '60s. Physicians passed out diet pills like Halloween candy, likely because there was such a high profit margin on them. It's estimated that more than two billion amphetamines were consumed annually during this time.[26] No wonder the waif look became a thing.

The body ideal of the 1970s wasn't nearly as iconic as the decades before and after, probably because of how distracting the bad hair and clothes were. Again, google it, you shan't be disappointed. Bell-bottoms! Crochet! Polyester! Patchwork! It was a Worcestershire-colored world back then.

When I really entered the weight-obsession arena in earnest, it was the dawn of the 1980s. Prior to that time, I'd looked at my body as a vehicle to climb trees and outrun my brother, a functional means of conveyance. The doughy, pasty, munchie-driven '70s were out, making way for tanned, aerobicized bods. The focus on my bottom's line couldn't have come at a more impressionable time.

I used to work out with my mom's Jane Fonda videotapes in our poorly designed family room. There were three different points of entry, and each one involved walking in front of the television, so I was perpetually interrupted/mocked by my brother when I tried to exercise. Also, I spent the first five minutes waiting for the VCR to cue up from the previous session, as my mother feared its glowing buttons and would never rewind after use.

I was awed and intimidated by Jane's taut, sculpted muscles. Despite being three decades older, Jane still looked better than me, likely because of the outfit. I imagine her video series would be less impressive had she performed it in an oversized Rick Springfield concert tee and her brother's outgrown sweatpants pushed up to her knees. Every time I tried an upside-down move, I'd smother myself in loose cotton. Once in a while, I'd just lie on the couch with a Tab and watch Jane, figuring that counted, too. (It didn't.)

Although a toned body was important in the 1980s, the nation was again distracted by even more ridiculous hair and clothing. I was at my thinnest at this point in time. Also, I'd gained four inches in bangs height. And yet, I squandered my small, perky ass on oversized khaki Bermuda shorts, loafers with argyle socks that I pulled up to my knees, and crewneck wool sweaters with tie-on lace collars. Comedian Karen Kilgariff, of *My Favorite Murder*, described the 1980s aptly as a time when young girls dressed like they were doing middle-aged secretary cosplay. Barbara had become my style icon.

The 1990s ushered me into the concept of "heroin chic" and the age of the supermodel, with a side of *Baywatch*. What a time to be alive. To me, it seems like we've been stuck at this point ever since, striving for tiny figures, although we're periodically allowed to have some butt fat, thanks to Kim Kardashian and Sir Mix-A-Lot. I don't like to throw around the word "hero," and yet . . .

Changing standards of the ideal body have pushed Americans to be thinner and strategically curvier, and then thinner again, yet our country continues to get fatter and fatter. The disparity between the ideal and our reality is making most of us twitchy.

I had hoped to determine the cause of our national weight gain, and now my Google search history reads like an existential cry for help:

Why are we fat?

Reasons for my obesity?

What's with all the snacks?

Per the World Health Organization, 39 percent of adults aged eighteen years and older were overweight in 2016, and 13 percent were obese. Most of the world's population lives in countries where obesity kills more people than malnutrition.[27]

It's true, we *fat*. But honestly, I can't pin down the exact why.

The answer has to be more than a simple calories-in, calories-out equation, although that equation isn't insignificant. Other likely factors include genetics, metabolism, farming and ranching practices, food sensitivity, the list goes on and on.

As a kid, I wasn't dissimilar to Twiggy in that I ate everything and gained nothing. When I lived in Bergen County, New Jersey, I walked to school. I often walked home for lunch, so I clocked roughly four miles a day, five days a week. Sometimes I'd cut through the woods, in which case it was a three-and-a-half-mile trek. I had daily gym class where I was the reigning kickball queen, thank you very much.

I loved climbing trees and exploring on my bike and running around on local playgrounds. None of this felt like exercise or effort, it was just life. Sure, I watched some TV, but I was never super into it. Without cable or Netflix, my choices were pretty much *Gomer Pyle* or *Bewitched* reruns. Even at eight years old, I could tell you that Gomer was a rube and I didn't like when they switched Dicks, *like we weren't supposed to notice.* My mom would kick us out of the house in the morning and we'd spend the day outdoors; I was in constant motion. Also, Mom was a hippie, and we rarely had good snacks in the house. The only thing she feared more than salt was sugar.

She considered an apple a delicious treat; I did not. I also was not in charge of stocking our pantry.

But times have changed. I would have died for more than three TV channels. I *should* have died considering all the time I spent walking through the woods alone. Now, Bergen is full of kids whose parents commute to Manhattan. Kids are eating lunch at school all the time, they're getting picked up in SUVs at the end of the day. And I bet, when they get home, the after-school snacks that await them are amazing. They are also, on average, fatter.

In a *Huffington Post* article that explored the reasons for the rapid weight gain over the last forty years, the most significant finding concerned diet. "It's not *how much* we're eating—Americans actually consume fewer calories now than we did in 2003. It's *what* we're eating."[28]

The quality of our food has declined. Big Food products are made to be satisfying: crunchy, salty, sweet, and diabolical. They are pumped full of fructose. When you eat sugar, the excess is stored as fat. Sugar spikes affect insulin production, which throws the whole body into chaos. Sugar sends bat-signals to the hormone that causes satiety, leptin. Sugar skews cholesterol. Sugar is linked to diabetes, heart disease, and memory loss. Sugar impacts your joints, gives you zits, and rots your teeth. It tells your body to text your ex at two in the morning. It's your mean friend, smiling to your face while stabbing you in the back. Sugar posts bad Instagrams of you. Sugar drains the milk and leaves the empty carton in the fridge. Sugar steals your phone charger. Sugar never Venmos for their half of the bar tab.

Yet sugar is the building block of cake, so you can see the dilemma.

I've done a few rounds of the Whole30 plan. A thirty-day elimination eating plan, Whole30 was created to suss out food sensitivities.

(It's since evolved into a way for your enlightened neighbor to broadcast their virtue.) The plan forbids sugar, dairy, alcohol, corn, legumes, wheat and grain, soy, and fun[29] for one month.

The first month I voluntarily took on this plan, I ate a variety of organic fruits and vegetables, grass-fed or pasture-raised meats, nuts, and other healthy fats. I didn't measure or portion anything, just participated in thirty days of clean, expensive eating. The plan's author insists Whole30 is not for weight loss, although weight loss can, and generally does, happen.

I had to read every label for a month. Trips to the grocery store took hours. I wandered the aisles, glaring at the tiny print on bottles through my reading glasses, floored by all the places sugar had weaseled its sweet way into. I discovered sugar in my *bacon*.

In my opinion, bacon doesn't need sugar, because it's *bacon*. It's already perfect.

I guess my mother was right to be frightened. Sugar is *everywhere*. It's in mustard and salad dressing and tomato sauce. I must have looked insane that month as I perused the aisles, shaking my fist and shouting "Cane sugar!" at random bottles of kombucha.

Many critics have blamed Big Food for the world's widening waistlines. Per the WHO, the global rate of obesity has almost tripled in the last four decades.[30] What's troubling is that while children's weights are increasing, they're still often lacking in critical nutrients. Turns out, malnutrition and obesity are not mutually exclusive.

So what is driving this trend toward food that doesn't aim to nourish? In a report by the Lancet Commission on Obesity, they charge Big Food with global obesity, malnutrition, and climate change.[31] The Big Food lobbies, including companies such as Nestlé S.A., the Coca-Cola Company, and McDonald's, are potentially influencing nutrition advice, and that's a large part of the problem. With unlimited resources, it seems as though they can fund unlimited studies to negate hard and fast nutritional truths. And no one's stopping them.

The food and beverage industry spent $21 million on lobbying in 2018. For perspective, the NRA spent $5 million lobbying for gun rights in 2018, [32] while the Everytown for Gun Safety opposition put forth less than $2 million.[33] It's not politically advantageous for our elected officials to call for healthier living standards. Big Broccoli just doesn't have the clout. So it stands to reason that the deck is stacked, but I can't pin all the blame on Big Food. Food and beverage lobbyists aren't the ones pouring us midnight bowls of Cap'n Crunch.

The trick to reducing my overall panic and worry about weight hasn't been about starving myself into a form that will satisfy whatever arbitrary societal norms are coming down the pipeline. The key has been finding a way to be happy with myself, regardless of what the scale says.

Acceptance hasn't come easy. The second my curves filled in, I started chastising myself, but I didn't realize exactly how much contempt existed outside my purview until I put myself online. I had one of the first mainstream blogs, long before I learned they were called blogs, back when I documented losing my executive job in the post-9/11 dotcom crash. I was a social media pioneer.

The first picture I ever posted of myself was a wedding portrait. I loved how I looked in that photo, thanks to the ministrations of talented hairstylists, makeup artists, and a seamstress, as well as a professional photographer, and, you know, being in love.

I was excited to share that version of myself with the world, but I was stunned by how quick people were to call me disgusting, to say I was an enormous pig, to tell me I had no right to exist. My writing, my ideas, were immediately—and loudly—dismissed because I didn't conform to an ineffable body ideal.

Anonymous fat shaming became a *thing*; turns out I was a pioneer for that, too. I despised reading hurtful descriptions of myself, but I refused to let that stop me from writing. I aspired to become a professional author. I figured I wasn't too fat if my fingers weren't too rotund to mash individual keys on the keyboard.

So I doubled down. I used those arbitrary opinions about my size to fuel my drive. Instead of skulking away, I worked to have my writing—along with that headshot—seen as much as possible. I refused to be invisible. If that led to personal attacks, so be it. When a stranger called me a fat bitch on a public bus, I channeled my anger into my work, and that moment became the opening chapter of *Such a Pretty Fat*.

One may think that with our increasingly PC culture, people would stop judging others by their size, but one would be wrong. Prejudices don't disappear so easily, especially when they're based on what scares us most. Right now, our nation is fat-phobic AF. In the last hundred years, societal pressure to conform to media-induced norms has conditioned us to deny our genetic code. That causes dissonance, and dissonance squirts out in all sorts of unpleasant ways, such as saying rude shit to strangers online *who are totes cute in their wedding pics, FYI*.

My weight, I decided, didn't automatically signal that I was lazy, and I intended to prove it. Did I appear at my first book event in a Lane Bryant dress? Hell, yes, I did.

Unfortunately, it's not only miserable internet trolls who are fat shaming our society. That judgment comes from all sorts of unlikely places, and one of the most dangerous sources wears a white coat and wields a medical degree.

It turns out that physicians aren't often willing to look past BMI, and that discrimination can lead doctors to provide their heavy patients with improper diagnoses. That's not to say that weight is something that should be left outside the exam room, and docs aren't doing patients any favors by *not* pointing out excess weight, as obesity can often contribute to morbidity and mortality.[34] But there needs to be a balance between healthy advice and taking patients' symptoms seriously. While it's not happened to me, I've had friends leave their doctors' offices in tears, their real symptoms dismissed with a suggestion to join Jenny Craig.

There is more than enough debate around fat discrimination, but the simple fact is that it's not a silver-bullet diagnosis. Fat people can be healthy and skinny people can be unhealthy, per *Harvard Men's Health Watch*[35]. But the obsession and the shame around weight has reached an undeniably unhealthy level. Regardless of size, shape, race, religion, sexuality, political affiliation, or any other thing society uses to set us apart, we all deserve respect and common courtesy.

Social media makes achieving that ideal more difficult. The internet is just one big venue for anyone to say anything to anybody—without personal consequences.

Listen, we're all afforded the right to free expression, and it's unrealistic to expect people to change their bigoted thinking en masse. Never gonna happen. And although we are in control of our thoughts about ourselves, we're up against a mounting onslaught of unrealistic images.

Selfie culture is causing our collective body dysmorphia to get worse, not better. Angles and filters are putting Photoshop at our fingertips, and now it's easy to change what we don't like about ourselves with a few taps and then broadcast that unrealistic image to the world. *JAMA Facial Plastic Surgery* is aware (and, ostensibly, loving the business it generates). "Overall, social media apps, such as Snapchat and Facetune, are providing a new reality of beauty for today's society. These apps allow one to alter his or her appearance in an instant and conform to an unrealistic and often unattainable standard of beauty."[36]

The notion of being able to "fix" what's wrong with us is causing a huge uptick in body dissatisfaction.

It's not new that we're tortured about our appearance—our size, our features, our everything. We've been stressing about this type of stuff ever since artists could present a beauty ideal. That anxiety has only been ratcheting up over the last century. I think what makes the anxiety next-level now is that we compared ourselves only to celebrities prior to the advent of social media. Sure, stars were perfect, but that was their job. What's more unsettling is seeing real people—those with the exact tools we possess, and in the same circumstances—become internet famous. How's a poor postpartum new mom supposed to feel good about her changed shape when she follows another new mom online who's faced zero issues getting back to her pre-baby bod?

However, there's hope! And it doesn't only involve clapping back at internet strangers.

Slowly, more body diversity is creeping into the media. Shows like *Dietland* and *Shrill* are reflecting a more accurate range of sizes in our society. Online retailers are providing a variety of models to demonstrate what their clothes might look like in different sizes. This is a huge step forward, proof that not everyone has to be built like a Barbie doll to find happiness in the world.

Hell, even Mattel diversified their program, introducing a line of Barbie Fashionistas, where the limbs have been shortened and the waists thickened. Some dolls are tall, some petite. Some have different hair textures. The curvy red-headed Barbie, clad in a tasteful "Girl Power" T-shirt and modest leopard-print skirt, was the bestselling doll of 2017.[37]

Does having a plus-size Barbie mean that obesity should no longer be a concern? Of course not. But with everything little kids worry about today, from school shootings to melting polar ice caps—issues that never crossed my mind as I traipsed through the forest alone—can't we please let them have the win? Allow them a minute to see themselves reflected in a toy? If we start introducing healthy, beautiful body diversity early enough, maybe we can begin to curtail the issue of body dysmorphia and untangle the idea that thin equates to healthy and any type of plus-size figure is hurtling toward an untimely death. Because this narrow definition of health and beauty is an issue, and it's making us stress eat. (Wait, just me?)

What gives me the most hope is the HAES (Health at Every Size) movement. The idea is that health is determined not by numbers on a scale, but by good habits. HAES advocates fat acceptance. It's based on the notion that the line between BMI and health isn't as clear cut as the medical industry once imagined, that a person can truly be healthy and overweight.

I support this idea because I live it.

Years after I wrote *Such a Pretty Fat*, I decided to try to lose weight again. I wasn't looking to become an Instagram booty influencer—yes, these exist, and that ship has definitely sailed for me. And sunk. What I wanted was to fly on a plane without worrying I'd need to request a seat belt extender. I'd created a nice life for myself with Fletch, and I wanted to live long enough to enjoy it.

Instead of concentrating on the usual gym-starve-gym tactic, I started to consider some different aspects of wellness. Fitness is only an eighth of the pie that determines wellness.

Taking a more holistic approach, I decided to improve those seven other slices, including aspects like spiritual, social, and intellectual fulfillment. The approach was pretty far outside my comfort zone; I'd been putting those areas of my life on hold, instead trying to find satisfaction through the narrow channel of diet and exercise.

Regardless of the success I'd had, I secretly believed that I couldn't truly be whole until I was smaller. Yet I made a list of all the things I wanted and decided to plow through them anyway. So I got busy. I started a side business refinishing furniture. I improved my relationships. I learned Italian, which gave me the confidence to travel to Italy solo. When my husband joined me in Rome, he was blown away by a simple conversation I had with a shoe salesman as we debated if Fletch would look cute in blue loafers. (Consensus? *Sì!*)

I found that the fuller and richer my life became, the less I looked to food for comfort and entertainment.

Huh.

Months passed while I worked on everything except the physical aspect of weight loss. I walked a lot, but that was only because I needed to calm Hambone, my anxious pit bull. Tired dogs are happy dogs. I didn't set foot in the gym until almost a year into my quest.

You know what?

I actually enjoyed exercising without the pressure of meeting an arbitrary goal. After a year of concentrating on wellness, I started working with Brett, a nice trainer who pushed me enough that I started to see progress, but not so hard that I plotted his demise between sessions. He's since become a great friend.

As for diet, I ate whatever I wanted; I just learned to indulge in moderation, and to stop obsessing about food—what I was or wasn't eating. And I gave up sugar, save for special occasions.

Eventually, I'd lose eighty pounds . . . and would still be considered fat. But thanks to the loss, I was taken off blood pressure meds; I didn't need them anymore. My bad-cholesterol numbers plummeted. I could run a mile—a distance that was beyond my reach long before I needed my 14/16 jeans. My numbers said I'd become healthier than I ever was when I was thinner. When my (awesome) doctor deleted the Lisinopril from my meds regimen, he shook my hand and said, "Congratulations! You've just added years to your life." That felt good.

I'd love to say that, on this side of the journey, I'm completely satisfied, entirely and deliriously happy. Honestly, there are times that I still struggle to feel content with myself at this size. Some days, I feel irrational anger at my pants. The pressure to conform to a smaller standard is powerful.

Yet I've gained the tools to view myself more objectively. I'm better about focusing on what I like about myself and my life, as opposed to obsessing over the areas that need improvement. Mostly, I see achievements, not failures.

Unless trends change dramatically in my lifetime, I'll likely never conform to society's ideal body. What I can do is work toward remaining healthy, but I'm done with obsessing over those ideals, jeopardizing my mental health. And I've gotten much better at laughing those cringe-inducing moments off, being kind instead of cruel.

What scares me now is that if I were starting over, depending on social media to give me the boost I'd need to become a professional writer, I'd likely fail. Fifteen years ago, words were the most important thing one could offer on the World Wide Web; today it's image.

If you're struggling, my advice is to be more kind and less critical toward yourself and others. Find a doctor who cares about your overall health, not just your number on the scale. Insist that the people you employ are respectful toward you, understanding and reasonable and not interested in doling out doses of shame.

Remind yourself that many of the images in the media and even on social media are filtered and retouched and otherwise unreal. You're seeing the best shot out of hundreds. And the fact that these folks' looks are on trend is temporary. There will always be someone younger and thinner, but they don't have your sense of humor, your ability to stay steadfast in the case of emergency, your uncanny knack to call your friends the minute they need a boost.

It's a process, but take those little steps toward treating yourself fairly, embracing body positivity, and celebrating what is unique and wonderful about you, and I promise you'll feel a break from all the tension.

As for me, I'm done worrying about size.

Mostly.

Unless there's bread on the table.

Again, it's a process.

FASHION FORWARD

As for clothing, I wrote the book on fashion.

Okay, I wrote *a* . . . eh. I suppose I can't open every chapter with a hard sell of one of my previous books. Suffice it to say that fashion has been a driving force in my life. My desire for alligator shirts in high school compelled me to build a babysitting empire. I earned enough commission to branch out from alligators to some shiny Tiffany silver, which spurred me on in my professional sales career. The possibilities were endless. I'm still striving for the Hollywood film that will bring home a Birkin.

I'm a cautionary tale on loving clothes, shoes, and jewelry too much. I learned the hard way that you shouldn't carry a Prada bag to the unemployment office. Substituting designer goods for self-esteem usually ends badly.

Long before I discovered the power of labels, I gravitated toward items that made me feel good—bright, color-coordinated pieces in unnatural fabrics. Think Garanimals—cute, simple, affordable sports-wear pieces. Once adorned exclusively with baby animal logos, today Garanimals include jaunty nautical stripes and pithy sayings. I heart-ily approve. They're now owned by Berkshire Hathaway, and Warren Buffett does not make mistakes. However, Garanimals proper didn't hit mainstream children's clothing until after I'd sized out of them.

Instead, when I was a child, my mother sewed most of my clothes. (Hippie.) I didn't own any jeans. The Toughskins dungarees available at Sears were too scratchy for my liking.

My go-to look in 1970s New Jersey included homemade plaid A-line knee-length skirts or snappy culottes. Never one to waste, my mother would use excess material to make matching shawls and capes. She'd cut the remnant into a triangle and finish off the edges, which I'd wear tied around my shoulders.

It's called fashion, *Susan*.

To complete the look, I'd add a solid-colored top, coordinating knee socks, and leather clogs with a low, sensible platform heel. The socks and blouses were swapped for turtlenecks and tights in the winter. It was my version of Garanimals. On days I was feeling sassy, I'd toss a fringed poncho over the whole ensemble. Eat your heart out, Diane von Furstenberg. I rocked the runway of the Lincoln Elementary School halls.

On Wednesdays, I wore my Girl Scout uniform, which included a Kelly-green-colored shift dress layered over a white cotton trefoil-print button-down. I accessorized that with a red snap-closed tie, a jaunty beret, and a sash boasting all my medallions.

So began my love of accessories, which would eventually lead me down the wrong path. I guess it all started when I used to try to snatch beads off senior citizens as a toddler. The old gals thought it was cute, but it was a clear warning sign.

Soon enough, the sash felt naked with the scant merit badges I'd earned. I desired, nay, *deserved*, symmetry. Balance. So I doubled my efforts, collecting as many badges as I could, yet they weren't enough to fill the emptiness. My sash was top heavy, with a few token emblems floating above a vast field of green, its blank slate mocking me.

No, no, that simply wouldn't do!

My thirst for adornment was unquenchable. I morphed into a monster, a power-drunk three-star general, willing to sacrifice the troops in the hope of earning that elusive fourth star. I started half-assing the badge requirements to speed the process.

I discovered that my mother didn't question me when I asked her to sign off on multiple entries in my *Girl Scout Handbook*, especially if I hit her up while she was on the phone. She trusted my innate goodness. (Hippie.) Eventually, I started forging her signature. She never raised an eyebrow over how I'd managed to earn badges in metallurgy, alchemy, and necromancy. Odd.

I *should* explain how I feel terrible about this petty larceny, because what kind of sociopath was I to lie to the Girls Scouts of the United States of America?

A well-appointed one.

My comeuppance came when my father was transferred to Indiana. It was the 1970s, and no one cared about children's opinions, so our move (mid)west was not open to family debate. In my new town, the kids eschewed dressing up for school. No one wore skirts, and they sure as hell didn't mess with culottes. Suddenly my Matchy McMatcherson aesthetic was out of vogue. Designer jeans were *in*, and my mother didn't believe children should own status symbols. (Hippie.) Worse, my new Girl Scout troop didn't even *wear* uniforms.

My husband was born and raised in Indiana. Around the time my family moved there, he'd experienced his own fashion-related incident. His older sister had come home from California for the Christmas holiday, bringing with her the first long-sleeve Ocean Pacific shirt Noblesville had ever seen. Inspired by her new local surf scene, she suggested Fletch part his hair on the side, instead of down the middle, bringing him a little closer to the beachy vibe of La Jolla.

As Fletch gazed at the mellow pastel airbrushed artwork of a rape van emblazoned on cotton, he instantly felt at ease. Relaxed. Possibly even groovy. No worries, brah. The new year dawned and Fletch was a new man as he boarded the school bus to junior high in his stylin' California-cool top and fresh coif.

After the ass-whupping he received, he claims he barely made it off the bus alive. While Fletch is a shameless exaggerator, there's a reason they don't host fashion week in Indiana.

Meanwhile, two hours to the north, I submitted to peer pressure and pulled on a scratchy, restrictive pair of jeans. It was a slippery slope, and I soon began worshiping over the Holy Trinity—Gloria Vanderbilt, Jordache, and Sasson.

But a part of me still longed for the salad days of skirts and capes. I missed the color coordination. I missed the tailored-just-for-me fit. (Who among us would argue against bespoke?) What I missed most was that my matched outfits took the guesswork out of my mornings. With my skirt/culotte-cape combos, I had the confidence of a solid week's worth of go-to looks that had clear function and made me feel good, kind of like a uniform. Losing that blueprint suddenly introduced a before-school dressing stressor that had never existed. I boarded the bus hungry most mornings, not because I lacked access to breakfast, but because I wasted too much time trying to piece together an outfit.

In theory, *any* clothing should satisfy the basic need on Maslow's Hierarchy. Without elemental protection, we die. Biologically, given we have enough skins, vines, and leaves to insulate our exposed flesh, we should be golden.

I suspect Maslow never shopped at Nordstrom. If he had, he'd have understood that clothing can be a self-actualizing, hedonistic pleasure, eligible for much higher placement on his pyramid. Did he comprehend the delight of a new handbag? Could he grasp the joy incumbent in a freshly sewn cape? Maslow didn't have access to social media, so he wasn't hip to the siren song of influencers. If he had been, he'd totally have rearranged a basic-needs block or two.

As a grown-ass adult with real-life responsibilities, perhaps you don't know what influencers are. Good for you. I'm here to ruin that. Influencers are people who trend younger, connected by frequent social media interactions, with the power to impact consumer purchasing decisions, particularly in health, beauty, and fashion. Their influence stems from their ability to highlight certain objects, like handbags. They don't *make* handbags or *sell* handbags or *distribute* handbags; they just post in-depth vlogs about handbags because they're passionate about handbags, which gives me pause as to why I am not a "cheese and moderately priced Chardonnay" influencer.

Since writing the chapter where I stated that Froot Loops influencers do not exist, I've learned a thing or two. Lee, Gina's partner, is a popular DJ and event producer. He recently managed a seven-figure party for a cereal company looking to connect with influencers to help them roll out a new flavor.

Anyway, influencers are credible on social media because their presence on social media deems them credible. Are you imagining a snake swallowing its own tail? You're on the right track.

On her Twitter feed, actress Minnie Driver recently posted:

> *I just met an 'influencer.' What do you influence I asked her.*
> *I influence your decision about which handbag to buy. I said,*
> *I have handbags older than you. She said, great I'll tell you*
> *which bags are worth the most and you can make some money.*
> *I am now in a bar.*

I suggest you read this to yourself in a British accent for maximum charming and absurd effect.

While I would like to be best friends with Minnie, that's not my point. We live in an age where Instagram model is a job and influencers have become as significant in swaying opinion as people who have, say, resumes with zero bikini selfies on them.

My friend Karyn lives in an LA apartment complex where many influencers and YouTube stars reside. She has a bachelor's degree and legitimate employment, yet she's in one of the regular-priced studio apartments in the middle of the building. The influencers occupy the top floors, paying upwards of $10,000 per month in rent. To me, their very existence screams, "Screw you *and* your humanities graduate degree! You should have invested that tuition in ring lights and flattering backdrops."

While I can mock (or envy) the idea of influencers all day long, that doesn't negate their impact on the marketplace. *CBS News Sunday Morning* reported, "By the year 2020, *Ad Week* magazine says influencer marketing will be a $10 billion industry."[38]

The segment went on to recount how influencer Tina Craig of Bag Snob was seated in the front row at a fashion week show, across the runway from the editor in chief of *Vogue*. Craig was afforded the same amount of importance as cultural icon Anna Wintour, who'd taken her first job in fashion at a London boutique in 1964.

Miranda Priestly would *not* approve.

The clincher in the CBS piece was when Alex Bolen, the chief executive of Oscar de la Renta, explained that production for his company's bags was up 100 percent since reaching out via the influencer community.

Bottom line, brands have reason to believe in the power of influencers.

Ashley Dodd, a Chase Sapphire representative who works with influencers in campaigns to promote said card, explained the power of influencers, citing that "millennials and millennial-minded folk value experiences over tangible things. Instagram is a good platform to showcase experiences."[39]

I gather this means the scope of influence is largely generational, because it's not grown-ass adults buying enough lip kits to make Kylie Jenner a billionaire. I have a hard time seeing my middle-aged husband buying a power tool because some neck-bearded Navy SEAL posted a video on Facebook of himself enjoying his drill on a golden Saturday morning.

Wait, I totally can.

I run across images from influencers on my social media feeds all the time. I don't follow these people, but they show up anyway via retweets or likes. Carefully curated influencer pictures stoke my angst about aging, as though there's a dotted line connecting my not being youthful enough to shop for floral rompers to my own mortality. Thing is, I don't even *want* a goddamned romper, because I don't like stripping down entirely to take a leak in a public restroom. Yet the choice on social media feels binary—I can buy an off-the-shoulder Free People boho blouse or a silk-lined casket; there's no middle ground.

Influencer images subconsciously suggest that no matter how hard I try, I've lost the thread of what's current. While those of us in Gen X are deemed too old and irrelevant to influence fashion decisions, it seems we are far from immune to influence. Ironic, because per a study by American Express, "Gen X has more spending power than any other generation, with 29% of estimated net worth dollars and 31% of total income dollars."[40]

This past April, I flew to LA to meet with production companies for potential writing gigs. I spent ten months getting ready. The previous year's visit hadn't resulted in jobs or deals. I figured I needed to try harder. I prepped by taking every Second City screenwriting course and workshop, all taught by moonlighting film school professors. I developed four different series ideas, creating multiple scripts in three genres, each written and rewritten using all the notes I'd gotten from my millennial classmates to make sure my message wasn't dated. I'd even started to adapt some of my fiction. Instead of *telling* executives I could write for television, I'd *show* them.

In one meeting, I ate avocado toast at Joan's on Third with a Hollywood player. (Yes, you've seen her shows.) She mentioned a beloved series was slated for a reboot and told me about the uncredited writer she'd brought on to spearhead the project. During high school, that writer had found a pair of designer shoes abandoned after a big house party. They weren't her size, but the girl forced her feet into them because, Gucci. She was from a normal family, not rich or renowned, and yet Gawker society reporters spotted her wearing those shoes around town and decided that she was an "it girl." The site started to feature her. She became a proto-influencer, thanks to the scavenged shoes, and that opened doors for her in Hollywood. I mean, the producer loved the story so much, she *hired* the woman as a lead writer. Again, not because of training, but fashion.

I glanced down at the black Børn sandals I'd chosen in preparation to walk across studio lots all day. Perhaps I should have spent the year tightening up my footwear game, not my scripts.

So you can understand why I cheered on Payless ShoeSource after they duped a group of influencers. Freshly emerging from a 2017 bankruptcy, Payless needed to change consumers' perceptions about their brand, so they hired ad agency DCX Growth Accelerator. They rented an old Armani store in LA and created a fake Instagram account. Influencers were invited for a two-night event to celebrate the launch of the luxury brand "Palessi," where Payless's regular offerings were marked up more than 1,800 percent.

Doug Cameron, DCX Growth Accelerator's chief creative officer, explained, "Payless customers share a pragmatist point of view, and we thought it would be provocative to use this ideology to challenge today's image-conscious fashion influencer culture."[41]

The invited influencers raved about the shoes' style, quality, and craftsmanship, plunking down hundreds of dollars for their new "Palessi" kicks, which were placed on display like Louboutins. Cameras captured the influencers' reactions when they learned of the trick, making for a good ad and for even better schadenfreude.

I'm not surprised influencers were taken in by the cute items in that fancy pop-up store. Fast-fashion retailers like Payless routinely knock off runway styles, reproducing the looks on the quick and cheap. Scrolling through the Payless.com offerings, I can identify shoes that are clearly inspired by couture designers like Loeffler Randall, Jimmy Choo, and Gianvito Rossi.

The influencers, though, seemed to lack the basic ability to discern quality. There's a world of difference between premium bridle leather, hand stitched by master craftsmen in Italy, and man-made materials mass-produced in Chinese sweatshops. That these influencers couldn't detect the difference—*on the very products for which they influence*—called their credibility into serious question.

Days after the event, entrepreneur and writer at *Inc.*, Peter Gasca, predicted Payless's strategy, while a brilliant retail promotion, would fail. "By making a large number of influencers look foolish and boasting that the company will continue to use the prank for promotional reasons, it breaches any trust and respect these influencers may have had for the Payless brand—and that breach will get passed onto their fans."[42]

Gasca was right.

The brand recently announced they're liquidating the business, shuttering all 2,100 stores and closing their e-commerce arm.[43] So taking down a bunch of influencers may not have been the most savvy policy. Yet I respect that they did not go quietly into that good night; they went down fighting.

What the stunt shows—in addition to the dubious skills influencers have at recognizing craftsmanship—is the link between fashion and *confidence*, a feeling that is the antithesis of anxiety. A favorite piece can make us feel great, an exclusive brand gives our ego a boost, but is the opposite true? Can fashion worsen our feelings of anxiety?

Short answer? Totes.

Clothing was one of the first things my instructor Erin called out as important in stand-up class. She said stage wardrobe is a nonverbal representation of identity and will immediately color the audience's perception of a performer. My sartorial choices, I learned, must be a deliberate and accurate representation, unless the bit I'm going for has me trying to play against type. She explained that so many comedians take the stage in old tees, regular jeans, and Converse because it's the de facto comedy club costume; it establishes a credibility shorthand. It satisfies the audience's expectations and lessens their anxiety.

I scanned the room at Second City, deciding what everyone's outfit said about them. Sami's patch-covered work shirt and fishnets under torn jeans indicated, "I don't conform to conventional norms."

Max's growing-out high-and-tight haircut, combat boots, and loose sweatpants declared, "I'm fresh out of the military, and I'm confused as to what's next."

My skirted leggings, tunic sweater, and matching scarf announced, "I had a 20 percent off coupon at the Eileen Fisher outlet."

I spotted a millennial who was just preppy AF. His horn-rimmed glasses and layers of J. Crew–type items, all with flipped collars, were finished off with an outrageous pair of socks. My initial reaction was positive; he was the male version of me during my sophomore year of high school. Connor became one of my closest friends in the group. Had I reproduced, he's what I'd hope my own son was like.

As Erin spoke, a man cruised into class a couple of minutes late. He wasn't afraid to make an entrance and every eye was on him.

"Sorry!" he sang as he removed his coat, revealing a Harvard sweatshirt. "My Uber driver sucked."

"Hi, who are you?" Erin asked, glancing at the attendance sheet.

"Andre," he replied.

"Hello, Andre. We're talking about first impressions," she said. "Now, let's use you as an example. If Andre goes up onstage in a Harvard shirt, people will have certain expectations of his comedy, so—"

Andre didn't let her finish. "Oh, girl, I didn't go to Harvard. Uh-uh, no. I just wear this shirt so white people"—he looked over at me, raising an eyebrow—"aren't scared of me."

The millennials gasped in shock. I let out a single sharp "Ha!" that perforated the room before I could stop it. But I couldn't help myself—his punch line, his timing, his delivery, all of it, Italian-chef-kiss perfection. Andre was delighted to receive the first big laugh.

While showcasing his comedic skills, Andre was also immediately setting expectations of what he would and would not tolerate. From that class on, we were tight.

While Andre made a joke about his shirt that first day, he wasn't kidding. His clothing choices are deliberate, meant to shield him not only from the elements but also from preconceived notions. He feels obligated to dress in a way that makes allowances for other people's ignorance, and lessens his own fears.

A CalmClinic article laid it out: "What you wear (and why you wear it) can have a big impact on the amount of anxiety you have. Because of the power of first impressions, as well as how quickly visual information is processed, the way you present yourself to the world via your appearance will affect your relationships with others as well as how you view yourself."[44]

Andre had already proved to be a master class in predicting and preempting impressions when it came to how people saw him.

But, what about how we see ourselves?

The social comparison theory argues that people have an innate drive for self-evaluation; it's human nature. To satisfy this drive, we're compelled to consistently take measure of ourselves in relation to others.

So we base our own self-worth on how we stack up to others?

No stress there.

Festinger's theory leads me to believe that we're bound to be more anxious if we deem those around us to be, say, thinner, funnier, or better dressed. "Sure, there is no harm in looking across the room and comparing your outfit to another person's," the Elite Daily pointed out. "But, when we add social media into the mix with the social comparison theory, we ultimately set ourselves up for failure."[45]

That's why when I see how influencers carefully frame their lives, perfectly coiffed and dressed to the teeth, I remind myself that my track pants and paint-splattered sweatshirt aren't an apples-to-apples compar-ison. I'm judging my roll-out-of-bed choices against someone's carefully orchestrated highlight reel, not their day-to-day reality. I remind myself, yet I still allow the disparity to cause me stress.

Basically, I transferred the body image issues I'd assumed I'd out-grown to my wardrobe, which is problematic.

My dad is an inspiration in this area. Once, while on a family vacation, we bought souvenirs from an outdoor vendor selling Peace Frogs board shorts. The bottoms resembled flags from other countries. I picked the Australian flag (g'day!) and my brother opted for the Stars and Stripes. My father chose the flag of Kenya, equal bands of black, red, and emerald green, bisected with thin white lines, and accented with a shield and spear. He paired these with a navy and mustard striped rugby shirt and a tan bucket hat. He looked like a Mondrian painting about to go on a fishing expedition.

He could not be convinced that he didn't look fantastic.

"But it's all stripes," he argued.

He was right, but he was also very wrong. In a rare moment of solidarity, my mother, brother, and I banded together, refusing to leave for dinner with him until he turned the outfit down from an eleven.

While my dad was utterly content with the state of his closet and how he presented himself to the world, I suspect he'd have benefited from more of a Garanimals approach—where everything was meant to be mixed and matched. (Or possibly a color-blindness test.)

In fact, capsule wardrobes have been floating around in the fashion world ever since a London boutique owner brought the idea across the pond decades ago. Designer Donna Karan then took the idea into the mainstream with her Seven Easy Pieces concept that debuted in the mid-1980s.

Karan argued that women had mastered shortcuts when it came to family meal prep, but they often struggled to do the same with their wardrobe. So she designed a handful of key pieces that could be swapped up to create different looks along with a black bodysuit: a large scarf, a cashmere sweater, a chiffon blouse, a versatile skirt, loose trousers, a tailored jacket, and a white shirt.[46]

Basically, neutral Garanimals.

Would we feel less low-level dread if it were easier for us to dress ourselves? Would our lives be simpler if we took the stress of sartorial choices out of the equation?

For all the stressors in our world, those relating to fashion can be among the easiest to change. First, I'd like to urge you to stop measuring your outfit against others', and just as soon as I figure out how to do that myself, I'll report back. In the meantime, there are some simple steps to take.

If influencers are triggering your distress, mute them. (If we ignore them, I promise they'll go away.) Refuse to buy the goods they are "modeling." Stop shopping on Instagram.

If you're wrapped around the axle because your clothing doesn't fit, I can empathize. My resounding advice is to size up or down as needed. Trust me, a well-fitting 16 looks and feels a million times better than a too-small 12. Start to replace the core pieces in your wardrobe, and I guarantee that you'll start to—literally—breathe easier.

If you're unsure of what might flatter your figure, employ the free ministrations of department store stylists, or check out shopping services like Stitch Fix, who will pair you with stylists that send you suggested staples, and learn your taste as you decide to keep or return the pieces they select.

If your closet's too overloaded to make choices, be ruthless. Purge and donate.

If your budget's got you in a pinch, sell your unwanted items on reseller apps like eBay, Poshmark, or Mercari, where you can also buy new (to you) items at up to 90 percent off retail prices. Hit the RealReal if you want to splurge on authenticated designer items. Remember, there's zero shame in the very affordable thrift shop game.

Don't want to break the bank for a special occasion outfit? Short-term lease your couture from places like Rent the Runway or Style Lend. Want a constant variety of looks without the expense or commitment or ecological impact of filling your closet with fast fashion? Use subscription services like Le Tote or Gwynnie Bee. If your goal is a less stressful morning? Do what I finally figured out my senior year of high school—lay out your outfit the night before. This is far more appealing than showing up late and then listening to your stomach rumble until lunch hour.

Bottom line, clothes should make us feel good. We want what we wear to protect us, literally and metaphorically. Our garments should provide solace and happiness, should quiet our anxiety. At minimum, they should keep our bare asses from getting burned by the sun.

Try to cultivate your inner "my dad" and you'll care a whole lot less about external validation. FYI, you might need a few airplane bottles of Dewar's to aid in this process. Have Barbara pick them up for you if you're busy.

If you can't do any of the above, then please join me as I petition Warren Buffett to finally create Adult Garanimals.

Ideally, this new line will include many capes.

GIMME SHELTER

Close your eyes and picture the couch in your parents' house while you were growing up. Do you see it? My memory of our long, squared-off midcentury modern model is indelible. It had a low back and was upholstered in a navy-and-rust tweed. The couch weighed a ton and could have anchored a small yacht—a fact I rediscovered every time our German shepherd, Samantha, dropped her ball behind it.

Constructed on a solid hickory frame, the piece had been hand assembled and joined with dowels, a selling point my dad mentioned in lieu of helping me move it when I complained about how heavy it was. My parents had ordered it custom from somewhere in the Carolinas, right after they were married in the early '60s. Hidden beneath a cushion was a tag proudly proclaiming this fine piece of furniture was custom made for the Lancaster family of Wakefield, Massachusetts.

The couch followed us from our home in Wakefield, Massachusetts, to Randolph, Massachusetts, to Bergenfield, New Jersey, and finally on to Huntington, Indiana. Save for a trip to Disneyland when I was five, the couch was exactly as well traveled as I. Every time the movers grunted when they lifted that behemoth, I felt vindicated.

When I recall my childhood, this couch was a constant, bearing silent witness on sick days as I reclined with ginger ale and Bob Barker. From its vantage point, I witnessed so many of pop culture's highs and lows: President Nixon boarding Marine One for the last time as my mother cheered, Al Michaels shouting, "Do you believe in miracles?!" as the country cheered, and Michael Jackson moonwalking for the first time as the entire world cheered. That couch was there for birthday parties, Christmas mornings, weddings, funerals, and graduations; it was a member of the family.

There is a passage in *Fight Club*: "You buy furniture. You tell yourself, this is the last sofa I will ever need in my life. Buy the sofa, then for a couple years you're satisfied that no matter what goes wrong, at least you've got your sofa issue handled."[47] We had that couch for decades; our sofa issues were *handled*.

Notice that I have yet to mention comfort. My parents' couch was designed before people lounged for hours, Netflix-and-chilling. It was made for Mr. Cleaver to sit on, reading the evening paper in his business suit, while Mrs. Cleaver cooked a pot roast and Wally and the Beav tossed a ball on the front lawn.

(Note: Calling a bucktoothed kid "Beaver" is now considered bullying, a crime more damning than murder. Proceed at the risk of concerned internet strangers establishing a Kickstarter to pay for his orthodontics, which his aunt will then funnel into a secret account to purchase bigger boobs, a trip to Maui, and a motorcycle for her sidepiece.)

Anyway, the depth of the seating portion of Ol' Blue was the width and softness of your average bus bench, and the back was so low that to remain upright, you had to engage your abdominal muscles. It was the only couch in Christendom that would create a six-pack, instead of causing one to vanish. The position in which one could achieve a modicum of comfort was to sit with legs extended lengthwise, an impossible position as my mother, brother, and I had to share the space. There was a lot of kicking, on all our parts. No one was permitted to use my dad's buttery leather chair with its accompanying ottoman, and no one ever thought to question this imbalance of power.

The couch didn't face the TV—a deliberate choice on my father's part. He'd arranged the family room to be as unwelcoming as possible, a passively adverse environment where one would not want to linger. Like a bear in a den, he preferred to spend much of his time alone. We made too much noise. By "we," I mean my mother, whose constant need for attention caused her to narrate anything she saw on television. Long before surround sound was a thing, my father hung his Bose speakers upside down exactly twelve inches from the ceiling, and on either side of the television, for the best acoustics. He was surprisingly technically inclined when he stood to gain from the effort. My brother and I, though, would routinely smack our heads into the speakers—my mother was too short—and I believe that is the reason I still can't add fractions. My point here is, if anyone wanted to watch the color TV from the couch, they had to crane their necks at a ninety-degree angle.

The furniture in my grandparents' homes was equally iconic, but vastly more functional. My paternal grandparents' couch was a wide tufted kidney-shaped Danish banana model, covered in a pale green velvet. Nanny called it a divan, and she'd watch her stories from it. Everything about it screamed elegance and luxury, and she enjoyed entertaining company on it. That is . . . except for my mother. As for Noni and Grampa? Their sofa was old, red, and filled with enough horsehair and dust mites to set off an asthma attack in a distance runner.

As a member of Generation X, I grew up with furniture that was as permanent a fixture in my home as the tubs, toilets, and walls; it never changed. No matter what, the sun would rise, the sun would set, and anyone who wanted to watch a movie in my family room would end up with a stiff neck.

Flash forward to now—I'm hard pressed to remember the couch I owned five years ago. I think I've been through a dozen of them since college between moving, upgrading, and redecorating. While no less expensive than the piece my folks had commissioned, home items now have planned obsolescence. Furniture's not built to last a lifetime, and even if it were, people wouldn't want it to. Our relationship to shelter has changed.

My parents still use much of the furniture and household goods they registered for when they were married more than fifty years ago. Some of their Tupperware is older than me. (God have mercy on whomever didn't return that big round bowl with a celery-colored lid after a block party.) That was how it worked for their generation; you got hitched, you received useful gifts, and you were set for the rest of your natural life.

Our physiological need for shelter demands protection from heat, cold, dampness, bands of marauders, and anything that bites. In theory, we should be happy with a safe, dry cave, a warm fire, and a bed of leaves. Yet the reality is that many homeowners are completely stressed out by how dated the custom cherry cabinets they had installed in 2009 look.

Even cavemen drew on the walls to add a pop of color.

In an article for *Domino*, Marissa Hermanson traced the relationship between cultural happenings and interior decorating over the past 100 years. Design was certainly a consideration in the art deco–influenced 1920s, and with the utilitarian silhouettes of the 1930s when interior design came into the mainstream as a profession. Hermanson quoted architectural historian Richard Wilson: "If you look at the average, [of how] Americans lived 100 years ago compared to today, there's been an upgrade in the type of home you live in. There is more economic wealth—and more of a middle class and upper class."[48]

The birth of the modern middle class has been attributed to two factors: first, the GI Bill, which not only allowed returning vets to go to college, but also provided technical school education for those who wanted to learn more hands-on skills. The second factor was the creation of the Federal Housing Administration, which expanded the average person's access to credit. In the *Pittsburgh Post-Gazette*, Mark Roth reported, "The Federal Housing Administration, which had been set up in the middle of the Depression, helped spur the construction of thousands of new suburban houses with its mortgage insurance programs, and those housing developments were increasingly linked to major cities by the fast-growing Interstate Highway System."[49]

Ranch homes became the standard in the 1950s, with a design that connected the outdoors to the indoors. While this connection is now all anyone talks about on *House Hunters* (well, that and proximity to "transport"), this shift must have caused some cognitive dissonance. We're hardwired to desire protection from the outdoors. I wonder if we get a subconscious burst of adrenaline when we spot something bitey on the other side of all that glass.

New building materials were also introduced, such as linoleum and wall-to-wall carpeting. A common home renovation show refrain is "Why would anyone put linoleum over all this gorgeous hardwood?!" They did this because it was modern, durable, interesting, and easy to clean. Rest assured that when the next generation renovates your house, they're going to be screaming about all the goddamned shiplap.

The '60s also ushered in the advent of one of the retailers that elevated the home decor game: Crate & Barrel. This Chicago entity was founded by newlyweds Gordon and Carole Segal, who'd met as students at Northwestern. Gordon had worked in real estate and Carole was teaching first grade when they honeymooned in the Virgin Islands.

While in the Caribbean, Carole noticed all the imported Scandinavian design elements, so she bought some pieces to take home, as the couple hadn't received much from their pricey Marshall Field's registry.[50]

They came up with the idea to bring affordable, aesthetically pleasing items to Chicago. So, with the bulk of their wedding cash, they opened a retail establishment on Wells Street in Old Town, housed in a rustic old elevator factory. The Segals negotiated directly with manufacturers overseas to buy interesting contemporary designs that they then sold in their 1,700 square feet of retail space. They merchandised directly on the packing crates and shipping barrels that had been used to transport those treasures.

What truly flipped the switch for the Segals was when Carole sent Gordon up to the North Shore suburbs to go door to door, soliciting for a charity. Though he was impressed by the homes' fancy exteriors in Wilmette, he was underwhelmed once he peeked inside. "I said, 'Carole, you have no idea how you inspired me. I went into more homes that I thought would be beautiful that were so ugly, and we have so far to go and so little time to do it.' In the late 1960s and early 1970s, America had so little good taste and so little home furnishings. People would spend a lot of money on the outside of their homes and their cars, but very little on the intricacies of their homes."[51]

C&B expanded. Today, Marshall Field's is long gone, Old Town is prohibitively expensive, and no one gets married without a pricey Crate & Barrel registry.

As amenities became more available in the home, our focus turned further inward. With microwave ovens, people could make meals more quickly, so conceivably there was less impetus to dine out. With the advent of VCRs, cable TV, microwave popcorn, and comfortable furnishings, such as the La-Z-Boy recliner, there was less incentive to leave the house to watch a movie. Once people realized they were staying home more, the upgrades began in earnest. So prevalent was the trend to stay in and make our lives cozy that my parents even retired Ol' Blue after almost forty years of faithful service in the early 2000s, trading her in for a white leather monstrosity that appeared to have come straight off the *Miami Vice* set. Progress! (Sort of.)

Faith Popcorn initially named the trend "cocooning" in 1981, and she doubled down on the idea post-9/11 in an interview with the *Chicago Tribune*, predicting, "We'll see increases in home delivery, Internet shopping, virtual travel and home entertainment so we don't have to go out . . . Sparsely populated, remote areas will become the next boom towns. People think, 'Bin Laden wouldn't be interested in this place.' We'll see more gated communities. We'll make our homes cozier than ever, but we still have to make a living. Telecommuting and 'cashing out' (opting for simpler living) were already trends, but now we'll see even more of them. So we'll buy more home computers, comfortable clothing, home office furniture."[52]

Popcorn was right about all of this. After the terror attacks, people took the money they'd planned to spend on vacations and used it to renovate, improve, and update their homes, concentrating largely on their kitchens.[53]

The logical progression from being home more led to the advent of a seventeen-pound Restoration Hardware annual catalog and a profusion of TV shows that centered on the home. The first one I recall seeing was *Trading Spaces*, which premiered in 2000, although I didn't start watching until after I was laid off in 2001 and found myself with far too much time on my hands.

Based on the BBC series *Changing Rooms*, with the help of a designer and a $1,000 budget, two families traded homes for the weekend to make over a room in the other family's house. The show was a love letter to particleboard. Viewers appreciated picking up tips and tricks on how to upgrade with minimal expenditure, but that's not why everyone watched. Everyone tuned in to see what sort of chaos the eccentric designer Hildi Santo-Tomas would wreak in the home she designed.

As problematic as social media can be, I wish it had existed back in the *TS* heyday. Oh, to have had access to a Twitter stream during the episode where Hildi painted the walls of a room like a circus tent and covered the floor with sand. One hopes the family did not have cats. Or what about the room where Hildi shitcanned all the reasonable furniture and swapped it out for items made of cardboard?

Home flipping shows quickly popped up on a variety of networks, where savvy real estate investors would slap on some paint, upgrade the drawer pulls, and plant a few daisies in front, then resell the whole thing for a massive profit after a sixteen-dollar investment. These shows made HGTV a major player. Yet the network remained a contender because they pivoted when the bottom fell out of the housing market; instead of house flipping, they segued into home renovating.[54]

Somehow, the idea of shelter as the most basic need has morphed into a tangible demonstration of our value as people and an important expression of our souls, greatly upping the ante in terms of stress. At the dawn of humankind, those who survived were the ones who chose the caves that didn't flood during the rainy season. Now, we feel like we're going to die if we don't replace that dated popcorn ceiling.

I blame Chip and Joanna Gaines for this.

If you're unfamiliar with these two, they're the couple that entirely transformed the town of Waco, Texas, via their wildly popular show, *Fixer Upper*. In Waco, once best known for the Branch Davidian stand-off between David Koresh and the ATF, Chip and Joanna have created a new cult, one of affordable design. It's estimated that more than fifty thousand tourists come to town every week to visit their refurbished silos with twenty thousand square feet of retail space, where visitors happily purchase Magnolia merchandise.[55] For comparison, the Vatican sees around 140,000 tourists per week during its peak season. While my math isn't great (*see* stereophonics, family room), I'd say that boasting a third of the Vatican's numbers is not insignificant. I wonder if Chip and Joanna personally bless all the items they vend, like the pope does for the souvenirs being sold within the confines of the city-state[56]. If not, they're leaving money on the table.

For the record, I hate shiplap. I said what I said. Don't @ me.

Anyway, while shows like *Fixer Upper* are inspiring, they're also addicting. They have amped up the stakes around shelter. Suddenly, it's not enough to *watch* a kitchen renovation, we want these upgrades for our own homes, especially when our social media feeds are full of people living so much better than we do.

The pressure to maintain a Pinterest-perfect home environment has reached peak levels. Almost everyone I know has been through a kitchen or bathroom renovation in the past seven years. What had been a trend has bloomed into a full-blown obsession. One of my friends lives in a suburb where renovations are so frequent, there's an ongoing signup list to bring dinners to whatever family is currently without a kitchen. (This list is also used when moms in the community have elective plastic surgery.)

And there is a clear risk involved in all of this upgrading. The *St. Louis Post-Dispatch* ran an article urging readers to ask themselves three key questions before deciding to keep up with the Joneses:

1. Are you ever going to move?
2. Will you need to finance?
3. Have you done your research?[57]

While personal enjoyment is a factor, it shouldn't be the only consideration, especially when so many Americans are underwater on their homes, thanks to the insanity of the housing market prior to the crash a decade ago. Yet that didn't stop Fletch and me from feeling the pressure to keep up.

He and I lived in rentals for most of our post-college life. Every time something would break, we'd shrug and call our landlord to fix it. Then we bought our house and we stopped shrugging. We've since learned that while it's nice to have pleasing aesthetics, square footage, and the latest tech, it would have been smarter to invest in infrastructure over upgrades. Also, new furnaces are expensive, and it's almost impossible to type up a new manuscript while wearing mittens.

My friend Stacey did it right. She lived on the bottom floor of a three-flat for twenty-three years before she had the opportunity to purchase the building, something she'd been dreaming about since the day she'd moved in her first milk crate full of albums a couple of years after college.

"I walked in and the building literally gave me a hug and whispered in my ear, 'You're home now,' in a way that was completely visceral," she told the *Chicago Tribune*.[58]

Instead of financing, she and her husband took four years to renovate the building into a single-family home, slowly chipping away at projects. Not to be morbid, but she plans to die in this house, so every detail has been planned to support the journey from middle age to end of life. She even installed an elevator and made sure the doors are wide enough to accommodate wheelchairs.

Stacey's a tremendous home cook and a well-known food writer. You've never seen a more Instagram-ready house. However, you won't see her Instagram-ready house because her feed is mostly ad hoc pictures of the weird food combinations she's developing for recipes, like her French-onion-dip pancakes. She didn't put all that work in to impress others; she just wanted a place where she and her husband could grow old. She's an inspiration.

So approaching renovations and redecorating with a little bit of common sense can help abate the stress we feel about our homes. But ending the discussion there would ignore the concern of almost every millennial I know.

An entire generation is putting off homeownership. They're marrying later, they're congregating in urban areas where property prices are astronomical, and they're mired in student loan debt.[59] Saving up the down payment is a huge barrier to entry.

Connor, my comedy spirit animal in the horn-rims and popped collars, is the only one of my millennial friends who owns property. The night we performed our first sets on the Second City stage, the class headed to his place in Old Town to celebrate, not far from the original Crate & Barrel location.

Fletch and I marveled at how nice his place was—the decor, the window treatments, the U-shaped couch. All of it, lovely and perfect. He even had art!

"Did we live like this in our twenties?" I asked Fletch.

"You had six cats in a studio apartment and a mattress you scavenged from the garbage when I met you," he replied. "So, no."

I guess that's why Fletch and I overcompensated when we bought our house. Sure, we had to have a fridge, but did we really need side-by-side Sub-Zeros? And those extra bathrooms? While the purchase made sense at the height of the market and my career, for the past few years, this place has become an endless financial drain and tremendous source of anxiety.

What should have been a slam dunk in terms of satisfying a basic need is now a perpetually unchecked box at the bottom of Maslow's pyramid. I admit it; I was sucked into the HGTV hype. Like Stacey, my goal was to die in the new home; I told Fletch this house was my Grey Gardens. But my concern is that if something doesn't change, the stress of trying to keep it all running is going to kill me instead. Some days it feels like I am one babushka away from becoming Little Edie.

But it's not just me feeling this way, I know that. So many of us are still no different than prehistoric man, metaphorically worrying about our spacious low-lying caves and rising rivers.

I wonder, how much of our basic-needs-based anxiety could we abate if we were just to pack up our capes and avocado toasts and couches and move to a smaller cave on less Instagram-ready higher ground?

For all our sakes, I hope there's no shiplap there.

PART III

SAFETY NEEDS: PERSONAL/FINANCIAL SECURITY, CLIMATE, AND FAMILY HEALTH

In Maslow's second tier of the hierarchy, he addressed the human need for safety and security, both physical and financial, noting that factors outside of what are predictable can be cause for anxiety.

No shit.

LIFE IS HAZARDOUS TO YOUR HEALTH

You are going to die because life is going to kill you.

Seemingly daily, researchers report on new and common substances that are hazardous to our health and have been proven to cause cancer in laboratory rats. Every damn thing has an effect on those poor little rodents, from cell phones to sugar to soda.

The message is clear: don't be a lab rat.

Medical science is taking the fun out of most things. The latest study shows that the consumption of hot tea is linked to esophageal cancer; can you imagine anything less rock and roll than *hot tea* causing cancer?

Is cancer *specifically* targeting NPR listeners now?

The discovery of the tea-cancer connection makes me irrationally angry, as drinking tea is one of those acts I connect with proper health. What's next? Is yoga gonna give us all the clap? Might flossing bring on the herp? Will looking both ways before we cross make us go blind?

On the upside, this tea thing may explain why your sainted Irish gam-gam has passed and Keith Richards is still banging nineteen-year-old supermodels.

The research of the tea study, which was conducted in Golestan, a region of Iran, concluded, "As there is no known health benefit from drinking very hot beverages, it will be reasonable to advise people in

Golestan and elsewhere to wait for their hot beverages to cool down before drinking."[60]

It's tempting to live life according to the dictates in every study. Science! Advice! But the trick is to consider the source. Given enough financial resources, anyone can commission anything to prove or disprove findings that coincide with their bottom line. For example, the Parsnip Ranchers of America are never going to introduce findings on why we should eat fewer root vegetables. That said, I can't imagine that the iced tea conglomerates commissioned studies in Golestan on the benefits and drawbacks of scalding one's mouth, so I'm not going to question that one.

But I'm more willing to accept the link between cancer and voluntary/hedonistic/fun acts, like HPV and unprotected sex and cancer, or smoking and cancer, or the overconsumption of alcoholic beverages and cancer, or fatty fried foods and cancer. But Earl freaking Grey? Really? What's causing the next round of malignancies—cardigans? Sensible shoes? Reusable canvas tote bags? Come on! While I'm glad the medical community makes strides in improving our collective health, I don't want a two-hundred-year lifespan if that means two centuries of absolutely no pleasure. If I'm forced to add hot tea to the issues that keep me awake at night—the very thing I use to aid my sleep—I give up.

I do, on the other hand, appreciate medical researchers informing us and keeping us safe from what's completely stupid. For example, not long after Marie Curie discovered she could isolate radium salts from pitchblende, manufacturers started adding radium to everything—chocolate, water, toothpaste, et cetera—because it was supposed to possess magical restorative powers.[61]

Spoiler alert: it did not.

My good grandparents kept a radium-painted alarm clock in their bedroom, which eventually ended up taking residence in mine. It took decades for the country to completely discontinue all casual radium usage. Also, I'm pretty sure the radium is responsible for my inability to know where to place the word "only" in a sentence. Listen, I can only do so much, even with a copyeditor.

Additional spoiler alert: Curie died from leukemia, resulting from radiation exposure, thus proving radium is neither a suitable vitamin substitute *nor* grammar builder.

Radium isn't even the most outrageous substance medical science previously considered safe and healthful. At the turn of the last century, Bayer added heroin to a cough suppressant. *Heroin.* Can you imagine buying smack at Walgreens? "Say, Agatha, do you fancy chasing the dragon this evening?" "Why, sure, Theodore! Let us twenty-three skid-doo out of here and swing over to the apothecary!"

By 1906, the American Medical Association green-lit heroin for use in lieu of morphine, and soon there were more than 200,000 heroin addicts in New York City alone.[62]

Let's not forget that Coca-Cola derives its name from its original active ingredient, cocaine. When John Stith Pemberton created the beverage in 1886, his formula was three parts coca leaves and one part cola nut, and it was marketed as a substitute for alcohol.[63] So . . . the public had access to OTC cocaine-based products as well as those laced with heroin, all in the name of well-being? My God, can you imagine how annoying everyone must have been at parties back then? Laudanum used to be sold as a medicine. If you're unfamiliar, it's an alcohol extract *laced with opium,* marketed as a "veritable preservative of infants."[64] For every new mother who feels shame that she's not blending up her own farm-to-table, vegetable-based organic baby food in the Vitamix, remember that parents once thought it was a capital idea to dose toddlers with the big *O.* (Were . . . were they expecting their children to pen *Kubla Khan?*)

Other cough syrups once contained chloroform, which is an anesthetic. One chloroform-soaked rag and boom! Defenseless victim— according to *Law & Order.* I can't speak to whether or not the treatment rid people of their coughs, but maybe they just didn't care once they entered night-night mode.

Even after patients died from cardiac and respiratory complications from chloroform use back in the day, the FDA didn't ban it from human consumption *until it caused cancer in laboratory rats*. Dead people? *Meh.* Dead rats? *We'd best pass a law!*

My favorite of all the painfully unhealthy ideas was the *suppository* that contained Nembutal, a barbiturate. This medicine was administered to children to help them sleep and in stressful situations, with the bonus of no "morning-after hangover."[65]

Is anyone else surprised that humanity isn't already completely extinct? That our ancestors lived long enough to not win Darwin Awards is testament to our hard-to-kill nature.

I'm glad I was born when I was. Growing up in the 1970s, nothing was dangerous and the world felt free from stress. My brother and I were robust and healthy because my mom sprinkled wheat germ from the hippie commune on our cereal. Our generation felt safe because nothing ever seemed to happen. While all the good drugs had been pulled from the shelves, mine was a time of perfect stasis.

Lately, it feels as though everything is engineered to cause our demise. Anyone with an internet connection is suddenly an expert on longevity. God forbid a good Samaritan sees your sons and daughters consume from a BPA-laden bottle or ride their bikes to the end of the driveway without kneepads, elbow protectors, a helmet, and a mouth guard, because the onslaught of social shaming means you'll never be invited to the block party again. Permit your eight-year-old to walk Marshmallow, the family dog, around the block and completely within your line of sight, and someone *will* call the Wilmette police.[66] Try not to be stressed as you're investigated for neglect and abuse by the Illinois Department of Children and Family Services, 'kay?

What a miserable time to be alive.

My generation had it easier. When my friends and I were thirsty as kids, we drank from the garden hose, which was not only our primary form of summer entertainment *and* refreshment, but also our favorite weapon. The hose was all things to all people. Now kids can't confidently drink from the tap.

While *rates* of cancer diagnoses and cancer deaths continue to decline each year, the *number* of new cases and deaths is going up, per the CDC.[67] We're not yet out of the woods.

At my childhood home, we owned the same bottle of Coppertone SPF 8 for most of my young life. Said sunscreen lasted from 1973 to 1982, until my mother finally disposed of it, self-diagnosing her rash as an allergy to PABA and not connecting it to the fact that the bottle was vintage enough to be considered a collector's item. In my preteen years, I'd take my *Frampton Comes Alive!* double album, cover it in aluminum foil, and lay out holding it just so, reflecting the rays onto my skin—which had been coated in baby oil cut with iodine. Were it not for cosmeceutical science, my skin would now resemble a deflated kickball.

Neither my brother nor I were required to wear seat belts in the back seat when we were kids. Hell, until a recent Uber ride, I didn't even realize they *made* seat belts for the back of the Delta 88. Sure, now everyone's offspring can watch movies on their personal entertainment systems, but the trade-off is they must be strapped in Hannibal Lecter–style to do so. Still, I'd have taken that deal in a hot minute. You don't know boredom until your best option is to listen to a baseball game on AM as you traverse the surprisingly wide state of Pennsylvania.

The family took only one vacation that required airplane tickets, and that's because my father couldn't figure out how to drive to Hawaii. Maybe because his job required so many flights, there was something novel about piloting himself to a destination. In the car, we played by Ron Lancaster's Rules, which did not include "meals" or "biological necessity." Of course, when the only beverages in the car were a couple of lukewarm Tabs and a single diet tonic water, no one ever had to pee, so it worked out. The man did not believe in dawdling—ours was a singular goal: to get to our destination in much the same fashion as a long-haul truck driver.

We weren't the kind of family who'd make a sport of the road trip, singing songs or telling stories, although once my brother and I played a game of trying to catch a fly trapped in the car, assuming it was the only protein we'd get until we reached our destination. Mostly, we slept. My father was famous for announcing we'd leave at seven o'clock, then sneaking into our rooms, stealing our clocks, and hustling us into the car where some careless overnight DJ would announce it was three in the morning. My mother was never in on his plan and was perpetually furious about the ruse, but my father didn't care, as we were "beating traffic."

FYI, there's surprisingly little traffic between Huntington, Indiana, and Akron, Ohio.

Also, I suspect tired children are quiet children.

As a kid, my biggest dream was having a station wagon for these family trips, so my brother and I would have the luxury of stretching out in our own individual rows. What I would have done for a station wagon with optional third-row seating!

The larger station wagons—embellished with wood paneling, because what says "aerodynamics" like trees—used to have a jump seat next to the tailgate that could be folded up or down as needed. The seat faced backward and had no safety restraints or head support. To sit in the way-way back was to position oneself inches away from the potential of being showered with broken glass and punctured with jagged steel.

Also? Just imagine how it must have creeped out other motorists to see a row full of doomed kids staring at them.

When not on road trips, my brother and I flew around the back of the family car like howler monkeys hopped up on Pixy Stix, and no one found this problematic or dangerous. If we were truly badly behaved, engaging in our usual shouting and shoving (and biting—I was a biter), both my parents had mastered the art of disjointing their shoulders to smack us into compliance, their eyes never leaving the road. Try doing that now, I dare you. The state troopers would have you facedown at gunpoint faster than you could say "corporal punishment."

Ultimately, children weren't much cause for concern during my childhood, save for one specific and puzzling preoccupation of my mother's. On outings, my mother would stake herself in front of the men's room, as she was paranoid that someone would, argh, how do I say this, *emasculate* my brother, leaving him a eunuch, left huddled in a stall, surrounded by a puddle of his own blood. So instead of the real possibility of the molestation, abduction, or murder of an unaccompanied minor male in a public restroom, she assumed the bad guy would just . . . take a to-go bag with him for later?

While my mother was emotional, she wasn't irrational, so I assumed there was a basis for her paranoia. People couldn't verify specious information in the 1970s. We didn't have Wi-Fi. Our best defense was the phone number to the library. In Bergenfield, reference librarians were on standby, waiting to resolve dinner-table arguments. We never did think to call about the bathroom thing, though.

Recently, with no small amount of fearing that the search might put me on a *list*, I googled the castration story anyway, assuming it had to have come from somewhere. Turns out, the slashing trope has been a common concern for decades, with origins in . . . wait for it . . . systemic racism!

In each iteration of the fable, the attacker was a minority, taking part in a gang initiation. In fact, a version of this story dates to the fifth century AD, when European versions had Jews torturing and killing a Christian child. This dovetails into the "Blood Simple" legend, wherein minorities were out to torture the helpless. Per folklorist Jan Brunvand, "As we observe many times in folklore, the prejudices and stereotypes that people are reluctant to voice in direct terms will often surface in very obvious ways in their oral-narrative traditions of joke or legend."[68]

Please note that no one—of any color—ever touched my brother's ding-dong, and I'm sure he appreciated my mother's misguided vigilance in retrospect.

Maybe life seemed so much less stressful back then because we only feared the random bathroom slashers turning our brothers into geldings. Having been a nation at war for so long at the end of the Vietnam War–era, the country had shared a common enemy for decades. Once we settled into peace, we'd become so accustomed to conflict, we turned our hatred, fear, and suspicion on each other.

What gets me is why this bathroom degree of caution didn't apply to more plausible situations when I was growing up. Kids were by themselves all the time. Mine was the first generation of latchkey kids, referring to Generation Xers whose personal identity was, in part, shaped by the independence their working parents fostered when they left us alone after school.[69] In the state of Illinois now, I'd have to be fourteen years old before I could stay home alone. At fourteen, I was a freshman in high school, earning a dollar an hour to watch other people's children. By the time I was sixteen, I earned the big bucks staying with kids all weekend while their parents were out of town.

But the lack of supervision was also systemic. Every fall, students were tasked with going door to door for fundraisers—hawking gift wrap, popcorn, and candies. What could possibly go wrong with sending unattended fourth graders to hundreds of strangers' houses?

I lived in a town called Randolph in first and second grade. My house was three-quarters of a mile from a corner convenience store, next to a busy road. The minute I scraped together twenty-five cents, I set off on my own to buy candy. Occasionally, when aunts and older cousins would visit, they'd send me out to pick up cigarettes, as everyone born prior to 1965 was required by law to smoke then. People did it everywhere—I'm talking hospitals, restaurants, and churches.

Sometimes I'd go to the grocery store with my dad on Saturday, and he'd smoke in the aisles as we shopped. People lit up at their desks in office buildings. I recorded an audiobook recently in an older building on Chicago's Wacker Drive. There were still ashtrays built into the wall in the ladies' room. Cigarettes were once so ubiquitous, they required accommodations for smoking on the can.

Anyway, the clerks at the corner store always sold me cigarettes. Let me reiterate: *they sold cigarettes to a seven-year-old in 1974.* It's possible I had a note with me, and everyone knows that grade-schoolers would never forge documents to their own benefit. I didn't care. I was happily complicit because I was allowed to put the change toward a 3 Musketeers bar.

Were children simply more expendable back then?

Of course, Noni and Grampa couldn't believe how coddled my generation was, considering no one forced us to work in button factories to help feed the family. The Fair Labor Standards Act wasn't passed until 1938, and this set the criteria for both allowable hours and ages of workers.[70] Said laws didn't apply to my husband at ten years old, because he was forced to help at his dad's second job excavating in the 1970s. He'd scoop dirt out of crawl spaces with a coffee can, as he was the only one small enough to climb into the tight spaces under rickety old buildings.

Expendable.

After we moved to New Jersey, my family used to road-trip in the summer to visit Noni and Grampa in the Boston suburbs. Often, other relatives would be there, too, as they all lived locally. I was always most excited to see my cousin Nicholas. He was eight years my junior and profoundly beautiful, one of the most gorgeous kids I've ever seen, with an equally lovely temperament.

Nick had a glossy brown bowl cut, huge almond eyes, and lashes that bordered on ridiculous. He should have been in commercials because the whole world would have bought whatever breakfast cereal he was hawking. He was the youngest cousin from a family of eight siblings, so given his tender age, his looks, and his sunny disposition, the whole extended family adored and indulged him.

When a group of us would go to the Montrose in Wakefield to pick up ice cream, Grampa or Uncle David would sit baby Nick on their laps in the Thunderbird and allow him to steer because he got such a kick out of it. Forty-plus years later, the thought of this gives me hives. On what planet do we allow a two-year-old to navigate? No one ever deemed this a terrible idea, including his parents *who were Harvard educated.* Other motorists, including law enforcement, would smile and wave, charmed by the notion of allowing a baby to drive.

It may be germane to mention that Wakefield, where I was born, had a massive Hells Angels presence. A couple of days before my second birthday, 25,000 Hells Angels gathered on the town commons to rally in support of the Vietnam War (not a typo, many were vets), a block away from my house. A pair of Hells Angels almost ran me over in the street during a drag race. Please note the dual mantle of responsibility here, as I was a toddler *playing in the street.*

Speaking of childhood recklessness, hitchhiking was another totally normal activity in the 1970s. Everyone did it. My parents had only one car, and occasionally my mother would thumb us a ride home from downtown. She stopped this practice by the time I went to grade school, but I distinctly recall being in a stranger's Country Squire, pissed that I wasn't offered the optional third-row bench seat.

What's funny is that everyone's so appalled by the notion of hitch-hiking now, yet it's totes fine if we pay five dollars for the privilege of riding in a stranger's Lyft.

All of this brings me to my point that the need for safety is the second tier of motivation in Maslow's Hierarchy—personal, emotional, and financial security, as well as health and well-being. Per the *Washington Post*, there's never been a safer time in America to be a kid.

But that begs the question—are kids safer now because parents are hyperprotective or are parents hyperprotective to keep kids safer?

However it works out, child mortality rates are at an all-time low. In 1935, there were 450 deaths for every 100,000 children between the ages of one and four, and now, it's more like 30 per every 100,000.[71]

Even though children in my generation were allowed—sometimes even encouraged—to find ourselves in safety-compromised positions, the only real effect was our becoming independent. Oh, and cynical. Also, super anxious.

(It's possible free ranging wasn't the best parenting call.)

Maybe my generation's parents were less cautious because they didn't spend $100,000 to get us here. Now, with parents having fewer children and getting pregnant when they're older, it makes sense that each kid is a little more precious. This makes me think of the Birkin handbag that comes with a little raincoat to protect the leather. Owners carry these plastic covers at all times, slipping them on the second it looks like rain. No one wants to carelessly ruin a purse that starts at $10,000. Perhaps this is the same concept with kids.

There was a time that a chart-topping concern moms and dads had was their children falling into a well, à la Baby Jessica, the event that helped put fledgling new network CNN on the map.

What changed?

Are there fewer wells?

Was it Adam Walsh, whose kidnapping and subsequent murder spurred the creation of the show *America's Most Wanted*? Was it Polly Klaas, who was abducted from her own slumber party, with her entire family under the same roof? Or was it the still-unsolved JonBenét Ramsey case, where the child beauty queen was thought to have been taken from her home, but was instead found dead in the family wine cellar?

I can't point causality at any one incident. What I can say is these cases solidified my desire to not have children, because being a parent seemed way too scary as I headed into my peak reproductive years.

Of all the terrible child-murder cases, the JonBenét case impacted me the most. I recall buying every *People* magazine with her image on the cover. I wanted justice for her. I fell for what PBS's Gwen Ifill called "missing white woman syndrome": a disproportionate quantity of media coverage for upper-middle-class white women who disappear, like Natalee Holloway, Laci Peterson, and Elizabeth Smart, in comparison with missing men, boys, women of color, and people of lower socioeconomic status.[72]

Beyond the tragedy, the notion of child beauty pageants riveted the country. My God, that was shocking. I recoiled at the idea of little girls being forced into adult hair, makeup, and spangles, required to perform, even though that had all the earmarks of something I'd love. Lipstick, tutus, and cheering? Sign me up.

Maybe the JonBenét case struck home because the coverage was the most salacious, truly cementing the twenty-four-hour-news networks' newfound hold on the nation.

Regardless of how stunned we were in 1996, cultural norms rapidly readjust, especially when aided by the media. The pageant thing was featured so heavily and frequently in the JonBenét reporting that eventually viewers became desensitized, making way for the TLC show *Toddlers & Tiaras*. In the span of fifteen years, I went from scandalized to shouting at my screen when young contestants tried to skate through to the Grand Supreme title without wearing fake lashes or flippers (the row of small dentures made to cover up gaps from lost baby teeth).

Regardless of better or worse, change is both inevitable and hasty.

The paradox of living in the safest possible time is that those who suffer from anxiety aren't hardwired to take the win; we panic when things go too well.

In a *Huffington Post* interview, clinical psychologist Carla Marie Manly explained the physiology behind our brain's fear response: "The brain's fear circuit works very quickly, and it doesn't always pause to differentiate between good anxiety and bad. So, when something good happens, the physical symptoms you feel are similar to those that you associate with panic or fear. But even when you are able to distinguish between feelings of excitement (good stress) and panic (bad stress) following a dose of success, the climb down from Mount Euphoria can be an anxiety trigger in itself. When your body becomes accustomed to a chronic state of anxiety, the positive physiological changes that happen after good news can, paradoxically, trigger the sense that something isn't right—simply because you're not used to feeling good. As a result, your body never fully lets go of its hypervigilant state."[73]

This is also why your cat bites you during a blissful belly rub.

Like me, if you're already predisposed to anxiety, positive or negative stimulus on social media can make you feel worse, largely because of the algorithms. At its advent, all updates on apps such as Twitter were delivered chronologically and per our preferences. But now our usage data is measured and monetized, and algorithms put more emotionally weighted events in our timelines, such as engagements, births, and significant accomplishments.[74] Plus, the system gives us real time metrics about our own popularity, vis-à-vis likes, follows, retweets, et cetera. Again, this leads us to compare everyone's highlight reel to our day-to-day reality, and it's a drain on our mental well-being.

The phenomenon of "comparing up" on social media triggers two kinds of anxiety: trait anxiety, which entails persistent and lasting tension related to worry and fear, and state anxiety, which is a temporary response to what feels threatening.[75] Before the advent of sharing our lives via media, opportunities for comparison were far fewer. Our scope of influence entailed those who we ran into daily, largely coworkers, the occasional neighbor, and immediate family. Things only became competitive when braggy acquaintances would send out the annual Christmas letter. We looked forward to my mother's college roommate's card every year. My brother and I would fight over who'd read aloud that family's sterling accomplishments in the most derisive manner.

While I was better at pronouncing the SAT words, my brother could bring the drama.

There was a layer between us and our peers. We didn't measure ourselves against people on TV and in magazines. The untouchability of fame insulated us from its pressures. Now, with Twitter and Instagram, we can tweet at Kim Kardashian and there's a possibility she might react; the barrier has been removed. My theory is that with everyone on the same platform, there's an inherent assumption of equality, but when folks like the Kardashians post shots of buying Bentleys, we feel like we're not, in fact, keeping up.

On the upside, social media can make us feel less alone, providing a crucial shot of dopamine when we need a physiological pick-me-up, for example, when the whole world's reacting to *Game of Thrones* at the exact same time. (As I edit this manuscript, the Twitterverse is losing its collective mind over a Starbucks cup accidentally left on a table during the battle for Winterfell, and the "Coffee Is Coming" memes are perfection.)

On the downside, our postbaby bods are never going to look like Kylie Jenner's—ever—and there's a strong possibility we'll let this wear us down when we see it time and again in our feeds.

Because our emotional security is impacted by our sense of economic security, one of the best ways to mitigate stress is to get our finances in order. No small task, right? My expertise does not lie in crunching the numbers or what our country should do about the state of health care, but I can speak to *why* money triggers us: it's directly linked to our feelings of security, and these feelings impact our health.

The American Psychological Association has been charting stressors since 2007, and financial issues have consistently polled in the top spot since the inception of the study.

Per the APA, people are "putting their health-care needs on hold because of financial concerns. Nearly 1 in 5 Americans say that they have either considered skipping (9 percent) or skipped (12 percent) going to a doctor when they needed health care because of financial concerns. Stress about money also affects relationships: Almost a third of adults with partners (31 percent) report that money is a major source of conflict in their relationships."[76]

Health organizations have begun advocating for better understanding around the mind-body-wallet connection. *Forbes* reported that "chronic stress is linked to physical health issues. High stress causes a fight-or-flight reaction, releasing adrenaline and cortisol. These hormones can suppress immune, digestive, sleep and reproductive systems, which, if sustained, may cause them to stop working normally. Employees with high financial stress are twice as likely to report poor health overall and are more than four times as likely to complain of headaches, depression, or other ailments."[77]

So having our minds on our money and our money on our minds is degrading our health. In a newsletter from Goldman Sachs, financial coach Elisabeth Donati said, "Financial stress seems to trump almost every other kind of stress except health stress. When that drive can't be attained—you can't pay your rent, you can't pay for your car, you can't feed your kids—it compounds the stress."[78]

I don't have some magical key that will lessen our emotional connection to finances, and I can't offer suggestions to curb spending as a path to financial freedom, although those would be two outstanding solutions. (Perhaps you should have bought a book by Suze Orman instead of this one.) But I *am* an expert in worrying about the stress that out-of-control finances can cause.

Shortly after 9/11, my husband and I both lost our jobs, having just started to find professional success. As our financial situation morphed from annoying to dire, he sank into a depression deep enough to require medical intervention. While documenting this experience became my first memoir and changed the course of both our lives for the better, I couldn't think about the future: I was too busy trying to get him through the day to day.

Not getting stress under control can lead to serious consequences.

According to the Centers for Disease Control and Prevention, suicide rates increased more than 30 percent from 1999 to 2016.[79] The Aspen Institute further examined these numbers, finding "more than half of people who die by suicide do not have a history of depression or mental illness. Almost 30 percent of suicides occur in response to a crisis within the past two weeks and 16 percent occur in response to a financial problem."[80]

It's no mistake that Maslow's Hierarchy is set up as a triangle, with each level of anxiety sitting atop the last, like a mounting pile of concern. The issue of safety rests upon the basic needs like a sweet, smothering blanket. In modern society, our access to food, shelter, adequate sleep, and exercise are connected in a symbiotic relationship with our financial safety. They share deep roots in our anxiety. So while the Instagram posts and reality shows are creating increased envy and stress around food, weight, and homes, that envy and stress leads us to spend more, feel worse, and put our financial security at risk, which puts our mental health at risk. Again, it would help if we could just chill a bit and ignore some of the constant marketing and social pressure to be and have the most popular and sleekest basic needs.

Easier said than accomplished.

If we could just pour that same enthusiasm and competitive élan we use for accumulating things, renovating, or attaining better sleep into our savings accounts and FICO scores, we might start to undo that toxic connection.

Truthfully, I don't know how to break that cycle completely. But there is a possible, actionable work-around that can lessen the financial stressors and the anxiety and disharmony these cause. My chief suggestion is to think like a millennial and find yourself a rewarding side hustle.

A side hustle is any type of employment worked in conjunction with one's full-time job. Usually these gigs are freelance or piecework in nature, and provide a supplemental income.[81]

My Second City millennials introduced me to the term, explaining that it creates a cash-flow stream outside of their primary source of income. Some of them walk dogs, nanny, or drive for Lyft. In Connor's case, he side-hustles as an angel investor.

"So it's a part-time job," I offered. "Because then I've been side-hustling since I worked at the Olive Garden *and* Casual Corner in college. This is not a new thing."

Yet, it is.

The difference is that a side hustle is typified by flexible hours and spurred by passion. While I was an early fan of their unlimited bowls of salad, I have never defined the Olive Garden as a passion, nor was Casual Corner flexible, regardless of the relaxed-and-spontaneous-sounding store name.

Turns out, half of all millennials have at least occasional side hustles.[82] Young people all over are reselling items on eBay or fixing up a spare room to rent out on Airbnb. If you're in a pinch, it's worth a shot. If you love films, maybe you find a side hustle as a movie extra. If you're into writing, consider publishing your own e-book. If you're good at something—and you want to increase your monthly income—follow the millennial example and give yourself a cushion doing that which you enjoy, on your own timeline.

If there's any antidote to stress about financial security and its resulting impact on health, I'd say earning money while finding purpose and meaning would be right at the top of the list. So why not start marketing those cute animals you've been felting out of dryer lint on Etsy? Find driving meditative? Do a few hours of Lyft a week.

The bottom line is that stress is going to kill us, so we need to find better ways to manage it.

Whatever we can do to be healthier and more secure now, it's worth the effort . . . before medical science discovers that tacos and bulldog puppies are linked to obesity and they ruin every damn thing yet again.

GLOBAL WARRING

When I was a kid, the only mention I recall of the environment—referred to as "ecology" back then—came from a Keep America Beautiful public service announcement. In the television ad, a Native American—referred to as an "Indian" back then—paddles his canoe through the wilds of nature, to the sound of tribal drums beating. His face is weathered and wise, his gaze gimlet. Clad in head-to-toe buckskin, his long black braids hang down to his beaded belt. As he navigates the ancestral waters, the fringe from his sleeves flaps in the clean, crisp breeze. Just the white man's central-casting ideal of how an indigenous person should look.

Clearly this man in fringed everything is a pro, as he's not completely soaked from getting dumped into the river fifteen times over the course of his trip, unlike every other person who ever thought it could be "fun" to rent a canoe for the day.

As he travels, the music's intensity increases and the horn section joins in. We see debris accumulating in the water by his paddle. The first bit of garbage appears to be a floating pamphlet. Since the PSA's intent was to amp up our interest in receiving ecology pamphlets, I wonder that no one caught this irony in the editing process.

The music swells as he paddles into a bay, passing factories that spit toxic smoke into the air. Hulking container ships loom ominously at dock in the background. The scene is a post-apocalyptic hellscape. Pollution aside, this location is not ideal for recreational small-craft boating.

He makes his way to the shoreline and disembarks on a rocky, filthy beach, completely strewn with water-logged garbage. A narrator begins a passive-aggressive voice-over about how *some* people have a respect for the country's natural beauty. He says this in the same tone you'd use in your office's kitchenette, where you point out that *some* people refuse to rinse out their yogurt bowls, leaving the crusty relics in the sink for days, when we all know good and goddamned well it's Susan, and she's just sitting there, feigning innocence while playing solitaire on her phone, as though she's never even *heard* of Activia.

The canoer loiters silently by a busy highway, choked with huge gas-guzzling automobiles, whipping past him at dizzying speeds. A careless passenger tosses a fast-food bag out of the window, and the sack lands with a wet splat on the guy's moccasins—particularly hurtful when you consider how difficult suede is to clean.

We pan up, only now taking in with full appreciation the kind of pants that David Lee Roth would die to wear onstage a decade later, coming to stop on the man's expression. There's a single tear about to stream down his noble brown face as the narrator says, "People start pollution; people can stop it."

I was three or four years old when the PSA started airing, and that shit was sadder than when Bambi's mom died. All I wanted to do was watch *Sesame Street* and maybe have a nonlethal vampire teach me how to count to ten, but nooooo. Instead, I bore witness to man's inhumanity toward man and Mother Earth and suddenly everything felt meaningless, and just like that, I turned into the world's youngest nihilist.

On the bright side, while littering was commonplace in the late '60s and early '70s, this commercial set forth a guilt that thrived in me, and to this day I always put my trash in a can. It's also why I will eventually get stabbed in the neck for chasing someone down, saying, "Hi! You dropped this!" while handing their discarded Starbucks cup back to them.

Had more PSAs been made, had the concept of protecting the earth been emphasized with more frequency when I was still impressionable, I may have joined Greenpeace, or at least I would have taken environmental concerns far more seriously, far sooner. But nobody did, save for one of my cousins. Instead, what came out was that Iron Eyes Cody, the actor who claimed parentage in a few different tribes and played the PSA's Native American, was Sicilian.

So . . . Native Italian.

For me, my environmental gateway drug was Hurricane Harvey. Prior to that horrific event, I wouldn't say I was a global-warming denier, so much as I assumed cleaning up after myself and being child-free was the entirety of what I was willing to do about that whole carbon footprint business. Also, I couldn't help wondering how recycling my four Tab cans per week could counteract the pollution damage from hundreds of thousands of Chinese factories. I'd say to myself, "Environment? That sounds like a *you people* problem."

I moved about my life, driving my SUV, mixing all my garbage in a single trash bag, and keeping my home and pool chilled or heated to my specific comfort levels. If I wanted to wear a sweatshirt indoors during the summer, or a T-shirt in winter, that was *my choice*. I wasn't loading up the earth with four kids' worth of disposable diapers and Go-GURT tubes.

My environmental considerations were driven entirely by geological disaster movies such as *2012*, *Armageddon*, and *The Day After Tomorrow*. Flooding footage is my fave, and I'm still mad that the Rock never took off his shirt during *San Andreas*. That was the *real* disaster, in my opinion.

Then Harvey hit and my perspective shifted.

While the content scrounged up to fill the twenty-four-hour news cycle is a tremendous source of our collective stress, there was nothing manufactured about the storm that caused $125 billion in damage, making Harvey the second costliest natural disaster in American history. Harris County (home of Houston) Flood Control District meteorologist Jeff Lindner estimated that 70 percent of the 1,800-square-mile county was under a foot and a half of water.[83] In Southeast Texas, the flooded area was equal in size to the state of New Jersey.[84]

Picture it—the whole Garden State submerged, from Paterson to Camden to Cape May. Geophysicist Chris Milliner said the weight of the water "flexed the earth's crust," causing Houston to sink two centimeters.[85] I imagine him standing there at a press conference, maybe with a big ol' belt buckle and cowboy boots, saying, "Y'all, this storm *literally* broke a damn piece of the planet." To my knowledge, this never happened, which makes my speculation on his diction and sartorial choices just that—speculation. Also, he did state that the land would snap back after the water receded. Finally, he works in Pasadena, California, so there's no reason he'd go full-on Texas stereotype when discussing a Houston event. Still, I picture Josh Brolin playing him in a movie.

While my central theme to our current state of anxiety is that we don't actually need to worry about nearly so much, a glaring caveat may be the environment.

Listen, I completed my last science class in 1982, where we mostly watched my freshman biology teacher dissect the lambs that died on his sheep farm. Historically, I've been the least likely person to discuss all things STEM. If you'd previously desired specifics on global warming, I would have advised you to consult your average sixth grader; they'd have been far better acquainted with facts and figures than I was.

So my newfound environmental anxieties threw me for a loop. I was underprepared to manage them. I decided that I needed facts, to educate myself with source material beyond Facebook shares that ran the gamut from "the sky is falling and we're going to die, like, tomorrow" to "the environment is a Ponzi scheme cooked up by Ed Begley Jr."

While the term "global warming" wasn't first used until 1975, alarm bells about global warming started to sound more than fifty years ago. What kicked it off was a report called *Sources, Abundance, and Fate of Gaseous Atmospheric Pollutants*, and if Michael Bay doesn't option those film rights, he's leaving money on the table. The report, which detailed the problem with rising CO2 levels, was issued by the Stanford Research Institute and delivered to the American Petroleum Institute, a fossil-fuel trade consortium that *definitely does not* sound like a group of Bond villains.

When the report was written, CO2 levels in the atmosphere registered at 323 ppm. They have since risen to 369 ppm, which means there's been "a temperature increase of nearly half a degree over pre-industrial averages."[86]

This seemed like good information to know . . . had I any idea what it meant.

Was a half degree a big deal? Or was it like gaining half a pound? Was it like when a packaged food's label boasts "No Trans Fats" even though the food, by nature, has never had trans fats in the first place? Was the world about to end in fire? Or ice? (From what I've tasted of desire, I hold with those who favor fire.) And should we have been talking about this stuff in my biology class, instead of poking around in a sheep's kidneys?

As I don't know any sixth graders, I had to turn to NASA for an explanation. Bob Silberg of NASA's Jet Propulsion Laboratory wrote: "The European Geosciences Union published a study in April 2016 that examined the impact of a 1.5 degree Celsius vs. a 2.0 C temperature increase by the end of the century, given what we know so far about how climate works. It found that the jump from 1.5 to 2 degrees—a third more of an increase—raises the impact by about that same fraction, very roughly, on most of the phenomena the study covered. Heat waves would last around a third longer, rain storms would be about a third more intense, the increase in sea level would be approximately that much higher and the percentage of tropical coral reefs at risk of severe degradation would be roughly that much greater."[87]

Nutshell version, per Silberg?

A half-degree shift can mean *as much as a ten-degree variation* in some places and can be incredibly problematic where crops are already being grown at the height of their threshold for heat. And PS, this shift doesn't even account for the bugs and bacteria that could thrive and multiply at higher temps. (I smell a sequel here, Mr. Bay.)

In a smaller nutshell? This shift could prevent breadbasket crops like corn from growing, and then what are we going to serve as a side dish at our Labor Day cookouts? You don't make friends with salad.

As you can imagine, the American Petroleum Institute met the report about CO2 levels with the exact level of enthusiasm and acknowledgment as I receive when handing a stranger back their empty Frappuccino cup. The report was silenced under oil execs collectively clamping their hands over their ears.

Faced with the advent of an international treaty to reduce greenhouse gas emissions, the Kyoto Protocol, the API created the Global Climate Science Communications Team Action Plan. (I'm not on the payroll, but I strongly suggest this team wear matching jumpsuits, Mr. Bay.) Their purpose was to create public "uncertainty" about climate policy, specifically targeting media, policy makers, and science teachers. There was literally a document they created, commonly referred to as the Victory memo, that contained bullet points about the measurable goals of the plan.[88]

While these actions strike me as unconscionable, I'm also loath to think of the immediate chaos that might ensue if a harsh and immediate crackdown on greenhouse gas emissions went into effect and set off an oil crisis like the one we faced in the 1970s. In 1973, odd-even day rationing was introduced, and the speed limit was dropped to fifty-five miles per hour.[89] Nixon signed the Emergency Daylight Saving Time Energy Conservation Act of 1973 to deal with the massive gas shortages. So when you're groggy and cranky for two weeks after the Spring Ahead, and your kids won't go to sleep when they're supposed to, and you're sitting in a line that snakes around the block to fill up your car, that's just a small taste of what could be to come.

Again, it feels like we're choosing between fire and ice. Do we want the game over for the planet in twenty to thirty years, or the potential for eventual salvation but riots in the street right now?

Some oil companies, such as Exxon, did start finding ways to cut emissions after their own internal climate modeling verified the initial report. Lest we give Exxon a trophy, Richard Wiles noted that they also spent $30 million on ads and climate-denying pseudoscience post–Victory memo. They covered every base.

Also, keep in mind that the world's five largest publicly owned oil and gas companies spend approximately $200 million each year on lobbying designed to control, delay, or block binding climate-motivated policy.[90] They primarily contribute to Republicans, although plenty of Democrats benefit from their largess, as well.[91]

Senator Chris Coons, a Democrat from Delaware, received the smallest amount from the oil and gas PACs—a whopping two whole dollars. This fact delights me. Did the senator accidentally accept a Diet Dr Pepper from a lobbyist in the congressional commissary one day when he forgot his wallet in the office? Did lobbyists slip a bunch of nickels under his door? Did the intern who cashed a two-dollar check get fired? Was the Senator chased around by the paper boy in *Better Off Dead*, all, "Two dollars!" until he finally relented?

When people question the environmental crisis they often wonder why, if climate change has been happening for so long, it doesn't seem like anything is terribly amiss?

Public Radio International offered an analogy that addresses that perceived slow progression, explaining that global warming is like microwaving a bag of popcorn. Nothing seems to be happening in the first minute, and it's only during the second minute that things begin to pop and are forever altered. Scientists figure we're in "minute two" of the environmental crisis, explaining, "Thirty years ago we predicted it in the models, and now [we're] experiencing it. You see the fires in the western US and British Columbia. And [. . .] it rained three feet in Hilo, Hawaii, from [a] hurricane—that is a new record at the same time that we have droughts and fires, [and] over 300 people died in India from floods. We are not prepared."[92]

None of the articles or interviews I've read mention minute three in the analogy, when the popcorn blackens and then you never, ever get the stench of it out of the breakroom, causing every person who enters to say, "Who's burning popcorn?" (It's Susan, because it's *always* Susan.)

I read an article in *GQ* recently that, at first glance, I thought carried the headline "Billionaires Are Leading the Cause for Climate Change." *Yay!* I was finally about to read something heartening, along the lines of how Bill and Melinda Gates are working to wipe out malaria through their global health initiatives.

Nope.

After I put on my reading glasses, I saw that the article was about how billionaires *are the leading cause* of climate change. Big difference. It turns out that the *Carbon Majors Report* shows how a small number of fossil-fuel producers are responsible for 70 percent of global emissions.[93] These companies don't want to change or to comply with restrictions because those measures would be expensive and would cut into their bottom line. Instead of adopting measures that might make a real difference in the acceleration of global warming, some billionaires like Peter Thiel continue to deny climate change, yet have helped fund ventures like the Seasteading Institute, which aims to construct floating cities—a pursuit that could be incredibly lucrative if sea levels continue to rise.

Is this gross and callous?

Or is a company's sole responsibility to that of their shareholders, as they ain't running a damn daisy farm?

I don't know the right answer![94]

The more I learned about global warming, the more I found myself paralyzed by the findings. I yearned for the salad days of my willful ignorance before I'd been convinced that, yes, global warming is a huge issue, and yes, it's on track to change the world as we know it. Truthfully it's a Rubik's Cube of shitty outcomes. Plenty of people are also getting rich by capitalizing on the green agenda, in no small part thanks to federal funding. In 1993, the government put $2.4 billion toward environmental causes. In 2014, that figure had risen to $11.6 billion, with an additional $26.1 billion earmarked for programs and activities provided by the American Recovery and Reinvestment Act of 2009.[95]

(Are you exhausted yet? I'm exhausted.)

What I've come out understanding is that lots of people have vested interests in denying the green agenda, and others are Team Climate Change Chaos, because a global-warming crisis will pad their bottom line. And there's data that shows how global warming has decreased the wealth of the poorest countries by 17 to 31 percent, while enriching the wealthiest.[96]

Everyone has a dog in this fight, and every agenda is different.

I became incredibly frustrated trying to sort it all out.

So how could I not be especially anxious about the environment when I questioned almost everyone's motives?

Then I remembered my cousin.

In the '70s, my hippie cousin had big concerns about ecology, so he studied science and engineering in college and looked for jobs in environmental engineering postgraduation. His heart was in protecting the planet, due in no small part to that fateful PSA that ran during our childhoods. As his work responsibilities expanded, he traded in his bell-bottoms for Brooks Brothers and shaved off his sweet-ass sideburns. While he looked different, his commitment remained steadfast. In the early '80s, he started his own environmental firm and grew his business, cleaning up one polluted lot at a time, going from a single office with such a rickety staircase that the postman refused to deliver mail there to a $20 million company with projects on three continents. Eventually, his passion for the environment afforded him the opportunity to retire at fifty, with a nice home and a sailboat, thanks to his particular combination of hard work and strong ethics.

Protecting the earth *and* protecting the bottom line don't have to be mutually exclusive concepts. My cousin is a living example. Just knowing that lessens my anxiety.

So here's what I know: I can't change the whole world. My locus of control ends at my fingertips. I can only adjust my own behavior. After Harvey hit, I looked for ways I could be less of a garbage person regarding environmental issues and, ergo, fixate less on my actions. I lowered my thermostat in the winter and raised it in the summer, donning and removing sweaters as needed. I didn't fix my malfunctioning pool heater, which I'd melted the previous season, having heated the whole thing to bathtub temperature. I just let the pool be a seasonal cooling luxury. I walked more and drove less. I recycled. It was a start.

I'd taken my facts and turned them into acts, and that put me at ease.

What caused the true seismic shift for me was Burberry.

Yes, as in the plaid.

In 2017, the brand made the decision to burn more than $38 million worth of unsold products to prevent the items from being sold to the "wrong people."[97] Turns out, destroying surplus inventory is a common fashion-world practice. To prevent markdowns, counterfeits, and "grey-market transactions"—selling products at steeply discounted prices via an unauthorized seller—high-end brands routinely trash their pristine unsold inventory.[98]

As someone who's spent a lot of time conflating self-esteem with designer labels, I appreciated the gesture. My Burberry should mean something! As someone who didn't want to see Texas under two feet of water again, I was appalled.

I dug into other fashion-industry practices and was staggered by the amount of waste involved, such as the 2,000 gallons of water it takes to produce a single pair of jeans, between growing the cotton and processing the dye. Maybe I wasn't so wrong in hating dungarees as a little girl. (Remnant-sourced capes for the win again!)

Every single second, a truck's worth of fabric is dumped and burned, resulting in 1.2 billion metric tons in greenhouse gas emissions per year.[99] There is a claim that fashion is the second-largest polluting industry after oil and gas, and that claim, friends, is unverified. What *is* verifiably true is that the fashion industry produces 20 percent of global wastewater and 10 percent of global carbon emissions; these numbers are greater than those of global maritime shipping and all international flights. Combined.[100]

When I thought I couldn't do anything about reducing carbon emissions in China? I was wrong. The staggering figures around the fashion industry that I love so much clashed with my newfound desire to reduce, reuse, and recycle. That is, until I discovered sites like Poshmark, the online secondhand clothing retailer. In a three-year span, I'd been six different sizes, so I found myself with a ton of items both too big and too small. While I'd donated most of what I could no longer wear, I still had almost one hundred items that bore their original tags . . . but I still felt like I had nothing that fit.

My issues were twofold, both environmental and financial. I wanted some new pieces, yet I knew that would be supporting the fashion industry's poor practices. But if I were to buy more, I needed to recoup a portion of the purchase price from my old stuff—that stuff was expensive and in perfect condition. I'd recently changed publishers, and I was staring down a two-year gap between paychecks, so any cash flow was welcome.

I seriously considered opening a storefront, but shied away from that option largely because I was afraid of the optics. What would my social media followers say? The idea of reselling made me anxious. My writing career started inadvertently when I wrote about having to sell my designer bags to make rent after 9/11. To venture into this territory again made it appear as though I'd learned nothing.[101]

However, my comedy class friends were a constant reminder that there is no shame in working a side hustle, so I took my own advice about side-hustling and decided to offer some listings on a resale site.

I posted a pair of Fletch's like-new weightlifting shoes with a listing that read:

"I'm going to buy $200 Nike Romaleos 2," he said. "I'm gonna lift all the time!" he said. So, yeah. No. Nike Romaleos 2s, used twice. Please know the funds will be used for artisan cheese and craft beer.

I recouped 75 percent of the purchase price. Bonus? Funny listings proved to be great PR for my backlist of books.

I was surprised at how easy it was to sell online, nothing like the chore it was to sell in the early 2000s. And writing the posts turned out to be kind of fun.

The pieces sold faster than I'd expected. I found that selling was low stakes, and I liked styling the items for photographs. Every time I received an email that I'd made a sale, I felt an endorphin rush.

The average consumer is purchasing 60 percent more items than they did in 2000, and they are only keeping those items half as long. That means the market is red hot for resale.[102] Plus, having a side hustle gave me something to do other than worry about the state of, like, everything. There's something inherently satisfying about the quickness of online sales, especially since I was used to the glacial pace of an industry like publishing where it often takes two years between conception and having a finished product on a shelf.

Between writing my own books, I'd picked up a ghostwriting gig. In order to prepare for that assignment, I read Sophia Amoruso's *#Girlboss*. I was unexpectedly inspired by her success—the lady resold vintage items from her apartment and turned that hustle into a massively successful clothing company. I'd already sold all my unworn items, and I wasn't looking to launch the next luxury brand, but I did start looking for vintage and designer items that I could resell. Once I found some, I started listing them on luxury consignment reseller the RealReal. I was astounded by the amazing finds there were at thrift stores and estate sales; I felt like an early prospector during the gold rush. I educated myself on the high-end goods and learned that everyone hunted for well-known items like Burberry and Tory Burch, but no one looked for pieces from the more obscure but pricier fashion houses.[103]

For example, someone donated a $1,250 pair of Roger Vivier Chips d'Orsay ballet flats to a charity shop. That donor was able to write off their donation. I bought them for $50, which was pure profit for the charity who used those funds to support their cause. I cleaned up the shoes and sent them to the RealReal. The site verified the authenticity and marketed them for $400. Their customer paid 68 percent less than retail for that amazing designer find, so they were thrilled. My share of the sale was $200, so I was thrilled. The people who work at the RealReal get paychecks and benefits, so they were thrilled. And AT&T was thrilled when I used those funds to cover my wireless bill. (I might be stretching it here.)

Regardless of the collective thrills, the best part was that nothing ended up in a landfill. If there's a downside, I don't see it.

As a society, we eschew anything short of the latest and greatest. Department stores dump racks of clothes over the smallest imperfections. Recently, I bought a new-with-tags $300 Parker dress for $20 because it had a tiny stain on the bodice. I fixed it in ten seconds with a swipe of Dryel pen. I'm not complaining, but I would be if they'd taken that gorgeous piece and thrown it in a dumpster. I've also started snapping up items that require a bit of love, such as suede boots in need of buffing or handbags that have been discarded because of cracked wax seals on the handles. I taught myself how to repair and refinish them, turning respectable profits thanks to nothing more than a quick YouTube instructional video, an hour's worth of effort, and a ten-dollar bottle of Fiebing's Bag Kote, proving that it's possible to be environmentally conscious *and* build a bottom line.

If you're panicking about all things environmental, you're not alone. In fact, 72 percent of Americans say they worry about global warming and want to fix it.[104] The recent surges in natural disasters are impacting so many of us, and if your home or livelihood is affected—or even if you're just bothered by the increasing danger—you should act. By act, I mean take *real* action, not just a click, post, or like. Adopt a highway. Plant some trees. Recycle your wine bottles. Whatever works for you.

Call your legislators. Make your views known. Vote.

Vote with your dollar. Support those publicly traded companies on the Carbon Clean 200 list, as they're working hard to help prevent climate change. As a fashionista, I've started to support sustainable fashion brands, like Everlane, Boyy, and Eileen Fisher, and I'm also contributing to the resale economy. But there are endless ways to still indulge in your passions and support a more green future. Shopping for local fresh foods at a farmers' market, purchasing an affordable farm share, or adopting a meatless Monday into your routine can make a significant difference in your impact on the environment.

I'm starting to believe that I *can* make a difference with little changes. And the feeling of doing *something* has lowered my anxiety about the pending doom.

Now, if you're not into it, if none of this is your thing, if you disagree, if you have insight that calls the science into question, I'm not here to argue with you. I'm just calling it like I see it and speaking from my particular stress experience. If you're just calm blue ocean on the environment for whatever reason, great. Conduct yourself however you see fit, and I promise I won't be a jerk about it on Twitter.

Of course, I may chase after you with a coffee cup and silently judge you for making old ~~Native American~~ Italian men cry.

NEW SHERIFF IN TOWN

Gina and I were in her living room, preparing to record a few episodes of our podcast. We were each on our respective leather couches, trying not to move, because her partner, Lee, had already adjusted our microphones. I'd learned early on not to wear shorts to a podcasting session, otherwise Lee is forced to edit our constant skin-on-leather fart noises every time I move, followed by annoying giggling and denial.

Gina and Lee travel so often that I lose track, whereas I don't like to leave my house. I'd left my zip code—and put on something other than track pants—that day because Lee and Gina were preparing for another one of their glamorous getaways.

Lee was plugging things into the mixing board, so he was only half listening to our conversation.

"Where are you going this time?" I asked.

"Amsterdam," Gina replied.

"Nice! Did you finally do the Global Entry thing?" I asked.

A few years before, I'd applied for TSA PreCheck and Global Entry. I hadn't gone anywhere that required a passport since my first and only international trip in the 1980s. I was heading to Rome, so I wanted to find ways to streamline my overseas trip to eliminate stress. I'd become a master of continental travel, taking advantage of airline club memberships, the right luggage, and my pre-packed dopp kit—ready to go on a dime—but flying outside the country was getting the best of my anxiety. So I learned Italian, prebooked all my tours, and enrolled in Global Entry.

Once I landed in Rome, I bypassed the long queue of my fellow travelers (read: suckers), instead making a beeline to the expedited area for *special* people, like myself.

Andiamo!

That's when carabinieri guards with M4s strapped to their chest stopped me mid-exit, explaining in perfect English that Global Entry only worked when I was *returning* to the States. A series of rapid-fire questions helped them ascertain that I was merely stupid and arrogant, not a threat to anything but the country's gelato supply, and they sent me to the back of the line.

Idiota.

"Then they shouldn't call it 'global,'" I grumbled only when I was well out of earshot, as I did not care to spend my vacation in *prigione*.

The Italian guards had zero chill, I learned, because they have employed extensive detention, monitoring, and wiretapping systems, practices which far exceed the protections afforded to us here in America, thanks to our Bill of Rights, in order to guard against the type of terror attacks so much of Europe has experienced.

For example, Youssef Zaghba was one of the men who carried out that terrible London Bridge terror attack, where they first mowed down pedestrians before going on a stabbing rampage. Zaghba was a naturalized Italian citizen, born in Morocco. The Italian police suspected him of terrorist intent, having found ISIS propaganda on his phone. However, they didn't have the authority to arrest him, per Bologna chief prosecutor Giuseppe Amato, who stated, "In Italy . . . the fact of having common-source images that evoke radicalisation is not a crime."[105] While they couldn't imprison him, they barely let him leave their sight. I imagine it was kind of like taking your dad on a date with you—regardless of intent, no one dared make a move with him there.

When Zaghba traveled to England, Italian authorities forewarned the British government about his ties, a fact that Great Britain later denied. Yet his own mother, Valeria Collina, told the *Guardian* in an interview, "[The Italian police] would talk to him at the airport. Then, during his stay, police officers would come a couple of times a day to check on him. They were friendly to Youssef. They would say: 'Hey son, tell me what you have been doing. What are you doing? How are you?'"[106] She added that British officials never stopped or questioned him, despite Italy's warnings.

So if Italy has their own version of the Global Entry program, I imagine their interview process is a lot more like the rights-violating one in my twisted fantasy.

And I suppose Italy's refusal to recognize my Global Entry had its benefits.

"I got *my* Global Entry right away," Gina replied, flashing Lee the stink eye.

"Wait, does that mean you didn't?" I asked him.

He nodded, swapping a longer audio cord for a shorter one. "Yeah, I was denied because of my interview."

"You're kidding! Why?"

The final hurdle in obtaining Global Entry, after the background check, is an in-person US Customs and Border Patrol officer interview. I'd completely freaked out about mine beforehand. I was Cher Horowitz prepping for the DMV, changing my shirt again and again, trying to find my most patriotic outfit. But I also didn't want to skew too "God Bless America," because I thought that might seem fishy, so I removed my Old Glory eternity scarf at the last minute and left it at home. Grudgingly.

I expected the interrogation to take place in a barred, bleak room with a single bright light shining in my eyes. I was sure I'd be hooked up to a polygraph and then asked to answer long-form, blue-book essay questions about America and capital-*P* Patriotism, in cursive, and that

I'd eventually be turned away, them saying, "Well, she got the questions right, but she has the handwriting of a serial killer."

Turns out, the interview was in a beige, carpeted cubicle about twenty yards from the McDonald's in O'Hare's Terminal Five, so everything smelled like hamburgers and ~~French Freedom~~ french fries. Also, the officer had dated my friend Kevin. That's mostly what we discussed. Renewing my driver's license took more effort—there's an eye test and I panicked about having to stick my face against a View-Master that a million other dirty heads (with pink eye? Lice?) had touched. Everything from my neck up itched for days after, but it turned out to be psychosomatic.

Yeah, I don't like to leave the house.

Anyway, my Global Entry turned out to be based mostly on my ability to dissect a failed relationship. And I totally could have worn my 'Merica scarf.

I asked Lee, "How'd you get denied?"

"*Someone* thought he was cute," Gina teased.

"What?" Lee said, feigning innocence. "They asked me if I'd ever been arrested, and I had to be honest. I told him, 'I'm a black man in America; *of course* I've been arrested. Never charged, though.'"

Gina shook her head. "He couldn't just give his answer, he had to editorialize. Turns out, Homeland Security is not the place to make a stand about the state of policing in America."

"Maybe you should have mentioned you know Kevin?" I suggested.

Lee adjusted our audio levels, explaining that he eventually got his Global Entry pass, but he'd had to petition his senator and provide copies of his outstanding military service record along with letters of reference to make it happen. Meanwhile, I'd been equally glib during my interview and had passed through on stars-and-stripes-emblazoned roller skates.

"That doesn't seem fair," I said.

Lee laughed. "Welcome to America, you must be new here."

When she was growing up, Gina said, her parents had "the talk" with her early and often. In our post-Ferguson America, that talk has maintained its importance. There's even a children's book by Sanya Gragg, a former social worker, called *Momma, Did You Hear the News?*, meant to teach kids how to conduct themselves around law enforcement, using the acronym ALIVE:

A—Always mind your manners
L—Listen and comply
I—In control of your emotions
V—Visible hands always
E—Explain any movement[107]

Gina's parents' talk focused on how bias existed and how she should work twice as hard to compensate for other people's assumptions. Her father had been an active figure in the civil rights movement. As a professional musician, he came up during a time when he wasn't allowed to stay in the hotels he was paid to perform in. A smart-ass from birth, Gina said her folks spent extra care convincing her she shouldn't try out her best snappy retorts on law enforcement. At the same age, I was sashaying alone through the woods like I had Harry Potter's invisibility cloak, which brings me to my point—there's rising anxiety over policing.

In theory, no one should fear policing, because the need for protection feeds directly into our need for safety on Maslow's Hierarchy.

In practice? That's a different story.

Crime rates—I reiterate—are down universally since their peak in the early 1990s, even though many of us don't realize it. Yet, for fifteen straight years, the majority of Americans responded to YouGov surveys that they believed crime was on the rise.[108] Also, these respondents ranked New York as the second least-safe city, while naming Dallas or

Houston the safest, when, at the time of the survey, the converse was true: New York had half the violent crime rate of either city.[109]

Congratulations, Texas, everything *is* bigger down there.

There are a few theories of why crime rates have dropped so dramatically. In a piece for *Forbes*, writer Neil Howe speculated on potential causes. The notion that fascinates me the most is the "lead hypothesis," which links certain levels of early environmental lead exposure—from paint or leaded-gasoline exhaust fumes, for example—to violent crime.[110] A decline in crime levels coincides with the improvements in air quality that have occurred since the 1970 passage of the Clean Air Act, which is kind of a microphone drop for the good that can come from protecting the environment.

Another theory Howe highlights is the decrease in the use of substances that are linked to violent criminal behavior, such as alcohol and crack cocaine. But he speculates the biggest factor is a generational change, as millennials are the first generation to engage in less risky behaviors, owing to having been more sheltered while growing up. Howe explains that it *feels* like crime is up because when something happens now, the criminal behavior is much more publicized because we're societally less tolerant of it.

A constant cycle of like, share, forward, *panic*, if you will.

Technology seems to be accomplishing a couple of important things when it comes to our relationship with crime. There are meaningful advancements in policing tools and technology, such as upgraded and crosslinked crime databases and an enhanced 911 system. While Chicago leads the pack in murder rates, there was a downtick in 2017 that many have attributed to ShotSpotter, a tech that uses detection radar and cameras to pinpoint the origin of a gunshot, leading to quicker response times and an increased ability to identify a perpetrator.[111]

So there are ways that tech might be providing some relief from crime-related anxiety, but for each action, there is often an equal and opposite effect. Nothing ignites our nation—and a social media timeline—like a police altercation gone wrong that's been caught on tape. As sentient, sensitive human beings, it's impossible to watch body-cam footage and not have a visceral reaction. Whatever context we heard can't override what we *saw*. We've seen the facts, as reported by the *Washington Post*: Of those who died at the hands of the police, 51 percent were black, 28.1 percent were white, 19.3 percent Hispanic, and 1.7 percent Asian. White people make up 62 percent of the population and black people 17.9 percent.[112]

Yet, as juries have proven, five seconds of videotape do not a conviction make. These recordings, tools meant to make us less fearful, often have the opposite effect. No wonder so many live in fear that justice won't be served. Decent people want life to be fair, for the same rules to apply to all, and when judgments don't align with what they have witnessed, don't align with the numbers, they are hard to swallow.

I decided the way around this disturbing reality was to police my local police force. Fletch and I signed up for Lake Forest's ten-week Citizens Police Academy, something he'd been pushing for us to do for years. He thought that a) it would be fun, and b) the class would go a long way in quieting my home-alone anxieties.

I grew up watching too many horror films, and on the rare instances when I'm by myself at night, I psych myself out. Not long before we joined the CPA, while Fletch was out of town, I took a Xanax, an Ambien, and a Benadryl, and topped it off with a few glasses of wine in order to unclench my entire musculoskeletal system enough to doze off. Fletch correctly identified that the cure to my insomnia was thorough, but it might have resulted in my not waking up again. He wasn't wrong.

The police didn't cross my mind much as a kid, beyond the occasional road trip, when other motorists flashed their high beams at us to warn of upcoming speed traps. My dad, driving eighty-five miles per hour with a lit cigarette and two unbelted kids in the back seat, would take his foot off the gas. Crisis averted?

My perception, in that scenario, was that the police were out to get us.

My only face-to-face encounter with a law enforcement officer was when a cop spoke to my second-grade class on career day. My classmates were curious about the people he helped and how it felt to drive around real fast using the sirens. Were the bad guys mean? Were they fed bread and water in jail?

I cared not for their inane questions—I wanted to know about the sidearm, sitting menacingly at his belt. Couldn't he lock that thing in his squad car? What if it fell and went off? Were we prepared for this eventuality? I was already stressed every damn day at that school because my sadist math teacher perpetually threatened to cut off my legs and send me home in a paper bag. The last thing I needed was a sloppily handled service revolver.

I recall thinking that I was in *second grade*, and second graders shouldn't have to worry about guns in their classroom and, oh, was I before my time with that concern.

The officer explained that he only drew his gun to shoot to kill, which he followed with a tangent about life-and-death situations and the importance of getting home alive. He went into such detail that that afternoon recess turned into a PTSD support group for me and the rest of my class.

Did I mention we were *seven*?

Read the room, Officer.

In high school and college, I doubled down on my perception that police were there to mess with kids, to ruin everyone's fun. They only seemed to make appearances when we'd cruised the McDonald's too many times or were walking home after a night at the bars. I knew a lot of people at Purdue who considered driving under the influence safer than risking public intoxication with the arrest-happy West Lafayette PD patrolling. Not a joke. (Also, they were wrong.)

Eventually, I moved to a Chicago neighborhood where the police would simply not come, because the block was allegedly controlled by a gang. A state trooper lived a few doors down from me, and he was jumped one night when he was out walking his dog. While he lay bleeding in the street, his wife had to fight with the dispatch to convince an officer to report to the scene. She had to call in favors. For an assault.

So I was apathetic at best over Fletch and I joining the police class. I'd never been Little Miss Team Blue. And it turned out that many of my classmates were on the same page as me—they were there to make sure the LFPD was doing the right thing.

I truly believe that it is our obligation as citizens to hold our local law enforcement accountable. The converse of this is our local police should *expect* us to hold them accountable—they should solicit community involvement.

For example, the Lake Forest PD was excited about adding body cameras because they wanted the transparency. Those videos exist as much for their protection as everyone else's. One night in class, an officer showed us the dashcam footage of his takedown of a known armed and dangerous criminal. We witnessed this officer gesturing for others on the scene to silence the sirens and hit the spotlight, ensuring whatever happened was clearly visible and audible.

Huh.

Fletch and I began the thirty-hour course by learning how LFPD officers are hired. I was all, "Ooh, a session on HR? Tell me more! Can we pretty please cover supply chain management practices next?"

I soon realized I was wrong and their hiring practices were worth discussing. They're proud of them and they should be. The process takes a year from the initial application to a job offer. Much of that time is consumed by psychological testing and background checks to ensure officers are stable and won't act on biases. To serve in Lake Forest, just about every single person in that potential officer's life, from the past and present, including family, friends, coworkers, romantic partners, and neighbors, is interviewed in person. The process can take months.

Each potential candidate is given a weighted score, based on testing, physical ability, background, and staff interviews. Job offers are only extended to those with the highest overall ranking. A new recruit then enters three months at the police academy, followed by another three months working side by side with a training officer, before the newbie is officially considered a part of the force. I can't imagine most places have the resources to invest so thoroughly in the way they screen candidates. The trade-off for the officers is a starting salary around $70,000, before overtime, funded by onerous property taxes. I fully support healthy police wages. (I am less enthusiastic about our city sanitation workers earning $75,000 per year. They collect garbage in golf carts and get first dibs on all the best trash. Where do I sign up?)

The LFPD is diligent because our community is unique. A typical officer's shift can entail eight hours of what's essentially PR work—helping residents trap a duck that wandered into their basement (true story), or teaching little kids about safety at the annual bike rodeo.

We have a bunch of car thefts because residents are keen on leaving their cars unlocked with the key fobs stored inside. Often there's a wallet in there, too. The training officers explained that, with such comprehensive insurance coverage, residents tend to be careless with their property. I hate to victim blame, but . . . maybe my neighbors shouldn't be such soft targets.

There was an older man sitting across the room, who said he'd joined the class because he was worried about a potential crime wave. His son had recently had two late-model German cars stolen from his driveway. (Spoiler alert: both had the keys inside.) His son's cars, he went on to tell us, eyes wide with fear and outrage, were abandoned two blocks away when the thieves happened upon two *newer* Mercedes with the keys inside. Ruthless.

I tried to have a conversation with him after class, curious to know what drug combo helped him get to sleep when he was alone. Perhaps privilege is the panacea.

Anyway, sometimes top recruits bypass Lake Forest to work on other forces—for significantly less pay—because they're looking for more consistent and stable action. One of my favorite local officers is former NYPD and used to foot patrol the Bronx; there was never a dull moment on that beat. He found the change to protecting Lake Forest's ducks so abrupt that he once considered quitting to work for the Chicago PD instead. Cops in my neighborhood need to be agile; they routinely have to shift from patiently dealing with a resident who fat-fingered her complicated alarm system after drinking Tito's on the last day of her Whole30 cycle, to pursuing a stolen vehicle full of cartel-connected drug dealers down the highway that bisects town.

(If the Whole30 resident sounds too specific . . . all I can say is that I'll personally vouch for exactly how patient—and amused—these officers can be.)

Because of generous financial support from a fundraising entity composed of local citizens, the Lake Forest Police Foundation, training is ongoing for the entire span of the officers' careers and they're provided with the most advanced equipment. As use of force has come under national scrutiny, the officers continually receive education on de-escalation techniques and have six different Foundation-provided less- and nonlethal weapon options in their utility belts. When all you're given is a gun, that's your only choice. As my ride-along officer explained, "Everything we do is aboveboard because this is a great job and I want to keep it." My point is, if the LFPD were a little girl, she'd be the one who had her own pony *and* swimming pool.

The training in Lake Forest is not standard, because there is no national standard. If there were one national policing standard, the police would be considered a branch of the military, which would be a violation of the Tenth Amendment. With more than twelve thousand local agencies and six hundred different police academies, police forces are incredibly decentralized.[113] Every municipality sets their own standards and rules.

For example, the town just to the south of Lake Forest, Highland Park, is demographically much the same, but their approach to policing is entirely different. On ride alongs, my training officer pointed out how each HP officer was stationed on Highway 41, waiting to ticket speeders and arrest drunk drivers, whereas all the Lake Forest officers were slowly patrolling neighborhoods, in an effort to better police and benefit the community.

For many years, police were thought of as "warriors for" the community, meaning the police had the authority to act like soldiers in battle, where the rules of engagement could be fluid and the emphasis was . . . not on de-escalation. New York City's old stop-and-frisk policy empowered officers to question, search, and detain citizens for weapons and contraband on no basis, save for reasonable suspicion.[114] The rationale was that, by removing low-level criminals from the street and confiscating illegal weapons, crime rates would plummet. The reality was that the term "reasonable suspicion" was too vague, open to interpretation, and influenced by long-standing racial biases.

New York's mayor Bill de Blasio was elected in part due to his 2013 promise to end stop-and-frisk. There was a lot of fear that by stopping that policy, crime would increase. But it didn't. Even conservative publications printed articles about their dire predictions being wrong. In the *National Review*, Kyle Smith wrote: "Nevertheless, de Blasio was correct in saying the city could withstand a sharp decrease in stop-and-frisk. And he was right to draw attention to the social cost of the practice; more than 80 percent of those subjected to stop-and-frisk since the start of the Bloomberg administration were, according to the NYPD, completely innocent. That means hundreds of thousands of New Yorkers were unjustly subjected to embarrassment or even humiliation."[115]

To me, it sounds like the stop-and-frisk policies were most successful in increasing mistrust of law enforcement, which has only been exacerbated by every questionable police shooting and subsequent not-guilty verdict in the past few years.

Not long ago, the American Civil Liberties Union challenged Milwaukee's stop-and-frisk practices, pointing to evidence that ethnic minorities have been unfairly targeted, in *Collins et al. v. City of Milwaukee et al.* According to Nusrat Choudhury of the ACLU, "From 2007 to 2015, traffic and pedestrian stops in Milwaukee tripled from around 66,000 to a whopping 196,000. Expert reports released this week, relying on the city's own data, show that a huge fraction of Milwaukee police stops are made without reasonable suspicion as required by law and disproportionately subject Black and Latino people to stigmatizing police encounters."[116]

My first thought was, come on, Milwaukee—you have all that pristine lakefront and unfettered access to Miller High Life and cheese curds. Please be cool. However, I'd be doing a disservice if I didn't try to find out the other side of the story, and social media was the wrong place to search. I didn't want hashtags, I wanted facts.

Now-retired Milwaukee chief of police Edward Flynn gave an interview with Fox6 Now, explaining, "If you read the entire suit filed by the ACLU, you will see not one word about crime. If you cherry pick the disparity of what we do and where we do it to reduce the disparity of crime . . . you can say 'well, look how biased that is. They're not doing that here in the middle class neighborhood where absolutely nothing happens.'"[117]

In November of 2014, Flynn was speaking at a meeting with a civilian oversight board regarding a police shooting. His phone was open and he kept glancing down at it, and the more he looked, the angrier the crowd grew at his seeming disconnection.

Well, *yeah*, how could they not? Optics matter.

After the meeting, reporters grilled him about his "apparent" disinterest—what they didn't know was that during the meeting, a child had been murdered. The video of his response went viral as he explained he'd been keeping up with developments in the case of a five-year-old girl who'd just been shot in the head in a drive-by. He talked about how the greatest racial disparity in Milwaukee comes from those getting shot and killed, how 80 percent of his homicide victims are African American, as are 80 percent of his aggravated assault victims.

He told reporters, "We're going up there and there's a bunch of cops processing a scene of a dead kid, and they're the ones who are going to be out there patrolling and stopping suspects that may have guns under the front seats. They're the ones that are going to take the risks to their lives to try to clean this thing up. We're responsible for the things we get wrong and we take action. We've arrested cops, we've fired cops and so on. But the fact is that the people out here—some of them—who had the most to say are absolutely MIA when it comes to the true threats facing this community and it gets a little tiresome when we start getting yelled at for reading the updates of the kid that gets shot. Yeah, you take it personal, OK? Now no offense, but I'm going up there now."[118]

What this boils down to is a citizenry who's absolutely convinced the police are doing the wrong thing and a police force who's convinced they're doing right. Can there be a middle ground here?

Ultimately, the city of Milwaukee settled the ACLU lawsuit for $3.4 million and agreed to significant reporting on details for pedestrian and traffic stops, including demographics, location, reason for the stop, and results of the stop.[119]

I'd have liked to have seen this case go to court, as I keep hoping for an arbiter, someone who can say unequivocally what is right and wrong, but that's likely impossible in such a gray area. Just like I want someone to decipher why our stop-and-frisk mentality hasn't worked to prevent crime in the US, but the similar program in Italy has kept terror attacks at bay (as of this writing).

What's the political or judicial equivalent of speaking to the manager? I feel like we need this.

That moral morass is definitely contributing to an overarching anxiety. But my experience with the Citizens Police Academy made me hopeful for the future of policing. Sure, they have unbelievable funding and access to ongoing training. And it's true that we are far from adopting that as a national standard. But just seeing this tiny microcosm of the Lake Forest PD shifting their policing from "warriors for" the community to "guardians of" the community has been inspiring.

Lieutenant Chad Goeden of the Alaska Department of Public Safety Training Academy put it most succinctly: "If we're warriors, who are we at war with?"[120]

Across the country, changes are afoot. Police are actively increasing cooperation and trust with citizens, by inviting them in for things like CPA. On my ride alongs, I've witnessed people being treated equally and with dignity and respect; I've witnessed an emphasis on service as much as on protection. With a force that is trying so hard to be transparent to the community, I trust this wasn't just for my benefit. I later found out that everyone else's ride-along officer showed them how to detach the center-console rifle and protect themselves if shit went sideways, whereas mine demonstrated how to work the radio to call for backup. So I suppose they were tailoring the experience to some degree.

Police forces in many parts of our country are updating their procedures, trying to better serve the community. Some carry trauma kits with hemostatic bandages that can prevent gunshot victims from bleeding out—a policy notably not in practice in the high-profile shootings of Philando Castile and Laquan McDonald.

Jim Bueermann, retired police chief and president of the Police Foundation, said, "I'm not sure that this is completely anchored in the culture of policing yet, but once a shooting occurs and the officers are safe, they should be administering emergency first aid as fast as they can. When they don't do this, or when officers leave a wounded or dead person uncovered on the ground, as they did in Ferguson, it inflames people."[121]

In Philadelphia, police take shooting victims to the emergency room instead of waiting for the ambulance. In 2017, one-third of Philadelphia's 1,223 shooting victims were delivered to a city trauma center in the back of a police cruiser or wagon.[122]

What I've come to understand is that what's reported often isn't the entire story. The most common, compelling narrative now is that the police are always at fault, but again, this is a gray area. The relationship between law enforcement and the media feels tenuous at best.

One of my CPA classes was taught by Sergeant Kevin Zelk of the Lake County Major Crimes Task Force. His team is called in to assist when the local PD can't handle the most heinous crimes, such as nonparental child abductions, homicides, and officer-involved shootings and in-custody deaths. He and his colleagues are the ones who investigate the evidence to determine culpability.

The night he led our three-hour session, he spent a lot of time discussing his definition of "force science." This is when the initial shot can cause the body to rotate 180 degrees, making it look like subsequent rounds were fired when the subject stopped advancing. When we see a not-guilty verdict for officers tried for shooting the unarmed, it often boils down to hours of forensic testimony that aren't recapped in the two-minute news stories. Zelk played a video to demonstrate just how quickly a retreating body can turn to brandish a weapon. We also engaged in Tueller drills, which show how fast the average person can cover twenty-one feet of distance.

It's 1.5 seconds.

However, Zelk began his talk by explaining that officers can make mistakes, especially when adrenaline is high. He said it's not uncommon for officers to freak out during an exchange of gunfire, and the only way to accommodate and adequately prepare to control that adrenaline surge is to drill, drill, drill. The practice of de-escalation is everything.

Andrew Fan of the Marshall Project, a nonprofit journalism site about criminal justice, explained that younger officers, with the least amount of training and experience, are the most likely to engage in overly aggressive policing. He found that the cops patrolling Chicago's Eleventh District, which has the highest murder rate in the city, are both the youngest and most inexperienced members of the Chicago PD. He wrote, "The average officer in the 11th joined the force 10 years ago; over a third of the district's officers have less than five years on the force. Meanwhile, most veteran officers with patrol experience in the late 1990s—the last time Chicago's murder rate was as high as today— work far from Garfield Park. Half a dozen miles to the north one of the city's safest districts, Jefferson Park, has only three officers with under 10 years of experience. Over half the patrol officers are 20-year veterans."[123]

Many of the terrible headlines we see stem from a lack of proactive training. In a study conducted by APM Reports, they "reviewed the training records of officers involved in 31 shootings of unarmed people, focusing on incidents in 13 states where the records are open to the public and where de-escalation training was not required for all officers at the time of the incidents. *In more than half the cases, the officers involved had obtained fewer than two hours of de-escalation training since 2012.*" (Emphasis mine.)[124] It's worth noting that the Chicago PD officer who shot Harith Augustus was still a probationary member of the force.

Looking at our troubled history, no one can deny that systemic and implicit racial bias can be a factor in these shootings. A researcher at the University of Colorado created and studied a paradigm called "the police officer's dilemma" using a first-person shooter game. The participants were faster to shoot armed black targets than white.[125]

So bias clearly plays a role.

What's not fair is to assume bias is the only factor. Every police force is different. There are a growing number of forces that find bias unacceptable and provide training to counteract it. And I support any group whose goal is to hold law enforcement accountable, especially in terms of systemic racism. If we don't want to self-destruct as a nation, black lives and blue lives mattering can't be a binary choice.

In a country where it is so difficult to prosecute police for unnecessary violence, public opinion matters. Social media matters, but the problem is, there are no controls on Twitter, no institutional ethics. And there's so much bad information out there.

Every time there's an incident, there's a barrage of misinformation, and suddenly some asshole from my high school who dropped out of junior college considers himself a constitutional scholar.

Ideally, our public opinion should be based on established facts. Would we feel less ill at ease if we allowed the whole story to unfold, waiting a beat before becoming judge, jury, and executioner? I suspect yes.

However, I live in a community where calling 911 for stray waterfowl is an acceptable practice and residents treat the police like ad hoc customer service agents. I cringe at the possibility of this town producing the next Permit Patty or BBQ Becky, self-righteously calling in some ridiculous police report on a harmless activity. I imagine she'd be crowned Lakefront Laurel, losing her mind over a person of color who just moved here not having a city sticker to park at the beach.

At least I have faith our PD would keep the situation from escalating, but despite the cute nicknames that follow these incidents, the threat of nosey, unnecessary whistleblowers is incredibly real in our biased country. Lighting a match and throwing it on a powder keg of a divided and scared nation is bound to end in horrific results.

Earlier this spring, my husband and I woke to banging on our door in the predawn hours. We assumed someone's car service had shown up at the wrong address. It had happened a few times before. We ignored the knocking; they could figure it out themselves.

Moments later, high-powered flashlight beams cut through the darkness. Fletch looked out the window and saw the house was surrounded by the LFPD.

Groggy, I asked Fletch, "What did you do?"

Here's the thing—I wasn't afraid. Of all the things in this world that frighten me, my local police aren't one of them, because I know and trust this force, entirely due to having gotten involved in holding them accountable. This, I imagine, is far easier to do in a cozy suburban enclave where the greatest crime is often wearing white after Labor Day.

"I was asleep!" he replied. "But something obviously happened. Maybe there's an escaped prisoner or a train full of chemicals derailed."

"Are you going to go out there?"

"Yeah, in a minute, as soon as I talk to 911 to see what's happening. Have you learned nothing from watching *Live PD* with me? You don't go running out there holding a phone; that's a good way to get shot. Hands visible and empty, always."

He called 911 and found out that four squad cars, a shift supervisor, and the fire department were surrounding our house because they'd been dispatched by a suicide hotline. Someone was threatening to kill himself and had given the hotline our address.

My anger vanished. There is a big problem with teen suicide in our town. If the local PD thought the best way to save a life was to surround the place, it was surprising, but okay.

By the time Fletch got outside, the police had already broken into our garage. The caller told the hotline he was in the car with the exhaust running. Unfortunately, the suicide hotline had somehow flubbed the address and the caller was seventy-five miles away in Rockford, Illinois.

The officer in charge of the operation was the man who ran the CPA program. He was mortified and apologetic, already coordinating the effort to have our door replaced on the city's dime.

As mad as I get over trivial nonsense, this whole ordeal made sense to me. I was glad the LFPD tried to do everything they could in that situation.

Gina was astounded when I told her the story over lunch.

"What you're telling me is the police broke down your door."

This is Gina's Jedi mind trick. She uses "what you're telling me" to repeat statements so ridiculous, her only recourse is to make the speaker listen to those words spoken back to them.

"Oh, don't 'what you're telling me' me. It was only the garage door. They tried to smash a window, but we have safety glass. One side broke but the other didn't. Like when that hawk tried to get at Chuck Norris [my cat] last summer and shattered one kitchen window pane, but the other stayed intact. They had to kick the door in, which was fine because Fletch only locked the knob and not the deadbolt. Damage is minimal, and we already talked to the town about fixing it."

Gina would not be dissuaded.

"What you're telling me is the police broke down your door," she repeated, stunned. "Then what did you do?"

"I offered to make the officers peppermint mochas because it was cold. I use nutpods creamer, so they're dairy-free but good. And Fletch got a bunch of selfies with one of his ride-along officers standing by the broken door."

She laughed. "Of course he did."

When I thought about it later, I realized that that situation, to most other people, would have been terrifying, especially as we've seen instances lately of police accidentally shooting innocent citizens *in their own homes*. Regardless of the steps taken, the playing field is still far from even.

Instead of fear, I immediately went into hostess mode. It didn't occur to me to be scared, for my mind to race over the ways in which the situation could break bad, to the alternate endings that those who don't live in my neighborhood or look like me so often experience.

In that moment, I was reminded that privilege takes many forms. Sometimes it looks a lot like offering Italian espresso-based beverages to the police officers who just kicked in the door.

ALL POLITICS IS LOCAL

The debate still rages about who should have won the 2016 election—the candidate with the most electoral votes, or the candidate with the highest popular vote.

Of course, the answer is obvious: the winner is Pfizer, the manufacturer of Xanax.

So much about our government feels both hopeless and broken right now, and that inherently makes us feel unsafe. There are no quick fixes to unify us, save for an *Independence Day*-style alien invasion. Everyone's convinced of their rightness, set in their position. I'm not going to change that, and it's fruitless to try.

That we're more polarized than ever isn't an opinion; it's fact. Zachary P. Neal, an associate professor at Michigan State University, devised a way to determine polarization by measuring the frequency of political parties working together and showing the ways they've grown away from consensus.[126] Spoiler alert? The teams aren't playing nice with each other, now more than ever. But anyone with a pulse knows that.

As profound as Neal found the divide in 2016, I bet he had no idea how 2019 would come along and say, "Hold my beer."

Before I proceed, full disclosure is necessary: I no longer identify with a political party. I don't want to be on anyone's team and I have zero trust in those who desire to lead us. Yes, I spent most of my adult life as a Republican, but to bastardize a Reagan quote, I didn't leave the Republican Party; the Republican Party left me. In theory, I'm a Libertarian, but until they find a candidate who didn't graduate from Hollywood Upstairs Medical College, I declare myself politically agnostic/independent and will hold my nose while I vote a split ticket for whomever I hate the least. As Plato said, "But the chief penalty is to be governed by someone worse if a man will not himself hold office and rule."[127] What he was saying is that the penalty for not participating is to be governed by your inferiors. He is also frequently credited with having said that only those who do not seek power are qualified to hold it.[128]

I feel like Plato might have been a bummer at dinner parties.

Anyway, last summer, I accompanied Gina on an errand to the South Side of Chicago. She pointed out Barack Obama's street as we drove through the leafy, green Kenwood neighborhood, lovely with wide sidewalks and elegant old houses set far back from the street. I voted against Obama, both times. But, oh, to have him now, his dignity and decorum like gold in my hands. As we passed the president's block, I felt a weight on my heart. I sighed and said, "I miss Obama." Gina, a lifelong Democrat, laughed and replied, "I miss Bush."

If I identify with anything, it's being an American, which is why I despise how badly we've splintered as a country. The divisions between us aren't new, but the ways we deal with them are. We've lost the social norm of civility. I suspect what's changed is the attitude that we're all in this together. Now it's a me-against-you mentality, and we've turned into a country of aggressively poor losers and bombastic, graceless winners.

Do we want a civil war? Because this is how civil wars are started. I'm operating on the dubious assumption that we don't.

With every passing year, I'm less concerned about my own interests and more concerned about what's best for society overall, *even when it's not to my benefit*. (Unless the interest involves a path to a Birkin bag.)

When I was younger, I never considered the world I'd leave behind when I died. My philosophy was "That sounds like a *you people* problem." I've shifted my position. I don't want future generations crippled by the mistakes and inaction of those before them. I hate seeing where we're headed, which is why I want to do what I can to bring people together based on commonalities. On what's still fun. I want my legacy to be that of a uniter, not a divider.

That said, I have only three suggestions to help lower the stress you surely experience when anything vaguely political pops up in your timeline or your life. I can't fix politics, but I can assist in them stinging a bit less. This chapter is a Band-Aid on a gaping wound, but it's all I have in my first aid kit.

I won't insult anyone by suggesting compromise or consensus, as what divides us politically is far too black and white. Tayari Jones, though, made a compelling case against the virtuousness of finding common ground. She detailed being raised as a child of activists, concerned about South African apartheid at the exact same time I was concerned about my mom buying me a Dancerella doll.

Jones was once heading to the zoo with a classmate when her friend's mom stopped for gas at a Gulf station. Jones explained to the mom that Gulf supported apartheid and begged her to fill up elsewhere. Because she was so young, she didn't grasp all the complexities of apartheid, but did know that kids who looked like her were being killed because of it, and that informed her passion. The mother explained that Gulf's gas was cheapest, so . . . she would not be going elsewhere. Jones exited the car and called her dad to pick her up, even though the easiest thing—and what she wanted most—was to suck it up and ride quietly along to the zoo. She did what she felt was right, regardless of personal cost.

Jones wrote: "The middle is a point equidistant from two poles. That's it. There is nothing inherently virtuous about being neither here nor there. Buried in this is a false equivalency of ideas, what you might call the 'good people on both sides' phenomenon. When we revisit our shameful past, ask yourself, Where was the middle? Rather than chattel slavery, perhaps we could agree on a nice program of indentured servitude? Instead of subjecting Japanese-American citizens to indefinite detention during WWII, what if we had agreed to give them actual sentences and perhaps provided a receipt for them to reclaim their things when they were released? What is halfway between moral and immoral?"[129]

A few years ago, I heard a fascinating story on *This American Life* regarding a study about influencing beliefs. The episode was called "The Incredible Rarity of Changing Your Mind," and one segment followed a research study about the best way to alter someone's deep-seated opinion on a controversial topic, such as abortion or LGBTQ rights.

Participants were first sent a series of questions about the topic. Then, canvassers went door to door to those homes to discuss how these very personal subjects impacted their own lives. For example, a woman who'd had an abortion would give a heartfelt explanation of why she made that choice. Researchers would compare survey results before and after the canvassers spoke with participants. The evidence overwhelmingly found that when presented with a personal perspective, people were far more amenable to changing their minds. In the abortion example, while the participant may have still considered the act morally abhorrent and not a choice they'd make for themselves, they were less likely to vote to bar access after listening to the canvasser.

Human connection is powerful.

The findings were a persuasive argument for the benefits of rational, nonconfrontational, face-to-face conversations . . . except the results were all bullshit because the person tasked with collecting all the data fabricated the results.

Ira Glass? *Not pleased.*

Over the next year, the show revisited this story and discovered a factual twist that's even better than the original fiction. When the study was undertaken again without cheating, researchers learned that "a single approximately 10-minute conversation encouraging actively taking the perspective of others can markedly reduce prejudice for at least 3 months."[130]

People who don't agree with you aren't inherently evil (generally). They just have a different perspective. Instead of filling your high school acquaintances' and extended family's Facebook feeds with links to articles that support your personal platform, you can choose to have an in-person conversation about how the view/right/need in question has impacted your life. While your chat might not change that person's mind, it could engender some mutual understanding. Plus, this approach is far less damaging and won't produce the bad will of an expletive-filled Facebook-comments screaming match, wherein all sorts of unrelated parties chime in with their two cents and everyone walks away infuriated.

De-escalation is not the same as compromise or consensus, but it doesn't need to be, especially if you're trying to preserve a relationship with someone you otherwise care about. This way, you don't lose out on the good things the person opposing you brings to the table. And wouldn't it be nice to have one Thanksgiving dinner where no one cries?

What if the answer were as simple as that—politely listening and processing, instead of trying to scream over the rhetoric? My concern is that one can only be outraged for so long before becoming numb. Hate is not an effective long-term solution.

Life After Hate is a 501(c)(3) nonprofit organization, founded to help people walk away from radical hate groups. The concept stems from a Swedish initiative formulated in the 1990s by sociologist Tore Bjørgo. Bjørgo's goal was to assist white supremacists in disengaging from their racist groups. People are often stuck espousing an ideology because doing so is the foundation of their social circle. Social needs are a driving factor of our lives—just ask Maslow. These groups are basically embracing identity politics with a dangerous twist.

The Life After Hate board is a mix of social psychologists, journalists, fundraisers, and . . . former white supremacists. They work to combat extremist rhetoric and to provide those who've been involved with these groups a way to break free—a virtual halfway house of a social circle as they deprogram and mainstream back into society proper. Reading the stories of those who've detached, I've found the message that comes up again and again is that pushing the counternarrative was not effective in stopping them. Yelling opposing views didn't work; it only served to strengthen their resolve. Hate becomes its own addiction.

Growing up in Massachusetts and New Jersey, I had friends of all colors, creeds, and religions. While it's possible I was too young to notice, I never heard racist talk until I moved to an all-white, all-Christian small town in Indiana. I couldn't understand why people despised those with whom their only contact was anecdotal.

(Ask me how popular I was for voicing these opinions.)

Anyway, per Tony McAleer, Life Against Hate board member and former neo-Nazi White Aryan Resistance activist, what changed him was connecting with others' humanity. As an anti-Semite, he'd feared what he hadn't understood, which neatly explains what I encountered in Indiana. As he transitioned away from that life, he became friends with a Jewish man and realized his dread and anxiety were based on lies and misperceptions.

Christian Picciolini, cofounder of Life Against Hate, spent his youth as a skinhead. His participation stemmed from having been disenfranchised as a kid. That's why hate groups are on the rise. People want a sense of community because they're disconnected, and it's easier than ever to form a community via social media. A study by sociologist Pete Simi of Chapman University concluded that what draws people into these groups is the social bond, rather than the ideology.[131]

In the Southern Poverty Law Center's Spring 2016 issue of *Intelligence Report*, Picciolini said, "Happy people don't plant bombs, and happy people don't behead people, and happy people don't paint swastikas on synagogues. It's just not the case. Disenfranchised, lonely, self-loathing people do that. There is something missing from their life, something that they didn't get."[132] What changed the narrative for him was people of other races showing him kindness—this new perspective created cracks and let the light shine in.

Communication. Connection. Kindness.

My question is, Why aren't our leaders advocating for conversation and understanding? DC has ceased to be that shining city on a hill, the very best representation of who we are as a nation. Shouting over others has become the political home-run swing. Has no one suggested we lock Congress in the employee breakroom and not let them out until they can be nice and find a way to work with each other?

Tip O'Neill's son Thomas wrote an article about when his father was Speaker of the House: "No, my father and [President] Reagan weren't close friends. Famously, after 6 p.m. on quite a few work days, they would sit down for drinks at the White House. But it wasn't the drinks or the conversation that allowed American government to work. Instead, it was a stubborn refusal not to allow fund-raisers, activists, party platforms or ideological chasms to stand between them and actions—tempered and improved by compromise—that kept this country moving."[133]

Is it impossible to hope we get back to the mutual respect these two opposing forces had not only for each other, but for the common cause and understanding of what was best for America?

Or is fostering division the ultimate ploy to create dependence and maintain power?

The media is just as complicit in highlighting our discord. I imagine that reporting on a nation at peace would be boring to cover twenty-four seven, so there's no impetus to bring us together—again, unless there's an alien attack. There's nothing exciting about nothing happening. Ad buyers want eyeballs on programs. Harmony doesn't sell; concord isn't sexy. For example, *Forbes* reported on the Institute for

Economics and Peace in their Global Peace Index ranking Iceland as the most peaceful country in the world—quick, tell me one thing you know about that place.

Wrong.

Iceland is green and Greenland is ice.

My point is, we don't know a damn thing about Iceland because there's no story there to tell. Plus, no one could spell their cities' names on the chyron under the breaking news crawl anyway.

In my three-pronged approach to worrying less about politics, step two is to stop reading political news on social media and to *absolutely* stop reacting to it. Per *Mother Jones*, "Nearly 70 percent of American adults say they get some of their news via social media."[134] That equals a metric shit ton of misinformation being disseminated every second, which means a metric shit ton of livid tweets and comments and angry-face emojis in response.

Let me ask, Has anyone ever resolved a political disagreement in a Twitter timeline? Has accord ever been reached in the Facebook comments section? Snotty, patronizing responses of "Let's just agree to disagree" don't count.

Further, do you want Zuckerberg's algorithms telling you what to think as they tailor your timeline to their predictions of what will prompt a response? Do you trust him? Did you even *see* his haircut while he was testifying in front of Congress? Why did no senator ask him to explain the '90s goth-girl baby bangs?

In a speech at Stanford, Chamath Palihapitiya, Facebook's former VP of user growth, told the audience, "The short-term, dopamine-driven feedback loops that we have created [at Facebook] are destroying how society works—no civil discourse, no cooperation, misinformation, mistruth."[135] When asked about his children's online habits, he added, "They're not allowed to use this shit."

Taking a step back from Facebook is a healthy idea, regardless of political spin. Researchers reviewed the online and in-real-life habits of thousands of adults for a two-year period, measuring self-reported aspects of life satisfaction, mental health, physical health, and body mass index.

They reported their findings in the *Harvard Business Review*: the more the participants used Facebook, the less positive they reported their well-being.[136] Facebook made them sicker and sadder and fatter. "That sounds great!" said no one ever. They found that the activity on Facebook was of little consequence—liking, posting, and clicking links all led to a similar result. The significant factor was the amount of time that they spent on the site.

I'm not saying not to use Facebook; instead I'm wondering if you're willing to place total faith in any organization whose motto has been Move Fast and Break Things?

Especially when what they broke was *us*.

A *New Yorker* profile of Mark Zuckerberg exposed a now-infamous memo that circulated after Facebook allowed a livestream of the shooting of Antonio Perkins, viewed by thousands. In the memo, a member of Zuckerberg's inner circle wrote, "Maybe it costs a life by exposing someone to bullies. Maybe someone dies in a terrorist attack coordinated on our tools. And still we connect people. The ugly truth is that we believe in connecting people so deeply that anything that allows us to connect more people more often is *de facto* good."[137]

If you need a second to delete your Facebook app from your phone, I'll wait. But if you want to keep it for access to recipes, book club posts, and cat memes, I'm behind that, too.

Basically, if you seek unbiased political information, please go to the source. Watch C-SPAN. It's definitely a fact that viewing may induce boredom cancer, according to Facebook, but you'll gain exposure to all sides of the argument before anyone can spin it to accommodate their own agenda. I highly recommend *Meet the Press*, too. Sure, it airs early on Sunday morning, but you can set your DVR or stream it online.

In terms of facts, we all know that Facebook permitted Cambridge Analytica access to the data of more than eighty-seven million people.

What they gleaned was in direct proportion to what we shared, liked, and responded to. We're the ones who got the Mogwai wet and fed him after midnight, and then we were all surprised when he turned into a Gremlin.

My husband thinks he invented the expression "If it doesn't cost anything, you are the product." I guarantee he didn't, but that doesn't make it less true.

Over the past few years, my anxiety over ending up in social media jail has led me to keep my thoughts close to the vest, so Facebook could only make predictions about me on my limited interactions. Based on the pet and book and snack information I fed them, their algorithm predicted my race, sex, age, and political affiliation wrong. How about this: How about we all give them less information? Because they proved they're not using what we're currently telling them for the common good.

My last advice about avoiding the polarizing, anxious anger that drives our relationship to government is the most actionable.

When someone comes at you with an aggressive political stance, and kindness and listening fail, I suggest you engage in the following steps, paraphrased from an article on wikiHow.[138]

- Do pay attention to the warning signs.
- Do exit before they can charge at you.
- Do back away deliberately if they become aggressive.
- Do keep calm. Now's not the time to lose your shit.
- Do seek medical attention if it comes to blows.
- Do not become hostile.
- Do not turn your back on them.
- Do not run away.
- Do not feed the beast.
- Do erect barriers whenever possible.
- Do inform the proper authorities if they remain problematic.

Granted, the wikiHow article was about how to avoid goose attacks, but it also works to fend off unwanted political dogma.

If there's any good news to buoy you, it's that commercial pilots and military personnel have reported an uptick in spotting unidentified aerial phenomenon (UAP) of late, noting odd flying patterns, advanced technology, and no discernable markings.[139]

Former deputy assistant secretary of defense for intelligence Christopher Mellon urged Congress to strategize a defense against the possible potential adversary with unmatched technical capabilities that has been buzzing our horizon.

Doesn't that seem more pressing than who said shit about whom in a poorly spelled tweet?

Of course, if said UAPs turn out to be an invading alien force and not something Elon Musk or Jeff Bezos cooked up, then it won't matter what side of the aisle lawmakers sit on when the House and Senate get vaporized *by little green men.*

Feel better yet?

PART IV

SOCIAL NEEDS: FRIENDSHIPS, INTIMACY, FAMILY, LOVE, AND BELONGING

The Beatles claimed that all you need is love. Later, they changed their tune to include a treatise on coming together, right now. Despite the portions of "Come Together" that veer into toe jam football and walrus gumboot, I feel like they were on the right track.

But Maslow? He begged to differ.

He thought that humans shouldn't concern themselves about love, belonging, and social connections until satisfying the first two tiers on the hierarchy. In his song, we'd come together only after the larder was full and we were safe from marauders.

On a somewhat related note, my grandmother was an infamous hoarder. Nothing that came into her home ever left; for example, her kitchen contained four refrigerators, only one of which functioned during my lifetime. However, the one thing she purged—and really, the single valuable commodity in the house—was my aunt's entire collection of original Beatles singles, which Noni burned in a barrel in the backyard.

Also? Aerosmith's version of "Come Together" was better.

That said, let's move on to the third tier.

But What about the Children?

I first noticed the change at the Whole Foods in Deerfield.

I was at the market to buy a pound of prepared kale salad. Kale had recently come into vogue and due to my FOMO, I didn't want to be the only person not embracing the trend. (These were the pre-avocado days of the early 2010s.) Kale's publicity team must have been working overtime, because I was convinced I'd be left behind if I didn't immediately embrace those stiff, waxy green bundles. Plus, Fletcher didn't despise kale, which felt like a victory after our recent brussels sprouts debacle that disproved my theory that he'd eat anything when smothered in enough bacon.

At the time, Whole Foods was the only spot that made a version of kale I liked. I did not enjoy chewing salads that had the consistency of parchment paper. But WF's prepared foods department did some magic with those leaves, so I routinely drove two towns away to buy it.

As I approached the prepared food section that day, a mother-daughter team cut in front of me with such grace and sense of purpose that I felt compelled to apologize for having arrived first. I took my place behind them in line and waited for my turn.

Mistake. Big mistake.

What I learned too late was that the little girl was a sushi aficionado and she had many questions for the *itamae*—which is the proper term for "sushi chef." While I was impressed that the kid knew the word, I was reminded of a blog post I read a number of years back when Paris Hilton's pet kinkajou had bitten her. The blog writer was aggravated, awed, and shamed that she didn't know kinkajous existed, while Hilton did. There's probably a great Japanese word for those concurrent feelings, as the language gave the world access to *tsundoku*: the act of buying so many books that they begin to pile up in a delightful mess.

The *itamae* was busy manning the entire sushi and prepared foods area while his coworker basted the rotisserie chickens. Too shy to verbalize her questions to the chef, the kid whispered them to her mother, who passed them on. The daughter's name was Margot, which I learned as her mother prefaced each of her Spanish Inquisition's worth of questions with, "Margot wants to know . . ."

Margot, it seemed, could have a brilliant career as a health inspector, what with the depth and breadth of her knowledge on food prep.

As seconds turned to minutes, I couldn't help but scrutinize the duo. I could have skated across the diamonds that hung on the mom's neck, ears, wrists, and fingers. Diamond sizes, I believe, exist in direct proportion to how often a spouse bangs the nanny. There was, in this case, a possibility this woman once *was* the nanny.

The color of her flawless hair reminded me I was running low on French butter. She was clad in equestrian gear, and not the never-once-touched-a-horse stuff Ralph Lauren sells at Macy's. I'm talking real-deal jodhpurs and riding boots, coated with a thin sheen of dust after she'd doubtless whiled away the day jumping rails in an indoor arena. You know who *doesn't* spend the day riding Thoroughbreds? Anyone with full-time employment. Aside from cowboys.

I felt slightly guilty about silently judging that mom within the privacy of my own head, but she basically demanded I do so when she cut in front of me. If I had a family crest, it would read Please Don't Make Me Be an Asshole.

After I'd grown bored with staring hot holes of hatred through that mom's bony back, I turned my gaze to Margot. The kid had her—equally blonde—hair arranged in a tight bun and was sporting a leotard, so she must have just come from ballet class and was feeling peckish.

She was wearing Dolce & Gabbana jeans. As I waited, I googled prices. One search string later and I discovered that the kid was wearing $300 denim. Let that sink in for a minute—$300 jeans . . . on a *six-year-old*. How her mom was not having an anxiety attack over whether Margot would ruin her pants with dribbles of soy sauce, I will never understand. If I'd ever been allowed to own something so precious, my mom would have held a tarp over me and the garment, protecting it like a Sartorial Secret Service agent, likely so I could eventually be married in it. I once dinged a pair of eight-dollar wooden clogs by wearing them on my bike, because the pedal ridges dug into the bottom of the wood. My mom was so mad at me—and not the manufacturer who used the cheap soft wood—that I wasn't allowed to wear my clogs for the rest of the summer. When I put them on again in the fall, I'd outgrown them.

I guess we all learned a lesson there.

Margot was also wearing a tiny North Face puffer jacket and carrying a Burberry purse. *What? No!* Why did she need a Burberry handbag at *six*? What was she carrying? Lipstick? Car keys? Plan B? I draw the line at kids carrying Burberry. That's a hard pass for me.

Here's the thing about being six—you can get away with anything under the guise of lacking necessary skills; it's the ultimate scam. Kids, please, let your mom pour your milk! Have your dad make your bed! Give them the privilege of drawing your bath! Being six is the closest most of us will ever come to understanding what it's like to have a butler. I made it to fourth grade before my mother figured out I knew how to tie my own shoes—I just didn't care for bending. Children should enjoy the few years of their lives when they can walk out of the house completely unencumbered by fifteen semiused Kleenexes, ten thousand keys, and that one time, a banana. (Wait, just me?)

Anyway, back to Margot. To complete her ensemble, she was wearing Hunter Wellington boots. The pair I own were a birthday gift from my college freshman roommate, Joanna. She endured me when I was seventeen; *she* is the one who deserves such a nice present, not me. I got them when I turned fifty. Per my calculations, Margot should have waited another forty-four years. Her Wellies cost as much as every pair of shoes I owned for my whole childhood. Combined. When I was her age, my kicks came from Kmart, Sears, or Thom McAn, just like everyone else's did. I assure you, Patrick Demarchelier never featured my adolescent choice of footwear in a three-page pictorial for *Vogue*.

PS, it wasn't even raining that day.

I guarantee Margot didn't need the boots to walk to school through puddles because 80 percent of third graders walked to school alone in 1971, but by 1990, that number had fallen to 9 percent.[140] Now, I bet it's more like 1 percent.

I think that enormous change was partially brought on by the 1979 abduction of six-year-old Etan Patz, one of the first missing children to appear on a milk carton. Patz disappeared on his way to the bus in New York City. His parents didn't know he never made it to school, because the administration didn't notify them. That was the norm. The principal's secretary was probably too busy churning out mimeographs that would be delivered to our classrooms, still warm and smelling like a photography darkroom. Once my mom took me out of school for a week to attend a wedding with her back in Boston. Only after five days' absence did administrators at my junior high school inquire on my whereabouts.

My anger about my free-range generation equals my annoyance at the backlash of overprotection. But neither of those feelings stopped me from coveting the wardrobe of someone who couldn't use an analog clock yet, or ever.

Also, when did kids start dressing better than me?

To clarify, I don't mean better than how I dressed in the 1970s, I mean how I dress *right now*.

Grade-schoolers used to wear whatever items their siblings outgrew. I didn't receive many of my brother's hand-me-downs, not because I didn't covet his supa-fly flat-front plaid pants and fuzzy knit vests, but because they didn't fit. Last year, Princess Charlotte wore Prince George's old jumper for the royal family's Christmas card photo. The British media went berserk, but I was charmed. *That's* how you normalize a monarchy and make them relatable. (Or, you marry Meghan Markle and invite Oprah to the wedding where you have a gospel choir perform, and please don't allow me to go off on a tangent about my royal love of royal love.)

Back then, everyone's pants had patches on the knees or little flowers embroidered over the holes on their sweaters. Items simply weren't considered disposable then. Friends with older sisters never received any firsthand clothing until they went to college. I inherited several funky items from cousins who grew up in the 1960s, so when I wasn't wearing homemade skirts and capes, I was rocking my cousins' old bell-bottoms and wide-collared velour shirts, just Jan Brady AF. My point is, no one was hitting up Neiman Marcus to stock their kids' closets.

Flash forward to today where it's nonstop fashion week for upper-middle-class elementary schoolers everywhere.

"People want to dress up their children to keep them fresh. Social media is making it easier to show pictures of your children, and parents and fashion labels are taking this demographic more seriously," according to David Park, an illustrator at *Complex* magazine.[141]

Of everything parents must worry about today, should "keeping their children's looks fresh" be at the top of the list? How about this—maybe get them vaccinated for measles before fretting about the sell-by date of their ensembles. Why don't we operate on the premise that at age six, kids don't need to establish a *personal brand*?

Regardless of my opinion, and thanks to platforms like Instagram, the children's designer clothing market is exploding. In 2016, the luxury category in the children's wear market constituted 4 percent; by 2018, it had grown to 11 percent.[142]

Another impetus for the major upgrade in children's clothing is that mothers want their kids' styles to coincide with their own. Originally, the drive to twin with children stemmed from the desire to demonstrate affluence. At the turn of the last century, only families with the highest income could afford to buy—or take the time to sew—matching outfits.

All of this concerns me.

The third level of Maslow's Hierarchy deals with community and the security of belonging; that's precisely why I'm not sure if my outrage is merited. I don't have kids, I'm not in the trenches, so I am only reporting as an observer.

I worry that kids will be ostracized if they aren't dressing like North Kardashian West before they can read a *People* magazine. Bullying is no joke. If a kid was mean to me in grade school, it occurred on the playground or in the lunchroom. With internet access, children are available to be hassled twenty-four seven. No wonder the National Survey of Children's Health found that anxiety diagnoses for kids between the ages of six and seventeen shot up by 20 percent between 2007 and 2012.[143]

Don't children have enough to worry about? They might be left behind if their folks don't have them training for the PSATs by their tenth birthday. Access to the best educational tools is already causing a division between socioeconomic classes. Are some children going to be excluded because their parents can't (or won't) buy them tiny Burberry bags in third grade? Will parents be pressured to give their kids what they need to fit in, budget be damned? Will we see an even greater division because of some arbitrary logo on a bit of PVC?

Personally, I wasn't aware of labels until junior high, and that was a game changer, but not for the better. Until then, I hadn't realized that my self-worth could be externally validated—or invalidated. I had a happy childhood without a ton of outside worries. Kids weren't considered consumers then, so the only ads that targeted us were for sweet cereal and toys. No one was capitalizing on the inadequate feelings of the most vulnerable in our society; corporations just wanted to sell us Sugar Smacks and Hot Wheels.

Studies show that by the time kids reach middle school, the typical child will have seen eight thousand murders and one hundred thousand acts of violence (including rape and assault) on television, the internet, and computer games.[144] Maybe Margot's mom is a bit more stringent with her media, but the point remains. Is it a given that we're handing our kids increased anxiety, and providing them with luxury items is a small way to mitigate it?

Searching for a root cause of the newfound attention the luxury goods market is placing on children, I ran across the Instagram of child fashion influencer Coco Pink Princess. To clarify, Coco doesn't just influence children, she *is* a child. She's eight. She lives in the Harajuku area of Tokyo, a place best known for its crazy, creative street fashion. Her profile has all the earmarks of being something that would cause me to rage. I see it as a violation of kids' privacy to post their images on public forums, and I seethe at the notion of children needing couture jeans to be happy, because I'm not sure Dolce & Gabbana denim in size 3T should ever have been on the table.

Turns out, Coco's taste is as exquisite as it is eccentric. She's a tiny iconoclast in coats that appear to have been constructed out of bathmats, or small hats with miniature veils. In some photos, she's a wee grunge queen, in others, she's Alice, just emerging after following a rabbit down a hole. Her outfits are more like costumes, and that delights me—what kids don't adore an element of fantasy when they're still experts in make believe?

The shot that won me over completely was of Coco clad in a pleated army-green skirt, with a matching military sweater, a tiny strand of pearls, a beanie, and wild-print knee socks, all by Gucci: it's like my id and my Girl Scout uniform hooked up in a fitting room at Bergdorf's.

Her parents, I came to learn, own a vintage store, and they sell the looks she creates, so they're not mortgaging the farm to afford her designer duds. So not only is Coco having fun, her internet presence helps the family business. Her aesthetic is exquisite, as the colors and textures she pairs are as much art as fashion. My money is on Coco growing up to excel at some sort of creative endeavor. More importantly, I suspect she's going to grow up *happy* . . . But alongside the total joy I feel while scrolling through her feed, I'm equally terrified that she might get abducted because her parents allowed her to have an internet presence.

In a perfect world, maybe Coco would have an emoji pasted over her face in her Instagram shots. Kids as young as five are being groomed on Instagram, and the number of children targeted by pedophiles tripled from 2017 to 2018.[145]

Even more shocking, by two years old, 90 percent of American children have had their likeness featured on social media sites.[146] For all the precautions parents exercise now, all the helmets and booster seats and sunscreen, wouldn't toddlers be safer without one million followers on Instagram? If nothing else, how can we keep our nation's kids from becoming assholes when thousands of strangers tell them how great they are every day?

I still think about Margot—who must be well into her teens by now. I wonder if she appreciates any of the stuff her mother lavished on her at six. It seemed that she'd been wearing the very finest garments since birth, and I picture her closet full of the brands I've toiled my whole adult life to buy.

In the attempt to give her everything, her mom, I fear, robbed her of the chance to realize the value of her own efforts.

I have issues with my parents, but their greatest gift was forcing me to produce my own results. Through the ups and downs of my life, my work ethic is my most prized characteristic. No matter what kind of pinch I'm in, I can fight my way to the other side with grit and determination.

And despite Margot's apparent determination that we all die in that line that day, she showed some stubborn promise, if not a total lack of respect for others and social awareness. I almost admired her when she started questioning the provenance of the "escolar"—I googled it, it's a snake mackerel. Then I googled snake mackerel, damn it.

But the entire incident had me questioning Margot's future, and alongside it, our youths'. For instance, her favorite food was sushi. All roads lead me to believe that's *because her mother wanted it to be Margot's favorite food*. Left to her own devices, any kid would likely choose chicken fingers and grilled cheese. I mean, who among us wouldn't? I can't see much upside to adults steering children toward an identity based on status and superiority—those things should creep in naturally during their insufferable teen years.

Buying a first grader $300 jeans as a status symbol just doesn't seem right. But what's more concerning is that here, in the new millennium, *the kid herself has become the status symbol.*

MOMMING SO HARD

As stressful as it is for kids today to grow up as status symbols who love tuna sashimi, parents are stressing about plenty on the other side of that relationship. In the 1970s, every adult had dominion over every kid, which meant every adult had carte blanche to shout at will. This was the golden age of "Get off my lawn," having been preceded by the "Get a haircut, hippie" heyday. Further, any grown-up was permitted to dole out corporal punishment—up to and including open-handed slapping—without retribution.

I wish I were kidding.

Once during a school assembly, I was standing for the Pledge of Allegiance. I noticed the auditorium chair lined up perfectly with the bottom of my butt, so I tried to prop up my cheeks like a scaffolding while remaining upright, in the name of science. Could I balance in such a way that I could lift both feet from the floor and experience the sensation of floating? I wasn't disrespecting the flag; I was genuinely curious about the physics.

My third-grade teacher thought I was trying to sit, and she grabbed me with her forefinger and thumb, pulling me close to her face so she could hiss that I should stand up straight. Even though she was ancient, that woman had the pincer strength of a mature Alaskan king crab. The next day, when I showed her the deep purple bruise I developed in the exact imprint of her gnarled forefinger and thumb, she replied, "Then I guess you won't do that again." FYI, my parents found no fault with Mrs. Manhandler's grip. While I'm not saying her behavior was out of step with the time, perhaps more women would have sought STEM educations if their early biomechanics experiments had not been so rudely thwarted.

When I was nine, my parents dropped off my brother and me at the theater so we could see *Star Wars* with our neighbors. The eldest in our group was twelve. We loved the movie so much, we decided to sit through another showing. In the lobby, we held up one pay-phone receiver reverse to another, so our moms could talk and coordinate pickups. As Luke piloted his X-wing starfighter on his way to destroy the Death Star, I rocked in my seat, simulating my own flight through deep space. The guy behind me kicked my chair and told me to knock it off. He didn't work there and I didn't know him. But I stopped, sitting frozen until the credits because I was afraid I'd get in trouble again.

If an adult yelled at another person's kid in a theater now, they'd end up in court.

Mine was an era of children having to accommodate, rather than being accommodated. No parents put their children's tastes and proclivities first. That's a relatively new development. Comedian Maz Jobrani said kids are running the show now, as when he was young, he was forced to play with his parents' friends' kids. Now, as a parent, he's forced to play with his kids' friends' parents.

When clans of yore went out for a meal in my day, there were no crayons, no sippy cups, no serving little Jennifer's unsauced spaghetti early. Generation X kids conducted themselves like tiny civilized sophisticates, because if we misbehaved, we'd enjoy a spanking for dessert instead of the triple-layer chocolate cake that was rotating in a glass case. No one blinked when a parent smacked their whiny kid at the

Cork 'N Cleaver salad bar. It wasn't abuse; it was *problem-solving*. I still recall how scandalous it was the few times children at other tables were permitted to misbehave. All the adults in the room would glower from behind their fondue pots, whispering into their Chablis glasses, "*They must be from California.*"

Since my childhood, the practice of spanking has gone out of vogue for many reasons. Corporal punishment doesn't provide positive guidance. It fosters mistrust. It damages mental health. It increases both childhood aggression and the likelihood for delinquency and criminal behavior.[147] But if you want your offspring to grow up to be cynical and jaded, prone to anxiety and depression, then by all means . . . swing away.

I'm in favor of progress, but there's been a backlash for Gen X, stemming from the fact that kids are now completely untouchable, all safe in their hermetically sealed Lucite bubbles. As parents, we allow children to operate with impunity, to scream at will, their personal riders reading like Van Halen's on their 1982 tour. Children today need not heed anyone's instructions, including those of their caretakers. They are confident in their position at the center of the universe. They have never received a disco-era whupping.

That said, there's so much more for the youngest generation to fear in our world. Providing a safe home and an adult-child relationship without terror is an understandable desire, but it translates to no discipline when out to dinner. I get it. If I don't like it, I can order delivery.

After being childfree for many decades, one of my friends had her first baby. She was used to taking her little purse dog out with her and being relegated to the patio—the only dog-friendly option. The first time she entered with her baby, she was shocked that she was offered a table inside.

Last week, Fletch and I had lunch at a casual chain restaurant, and he seemed surprised when a family with a toddler was seated behind us.

"Why would they bring her here?" he asked.

"Because it's lunchtime."

"But there's a bar," he argued.

"And a children's menu," I replied.

The little girl shrieked a few times, and Fletch started to twitch. "Don't worry, they'll bring her food out early," I promised him. And they did. "See? Quiet. She's eating mac and cheese and watching TV on her tablet. That kid is living *my* best life right now."

If hitting is the alternative, I'd rather see kids rambunctious out in public than damaged long-term. To clarify, I'd rather see them home with a babysitter if it's after nine o'clock at night, but if that fails, then I definitely fall in the camp that supports not spanking.

Still, nature abhors a vacuum, so society now makes up for our unimpeachable children by engaging in public parenting shaming.

I'm not quite done with Margot and her mother, yet. Neither had any concept that I'd grown old in line behind them that day at the Whole Foods. I never indicated or voiced my displeasure. They were blissfully unaware of my existence. A million snappy retorts raced through my head, but that's where they stayed.

It's human nature to have reactions to what we witness, and it's my job as a writer to call them out anonymously. Our brains are constantly processing sensory input, scanning for risks, informing our systems whether we'll respond with fight or flight. We're not in prehistoric times anymore, but maybe when they cut in front of me at the deli counter, my lizard brain perceived they were stealing the resources I needed to keep my family alive.

A few years ago, Fletch and I were driving next to a massive SUV. The car was a paean to safety with built-in booster seats riding high for the best vista, its gigantic steel frame lined with side-impact airbags. The woman in the car had a couple of small children tucked securely in the back seat, headphones on while they watched *The Little Mermaid* on their in-seat display screens. As we cruised down Lake Cook Road at fifty miles per hour, I noticed the driver, ostensibly the mom, thumbing through a recognizable social media website with royal blue borders and fonts.

I lost my mind.

There was no semiunderstandable rationale for her being on her phone, going that fast with a car full of minors. She wasn't googling the nearest hospital. She wasn't dialing 911. She wasn't even pulling up directions. She was reading other peoples' feeds, looking at their photos, and adding comments. I made Fletch sound the horn, and when she looked over, I gave her the "point at my eyes, then point at the road" gesture. Plus a bonus gesture for good measure. She was mad, but so freaking what? She was endangering not only herself and her offspring with her distracted driving, but every other motorist.

The mom put down her phone, sheepish, and peeled away. I wasn't out to shame her for life, to inflict long-term punishment. I didn't take photos of her, her car, or her license plate, and I'd never post them if I did. The honk and gesture served to snap her out of her temporary daze before she accidentally did something reckless.

Social media gives us the means to provide a virtual honk, an ad hoc "hey dummy look at the road" gesture. That practice, which likely started as an attempt to provide a quick heads-up to unsuspecting offenders, has led to mass shaming on issues not nearly as defined as violating a traffic statute.

Increasingly, every aspect of a parent's role is open to critique, and this has put our entire society on edge.

On the *Scary Mommy* blog, Kim Simon explained, "Our parenting beliefs are not as easy to hide as religion and politics, so we use them as weapons when we need a release. The Mommy Wars are collapsing our confidence one snarky Facebook comment at a time. We are breaking each other down because we're crumbling inside, our pre-motherhood identity slowly disintegrating under the weight of the laundry, the groceries, and the thirty thousand jackets and sand toys and leaky sippy cups that our kids have left in the car. Motherhood is hard."[148]

Everyone has an opinion on what's best, from birth plans to breast-feeding to sleeping techniques. It used to be just your mother-in-law forcing advice on you; now it's anyone with Wi-Fi. This constant swirl of unsolicited influence—available at the click of a mouse—serves to undermine most parents' confidence in their own competence. Nine out of ten experts may agree on one solution, but if another solution works for the family, then outsiders should stop insisting they know what's best for *every child*. What if it *doesn't* take a village to raise a child? It might just take one engaged parent. In the immortal words of Dr. Spock, "Trust yourself. You know more than you think you do."

Provided no one's endangering children, their own or others (*ahem*, trust vaccines), parenting decisions are nobody else's business. While it's human nature to form an opinion, so many people have forgotten that it's polite to keep their thoughts on pacifier use to their damn selves unless their opinions are requested. If we went back to talking behind each other's backs instead of posting comments, I imagine there'd be an immediate reduction in our overall stress.

Social media has turned motherhood into a competitive endeavor. It's invited the world in to critique individual decisions on child-rearing. And what do competitions have? Winners and losers. Our online relationship with parenting is setting clear stakes in doing better, being better, and knowing better than everyone else. The message boards are focused on psyching out the opponent. *Of course* others are going to tell a mom she's screwing up; if they don't, that mom might win! When parents listen to shaming commentary, they're ceding valuable yardage.

People's private lives are being invaded by the uptick in commentary, and the worst part is, we're so addicted to the instant gratification of feedback now that we have trouble turning away when it's not what makes us feel good. Nothing happens in a vacuum anymore. When an overreacting father forces his daughter to cut her hair because her mother took her for forbidden highlights, it's no longer just an upsetting family matter, because the ladies on *The View* are discussing it.

You're Doing It Wrong! Mothering, Media, and Medical Expertise researchers Bethany L. Johnson and Margaret M. Quinlan studied newspapers, books, and magazines of the last hundred years, and they found that the pressure to conform to an arbitrary standard has been around as far back as they could trace. Further, the idea persists that "the ideal mother is a cis, white, middle- or upper-middle-class, educated, and able-bodied female."[149]

Woe be to anyone who falls outside the arbitrary statistical norm.

Mom shaming isn't exclusive to women, as evidenced by the dog pile on Bravo host Andy Cohen after his baby, Benjamin, was born through a surrogate. Followers were up in arms about every aspect of his fatherhood, from letting his dog, Wacha, sniff the baby's nose, to how he held his child in a carrier, to allowing Anderson Cooper to wear his street shoes into the nursery. It's fair to say that Cohen's fatherhood has been under attack, and because he clearly doesn't fit that platonic ideal of a straight woman providing care for her child, the criticism feels particularly pointed.

In April of 2019, I'd been invited to interview Cohen as part of a charity luncheon. Prior to our interview, I was required to submit a list of potential questions for review by his team; that's how it works with celebrities. Trust me, Jimmy Fallon is not ad-libbing gotcha questions, because if he did, guests would never show up.

Cohen's people approved every single question, save for the one I'd proposed about his recent experience with dad shaming. When he and I chatted before the event, he told me that I could ask anything and no query was off limits. I assured him that I was not going to run counter to what his team wanted and that I'd stick with the approved list. (I didn't want to be Barbara Walters; I just wanted to be invited to the next lunch.)

He and I spent an hour onstage, while every single person in the audience sat silent and mesmerized by his charm and candor. I did not solicit his opinion on dad shaming, but I didn't need to. He gave the audience his everything, but behind the scenes, he was an exhausted and ecstatic single parent, completely overwhelmed by his love for his son and committed to whatever was in Benjamin's best interests.

Try to shame that, I dare you.

We talked about raising a baby in New York, and Cohen was adamant he didn't want to move to Connecticut; his support system lived in Manhattan. He also said he was way too tired to think about a brother or sister for Benjamin . . . yet.

Apparently, he's not jumping immediately into the other surprising trend in Manhattan: multiple children have become the newest status symbol for the elite. Per the *New York Post*, wealthy families in New York are opting to have three or four children, and raising them in the city proper in lieu of absconding to the suburbs to do it.[150]

In an essay for the *New Yorker*, Tina Fey wrote: "All over Manhattan, large families have become a status symbol. Four beautiful children named after kings and pieces of fruit are a way of saying, 'I can afford a four-bedroom apartment and a hundred and fifty thousand dollars in elementary-school tuition fees each year. How *you* livin'?'"[151]

In her memoir, *Primates of Park Avenue*, Wednesday Martin identified this trend early on, in 2016, when families were getting larger, and that size was projecting an elevated status. "Three was the new two, something you just did in this habitat. Four was the new three—previously conversation-stopping, but now nothing unusual. Five was no longer crazy or religious—it just meant you were rich. And six was apparently the new town house—or Gulfstream."[152]

Today, you'd have to be legitimately rich to raise multiple children. The cost to raise a single child is $233,610, and that's without Burberry purses or higher education.[153] For the price of two children with Ivy League educations, you could have a sixty-two-foot Prestige 590 yacht with three staterooms, which is the kind of vessel you wouldn't be ashamed to dock next to Leonardo DiCaprio in Cannes.

Historically, the highest earning and most educated women have had the lowest birthrates. As recently as 2011, the *Washington Times* reported that "new U.S. fertility data suggest that having a higher education isn't associated with having a big family: Women who are college graduates are likely to have fewer children—if they have them at all—than their less-educated sisters."[154]

Those stats have changed. A study found that fertility rates for women with advanced degrees have risen 50 percent since the 1980s.[155] Whereas fertility rates had been on a decline for these women for many years, a recent uptick has caused the graph to become U-shaped. There's now a clear correlation between the women who can afford additional childcare and the women having the most babies.

This just solidifies my assumptions about Margot and her mom. Status. Freaking. Symbol.

This trend also neatly explains why we're in the throes of the Operation Varsity Blues scandal, where ultrawealthy parents were bribing officials to make sure their children got into the top tier colleges, regardless of whether they'd be able to handle the curriculum once enrolled. In an email, Mossimo Giannulli, Lori Loughlin's husband, wrote: "We just met with (our older daughter's) college counselor this am. I'd like to maybe sit with you after your session with the girls as I have some concerns and want to fully understand the game plan and make sure we have a roadmap for success as it relates to (our daughter) and getting her into a school other than ASU!"[156]

Sir, you paid $500,000 to get a makeup blogger into a college that would impress your friends; maybe don't cast aspersions on anyone else's education here, okay?

The wealthiest families aside, birth rates overall are on the decline in the US. For four straight years, the number of births in the US have fallen, and we've just hit a thirty-two-year low for women having children in their teens and twenties.[157] Yet women in their thirties and forties have slightly higher birthrates than previous years—often buoyed by a deliberate decision and involving science and a five-figure check.

On Maslow's Hierarchy, the need for love and belonging motivates our behavior. While parents have always loved their children, something significant has changed in the parent-child dynamic since I was young. In *Psychology Today*, Dr. Steven Mintz raised the point that parents are much more sensitive to the risks that their children might face now. Thus, today's generation of children spend a lot more time indoors.[158]

Mothers in my era would have *lost their shit* over this. Kids in the 1970s trying to come inside during daylight were as wanted as a phone call from a telemarketer. I have clearly chronicled the time I spent traipsing through the woods as a child. My parents would have turned us over to the state if we'd been indoors, underfoot all day.

Unsupervised play outdoors has become an anachronism, only an expected choice for those parents society deem most neglectful. Author Kim Brooks left her four-year-old child—who protested coming into the store—alone in a temperate, locked car (but within her line of sight) for five minutes while Kim bought him headphones at a Virginia Target before their flight home. Only once she'd returned to Chicago did she learn that someone had recorded her behavior, causing her to spend the next couple of years on a legal odyssey, fighting neglect and endangerment charges that had been reported by a bystander. She was ultimately sentenced to one hundred hours of community service and twenty hours of parenting instruction.[159]

Talk about your mom shaming.

Anne Godlasky dissected the double standard of Brooks's conundrum in an article for *USA Today*. She argued that it was statistically less safe to drive the kid to the store than to leave him locked in the car, as hundreds of children are injured in car accidents every day while their parents drive, yet the number of child abductions is around one hundred per year.[160]

Perhaps the issue isn't judgment, it's perspective. People see kids riding in cars all the time, but seeing them *sitting* unattended in a car is an anomaly, ergo, cause for concern. Forty years ago, no one would have blinked an eye at an unchaperoned car full of kids—and that car would have been unlocked and running.

In the face of this scrutiny, Utah signed a bill into law—a bill that would permit free-range parenting. Governor Gary Herbert explained, "Utah's 'Free Range Parenting' law is a good example of common sense legislation. We believe that parents know and love their children better than anybody. We also believe that absent evidence of neglect, danger or cruelty, parents have the best sense of how to teach responsibility to their children. Responsible parents should be able to let kids be kids without constantly looking over their shoulders for approval."[161]

What I've noticed is that kids' opinions suddenly seem to matter. Children have attained suffrage. Gina is a C-suite executive recruiter, and she's lost many quality candidates for jobs that paid $500,000-plus per year, because the candidates' offspring didn't want to relocate. Could my brother and I have outvoted my parents on moving to Indiana? Instead of soliciting our opinion, my father promised he'd buy us horses once we lived in farm country.

There were no horses.

My father lied, and when pressed about this fib years later, his answer was "Jennifer, I don't negotiate with ten-year-olds." Respect.

But now, parents are perpetually leaving work early because their kid has a soccer match, even though that kid will ride the bench the entire time. None of my classmates had family that would rearrange their professional schedules to accommodate our amateur endeavors; it would have been weird.

Maybe childhood has changed because the way we look at parents has changed. While my mother had ninety-nine problems, worrying about how she measured up to other bitchy mothers wasn't one.

Probably because every person she knew wasn't scanning her social media feed on the reg and commenting at will.

The race to "mom the hardest" is running women ragged. Whose homemade organic baby food is the healthiest? Whose craft room is the most Pinterest-perfect? Whose kid is the biggest prodigy, thanks to a full-time job's worth of after-school activities? We can compare timelines to find out!

Mommy blogs sparked this trend in the early 2000s, when having a website became easier for people who weren't computer coders. Then, in post-9/11 America, many chose to rethink their lives. For some, that included starting a family. Manhattan experienced a baby boom, and the number of families with children under five rose by 20 percent between 2000 and 2003.[162]

The blogs began as an endeavor where mothers could connect and commiserate over the thankless chore of raising their children. (I had a mirror journey, connecting and commiserating over having lost my job.) Women shared their authentic joys and frustrations, and their blogs collected cult followings. I subscribed to tons of mommy-blogging feeds during the heyday, not because I was looking for toilet-training tricks, but because there were so many talented writers producing compulsively readable content.

Blogging quickly morphed into big business, as advertisers caught a whiff of the influence these ladies had on their audiences. Lots of women went from moms to moguls in the early days. And suddenly, those followers started to mean more than connection and commiseration; they meant cold hard cash. Instead of maintaining a supportive community, many bloggers shifted slightly to competing for the most lucrative marketing contracts. Being the best became a goal.

As new social media platforms came online, including YouTube and Instagram, savvy mommy bloggers extended their reach, like silent movie stars making the leap to talkies. When the emphasis switched from written storytelling to visual and from relatable to aspirational, I lost interest. I want to read your story; I don't care to see your #spon-sorednursery. But I was in the minority, because by 2020, social media platforms—ostensibly including mommy blogs—are expected to be a $10 billion industry.[163]

While I believe mommy blogging began as a noble endeavor, the new focus on mommy influencers has upped the collective anxiety level of far too many women, especially as the content is now driven by competition for sponsorship. The *Washington Post* attests: "It's beautiful. It's aspirational. It's also miles from what motherhood looks like for many of us—and miles from what the mommy Internet looked like a decade ago."[164]

For those mommy bloggers who didn't follow the trend, some resorted to oversharing not only the gritty details of their own struggles, but also those of their children, creating a digital footprint for their offspring that's everlasting, unaware or unconcerned that the internet is a bell you can't unring. When I was in grade school, my brother had a difficult time learning Spanish. Because I have always been the world's hall monitor, I wrote his teacher a letter, explaining how she could do her job better. I instructed my brother to deliver this note to her. He didn't. The Mrs. Cummings letter became family legend, and I never heard the end of it. If it had happened when my mother could have taken a quick snapshot and posted it online, it might have gone viral. Twenty years after the fact, potential employers would be confronted with the evidence of my unique personality before I even set foot in a job interview.

The parent-child immunity doctrine dictates that a parent can't sue a minor child in a civil matter, nor can the child sue a parent. But the subjects of these early mommy blogs are coming of age, so I wouldn't be shocked if we start seeing suits. I've got my money on a suit against Christie Tate, a mommy blogger who refused to stop sharing photos and stories, despite her fourth-grade daughter's pleas for privacy after finding way too much about her life on Google. Tate wrote an opinion piece explaining why she would not remove past content. "Certainly, my daughter is old enough now that I owe her a head's up and a veto right on the pictures or on portions of the content, but I'm not done exploring my motherhood in my writing. And sometimes my stories will be inextricably linked to her experiences."[165] I suspect if Tate finds herself alone at future Christmases, this will be why.

However, "sharenting" is becoming the norm: the average parent will post one thousand images of their first child online by the time they're five.[166] As a childfree adult, I have no frame of reference here. There are maybe twenty pictures of me from my childhood in total. I don't care how many pics people post to show family and friends, but I'm not struggling with infertility, so I'm not triggered when they fill my timeline.

The only parallel I can draw is when my husband was prepping for a colonoscopy, which involved a day of fasting. I could hear him cry out every time a food commercial came on. He stomped into the kitchen after a tuna commercial pushed him over the edge. "I don't even like tuna! And it's a stupid can, full of stupid herbs and spices that stupid Susan in your office would eat at her stupid desk because she's just so darned busy that she can't take a real lunch break! I would never buy that or eat that, but right now, it's the only thing I want in this world." He was livid and he was merely a day away from any type of sandwich he desired. If I'd spent years (and thousands of dollars) wanting children, only to come up empty handed, social media would be an exhausting minefield.

The competition to be a "bad mom" is surprisingly cutthroat, too. Recent films celebrate this phenomenon, depicting moms gone wild in the produce aisles. They're driving their kids to school in their jammies and sending packaged Oreos to the fourth-grade bake sale. They're swilling rosé from a sippy cup at soccer practice. They're badass moms.

I like this trend; it feels more authentic, which is what mommy blogs used to be. My friend Jen Mann made the leap from obscure mommy blogger to *New York Times* bestselling author, thanks to an off-the-cuff riff on the Elf on the Shelf. The small bit of holiday cheer had bested her. In the middle of yet another haggard holiday season, she read an overachieving mom's "101 Fun Ideas to Do with Your Elf" and completely lost her shit. Her screed became a rallying cry to over-worked moms everywhere and launched her writing career . . . and yet she's never posted a shot of her kids or given their real names. Team Jen for the win!

Honestly, from an outside perspective, parenthood seems too com-plicated now. Everyone's required to be so much more involved. When my brother or I had an issue with another kid, my parents weren't interested in solving our problems. We had to work it out ourselves. Now, one act of childish behavior on the playground requires a Strategic Arms Limitation Talk, with all members of opposing families duking it out like the Gambinos versus the Genoveses. Lawyers and law enforce-ment optional.

Parents having closer relationships with their children is a wonder-ful thing, but there must be some line where the closeness becomes too much. Schools are cracking down on parents for eating lunch with their children on campus, because it's becoming a problem. In fact, this happened so often in Darien, Connecticut, that the elementary school banned parents completely from the cafeteria.[167] Once upon a time, eating lunch with their kids at school would have been a punishment for parents, doled out by a capricious judge on a terrible sitcom. Now it's a treat. That's suspicious.

The rise in helicopter parenting, meant to keep kids feeling safe and loved, has created an unwanted side effect. Overcontrolling par-ents have had a meaningful impact on their children's lives beyond the schoolyard. One study found that "students who reported having over-controlling parents reported significantly higher levels of depression and less satisfaction with life. Furthermore, the negative effects of helicopter parenting on college students' well-being were largely explained by the perceived violation of students' basic psychological needs for autonomy and competence."[168]

Fletch says Facebook keeps suggesting he add his friends' kids to his buddy list, but he's not biting. "No," he told me in frustration, "I don't want to add them. I don't like them; they're the reason I haven't seen my friends in twenty years."

I admit, my perspective is particular. I decided to bypass parenthood. In the 1970s, only one in ten women was childfree; today the number is one in five.[169] Yet when I mention my choice, I've had moms look at me like I'm defective, or a unicorn, or a defective unicorn.

Keep your pity; I don't need it.

I knew early on that children weren't in my plans. I never once played with baby dolls. I preferred Barbies because it would have been illegal to dress up a baby for her Studio 54 date with Ken. I never felt a biological tug looking at children. It's not that I'm missing maternal feelings, it's more like they apply only to cats and dogs, possibly small monkeys. While I'm happy for everyone who wants a family, I look at the notion of having kids the same way I look at people who get tattoos on their faces, like, "Hoo-boy, that's permanent."

Also, the invitation to sniff a baby's head is lost on me; it's creepy and all I can smell is diaper.

Women ask me *all the time* if I feel like I made a mistake. This is rude. Of course, the best response to this question comes from Claire Underwood in *House of Cards*. When asked, "Do you ever regret it, not having children?" Claire answers, "Do you ever regret having them?" The mom shaming isn't relegated to those with children, I'm here to attest.

In truth, I've never had a flash of doubt. Once I was in a well-woman exam and the walls were thin. An odd throbbing sound came from the exam room next door, followed by yelps of joy and tears. I realized I was listening to a set of new parents hearing their baby's heartbeat for the first time. In that moment, I searched my soul and asked myself, "Am I missing out?" While their elation was contagious, my answer was still no.

It's possible I have the story wrong with Margot and her mother. Her mom might be a tech entrepreneur who retired early, based on her hard work, with the singular goal of being the best mother she could.

Margot's mom might have grown up dressing in nothing but the garments she received from the church donation bin, the subject of scorn and mockery on the playground every day. I have no idea what their story is—though I'd be happy to write it at least five different ways—but the point is that we all make decisions and have opinions.

The respectful thing to do is to keep our impressions to ourselves, but also second-guess them. The stories we create are often wrong.

Personally, I know what it's like to have a parent look to their child as a status symbol, and this is largely why I no longer have a relationship with my family. After I started gaining notoriety as an author, my mother found herself losing her scope of influence and she didn't like it. She was never happier than when Fletch and I were unemployed and had to ask her for help, and she relished the idea that we'd move in with her, as she was the only one in her family who didn't have an adult child living under their roof.

In my mother's mind, all I'd achieved was due to her, and not my own efforts. For example, when I was on *Oprah*, she didn't understand why she didn't get to sit next to me. Um . . . because it was an episode about dog rescue? The appropriate being—Maisy, my first pit bull—was by my side.

Eventually, my mother's behavior had spun out so much I sought an order of no contact against her.

I stopped speaking to her after she threatened to sue me for libel. While nothing I'd ever written had been libelous—in fact, she loved the book in question so much, she demanded I dedicate it to her—her threats cost me thousands of dollars as they came in during contract negotiations with Penguin Random House. Later, she almost cost me my career, thanks to a failed deal with Simon & Schuster.

Instead of backing down and apologizing, I stood my ground for the first time in my adult life. While I was growing up, my mother's behavior was so mercurial, I never knew what to expect, thus setting me on a course for a lifetime of anxiety. Having the one person I was supposed to rely on operate in a manner that was erratic at best, I was never able to let down my guard. The only way to make peace was to comply, regardless of the circumstances.

The problem with seeking an order of no contact was that I didn't know any lawyers other than the real estate attorney who helped us close on our home. I assumed that all attorneys knew all laws when I asked her advice, but I was way off base. Apparently our real estate attorney conflated the no contact order with an order of protection.

Big mistake. On all our parts.

Standing in front of a judge in a room full of abused women and their men clad in orange jumpsuits and shackles, I had to explain how my mother damaged my career by retaliating in ever-escalating shenanigans, such as sending the police to my house, leaving comments about me on the Facebook pages of authors I'd mentioned I'd read, maligning me to booksellers, soliciting Oprah to do a show to bring us together, and I believe, having someone falsify a sympathy note to make me believe my father had died so I'd be forced to call her.

My concern in court was her not being allowed to ambush me at book events. Again. I'd hoped to get the no contact order after her performance in Saint Louis. She'd showed up, having lied to my father about where she was going. On spotting me, she burst into hysterical tears, wailing so loudly that all the bartenders tidying up behind my signing table left the room because they were mortified. When she sobbed that she didn't understand what had happened with us, I explained that she'd threatened to sue me for libel. Changing tactics, she then demanded to know what number my book had debuted at on the *New York Times* list, had me sign a copy for her shell-shocked neighbor who stood there mute, having been inadvertently roped into her nonsense . . . and then gave me a framed picture of herself.

I can't even maintain a relationship with my father because she intercepts his phone, reads his mail, and hacks into his email to send me messages about how I'm ungrateful and should apologize and everything is my fault. To this day, she attempts to use social media to troll my readers and shame me, calling herself a victim, claiming she has no idea why we're no longer close.

Spoiler alert? We were never close.

I ended up telling this story one day in comedy class, as Erin didn't want us to be funny; instead, she wanted us to share something "real." I didn't realize how cathartic it was to tell that story until I'd finished. While I was tight with almost everyone in the class, I'd never formed a bond with Laura, the fourth-wave feminist exotic dancer. But after I spoke, she hugged me and said, "We have more in common than I thought."

Ultimately, I didn't pursue the order of protection, as I'd been misadvised by the person who reviewed my mortgage document for discrepancies. Go figure. My case worker said the best thing was for me to not show up in court and what I'd started would all go away. My mother still went to court, and afterward, she left me a message that the judge said he was very sympathetic to her and would have ruled for her anyway.

Right. I'll take "What Is Something a Sworn Officer of the Court Would Never Say" for $1,000, Alex.

My point is, parents would likely be happier if they concentrated more on their own achievements, and less on that of their children.

If there's any room for judgment in current parenting trends, it's that people put way too much pressure on themselves and others, while they are just doing that which humanity has successfully done since the beginning of time, long before seat belts or sunscreen or swimsuits with built-in floaties. And that pressure exists largely because they're worried about people like me assessing their every move.

Again, a mutual cease-fire would be beneficial.

Now, I'm not suggesting we start having our kids take the subway alone in first grade—which they do in Tokyo.[170] Nor do I recommend a parent park their sleeping baby in a stroller outside a coffee shop, unattended, in freezing temperatures—which they do in Stockholm to help babies' immune systems.[171] And I'm definitely not saying their junior high schooler should swill wine with the family dinner—which they do in Italy, to curtail the urge to binge drink later in life.[172]

But maybe they'd take a bit of pressure off themselves, their kids, and their timeline if they let a kid have chicken fingers occasionally after dance class. As a nod to health, they could serve them over a bed of kale salad.

The trick is to massage the greens first to make them tender.

FRIENDING IS NOT A VERB

Friendship was a given when I was in grade school, a guarantee. If I had neighbors approximately my own age, that was it; they were my tribe. We were bound together by shared geography.

Sure, I might have clicked with classmates, but if my mom had to skip her tennis match to drive my cape-wearing ass all the way across town to play Chutes and Ladders? Never happening. I could hang with the perfectly good kids next door, and I wasn't allowed to come home until dinner.

It didn't matter how weird anyone on my block was, how unpleasant, how combative, how they chewed the same wad of gum for two months and kept it in a dollhouse-scale cradle when sleeping (true story); if we had the same letter carrier, I was bound to Violet Beauregarde.

What's odd is, it worked.

Given no choice, I was obligated to navigate relationships with all types. If my neighbor Denise didn't like my Donny Osmond singles, then we'd listen to "Bohemian Rhapsody." If I wasn't into sharing a lump of bubblegum the size of a fibroid tumor, Violet and I would walk to the candy store, where she'd stock up on Hubba Bubba and buy Swedish Fish. As Sharon wasn't a Barbie fan, she and I would climb onto the slanted roof outside my bedroom window and dangle our legs off the sides. (No adult supervision in the '70s. None.)

Early on, kids my age learned the art of finding mutually amenable activities. Turns out, everybody loved making Shrinky Dinks. Sitting shoulder to shoulder, rapt in front of the oven window, watching those polystyrene creations contract and burst into brilliant Technicolor was a true bonding experience.

In Fletch's case, propinquity dictated that he hang with the boy across the street who only wanted to play "Dolly Parton" while Fletch hoped to run army maneuvers. They compromised by throwing rocks at the windows of the junior high.

Once Fletch got his big-kid bike, he left Dolly in the dust, vanishing from the relationship much like the man Jolene stole, but without any animosity. Fletch and his neighbor are Facebook friends, and that guy grew up to become a Dolly impersonator. He's met Dolly many times and his feed is full of photos of him beside her, a fact which delights me. Fletch is an army infantry vet, so I guess both of their dreams came true.

Anyway, during my childhood, we mostly just ran around outside with our immediate neighbors. Why go to the effort of walking three blocks when Violet B. was right there, two houses away?

Playdates as formal affairs didn't exist during my childhood—I lived in a neighborhood. No one's mom was involved, whipping out phones, attempting to coordinate schedules between all the after-school enrichment activities. I just knocked on the door and asked whoever answered if the kid could come out to play. The answer was always yes, because we never had more than half an hour of homework, and that was only when the narcs raised their hands to tell the teacher she forgot to give us an assignment. The big activity in my New Jersey neighborhood was TV Tag. Anyone who was not yet in college would play. It was a variation of Freeze Tag, only in order to become unfrozen, players had to yell out the name of a television show. There were so few shows to choose from back then that once we'd exhausted *The Brady Bunch*, *Good Times*, and *Happy Days*, players started getting picked off fast. I didn't realize I was a hypercompetitive douchebag back then. That knowledge hit me years later in spin class, where I determined that I would sooner die on that bike than allow someone ahead of me on the leader board.

But the trait had always been inside me, dormant and lurking. Before a game of TV Tag would commence, I'd quickly review all the listings in the *TV Guide*, as though I were cramming for the MCATs. I may be the first kid to ever have won a game by citing *The MacNeil/ Lehrer Report*.

I was not a gracious winner.

College turned out to be a lot like grade school in that I gravitated to those who lived close—either on my dorm floor or members of the same fraternity. Many of those friendships still stand.

After my third or fourth senior year, friend making became more difficult. All my besties had graduated and started their "real lives," so the leasing company put me with two roommates who were twenty-one years old to my twenty-five. For all we had in common, it may as well have been four dog years.

Generation Z would now call my old roommates "basic bitches." While they were tidy and sweet, their tastes were simple. They were fans of whatever the number one song was on the Billboard chart. There were no highs with them, no lows, just lots of pumpkin-spice-flavored middle. For example, while I loved the Canadian sketch-comedy show *The Kids in the Hall*, they preferred *Full House*. We didn't connect. They would cry-laugh every time Stephanie Tanner said, "How rude!" But when I'd show them a scene where Mark McKinney hid in the bushes, staring through his fingers pretending to crush the heads of Wall Street guys? Nothing.

Per Joanna, I'm dangerous because I remember every detail, like the day she said three snarky things (January 23, 1986). However, I'm hard pressed to come up with those roommates' names. Maybe they were both called Ashley. They were nice, but prone to the kind of small talk one expects from a dental hygienist.

One day, the Ashleys and I were at our building's pool. A girl from a different floor arranged her towel beside us. Ashley Blonde remarked on the girl's cute bathing suit. Ashley Brunette concurred; indeed, the suit was cute. I was reading and wasn't enticed to join the conversation. Beyond "I like your swimsuit" and "Thanks, it's from Ups 'N Downs," there wasn't much ground to cover. Yet the three droned on about swimwear forever, like they were on a corporate retreat for Speedo executives. They discussed the process of finding a suit that was cute, speculating on what cuts were the most to least cute, and debated where they liked to shop for suits that could be cute. The word "cute" was used no less than 426 times. They made plans to go back to our apartment to check out the tankini Ashley Brunette didn't wear that day.

It was cute.

I had to put on sunglasses so they couldn't monitor the frequency with which I rolled my eyes. Those three became best friends, and I moved into an apartment by myself the following semester. While I had fellow waitresses crash with me a few times over the next year, the Ashleys were the last roommates I had until Fletch and I moved in together.

Fletch was my boyfriend before it occurred to me that he'd become my closest friend. While many couples say that their partner makes them a better person, the reality is that together, we bring everyone down to our level, and that works equally well.

Making new friends as an adult can be hard and awkward because the stakes feel so much higher and we're set in our ways. For my girlfriends, I follow the hair extension rule. I had extensions put on once and they took most of the day, just me trapped in a chair, draped in a fancy garbage bag, having someone else's crowning glory glued to my own.

Stacey sat with me for five hours, sharing stories about Jewish summer camp and volunteering in Africa. Thank God for her, as the hairdresser spent the entire time snapping her gum. Stacey is the only reason I didn't end up on the news.

For my close adult friends, I want a person who can hang with me for the long haul of installing hair extensions without once saying "cute."

As adults, though, many of us default again to buddying up with those in proximity to us at home or work, which can be great, provided we like each other. If we don't? We're stuck with them anyway and every interaction becomes a master class in passive aggression.

None of my friends live closer than a forty-five-minute drive from me, and the rest of my tribe lives in different time zones, but distance doesn't matter. Whenever we get together, it's like no time has passed. While not specifically religious, I have faith, and in my prayers, I thank my Creator every night for the gift that is these women.

The key to keeping these later-in-life friendships is honesty. Gina knows there's no way in hell I'm doing something past ten o'clock, especially on a school night. I return the favor by feigning ignorance when someone asks me how old she is.

If I'm traveling with Stacey, her boundary is that we each have our own separate rooms *and* bathrooms. I could never sleep at slumber parties, and she doesn't wear pajamas, so no on both counts. With Tracey and Alyson, if they're at my house while I prep for a party, the rule is that they sit to the side and entertain us while Joanna and I whiz through the checklist in a well-coordinated dance. That no one's surprised by the other's wants, needs, and expectations eliminates potential stressors.

My mother never had close friends. She had chatty neighbors and tennis partners, but there was no one in our lives she was close to who wasn't a blood relative. In recounting stories about other women, she'd only highlight their faults—like the roommate who kept stuffed animals in plastic bags so they'd stay clean. While she received annual holiday letters from college friends, she never went on girls' trips or had groups over for dinner, where they'd drink wine and laugh and talk for hours. In her view, friends were how she'd kill time until she could be with her sisters again.

On the other hand, my father, an only child, was still tight with every single person he'd collected since his childhood. Overall, he was much happier, so his approach seemed better.

Friendship has a huge impact on well-being, during all stages of life. Scientists studied a group of grade-schoolers, looking at stress responses when a best friend was present versus absent. They found that having the kid's bestie beside them after a stressful time served as a buffer, lowering the cortisol stress hormone and increasing feelings of self-worth.[173]

Another study compared fifteen- and sixteen-year-olds who had close friendships to those who were popular, with larger friend groups but fewer close relationships—so the cheerleaders and partiers on the A-list. The study found that at age twenty-five, those who had fewer but closer friends had higher feelings of self-worth and less social anxiety and depression than the cool kids.[174]

The lesson here is you should never peak in high school.

For adults in the workplace, having a work buddy remains just as beneficial. A study found employees who didn't have a support network in the office were nearly two and a half times more likely to die over a twenty-year period.[175] Work is inherently stressful. No one would choose to be an HR generalist or tax attorney if those jobs didn't pay the bills. Having a kindred spirit there to lower your cortisol level is key. When Fletch worked downtown, he and Wes, his boss, would step outside a couple of times a day to light up a cigarette and shoot the shit for a few minutes. Once Fletch kicked the habit, he had no reason to tag along. After a few weeks, he decided to grab a coffee and continue to hang with Wes on smoke breaks. Turned out, the harder thing to kick was those moments of connection.

For the elderly, the risk of dementia increases when social attachments decrease. Researchers studied a group of Dutch senior citizens in 2012. None of the participants had dementia at the onset of the experiment. Over the course of the study, 13.4 percent of those who'd reported feeling lonely developed dementia, as opposed to 5.7 percent who had not felt lonely.[176]

As freshmen, lying in our respective dorm room beds before falling asleep, Joanna would tell me about her elderly aunts who traveled the world after their husbands passed away, riding camels in Egypt. We speculated that would be us someday. While we've yet to involve a dromedary, we take girls' trips at least once a year. I credit these times with keeping me healthy and sane.

Social media has changed the dynamic of friendship in positive and negative ways. An Instagram friend will favorite your post about bodybuilding; your real friend will help you move a body. But there's a place for online friendships. Social media alerts prompt us to consider our friends with every post. I might click over to Joanna's Facebook feed to see what cookies she's baking during the holiday season, or Gina's Twitter to see the trendy places she's traveling while I'm already in my jammies, so it brings us closer in some ways, but my communication with them is largely in person, through email, or on FaceTime. Social media allows people who'd have never otherwise met or who share specific interests to come together. If I were into something esoteric, like needle felting, instead of boring Fletch with all the fluffy things I wanted to craft, I'd find an online felting community. Online platforms are an excellent jumping-off point to meet folks of a similar mindset. My LA friend, Amy, met a girl in Texas in an online discussion group called My VW Jetta Is Trying to Kill Me. They discovered tons of shared interests, and now they visit each other all the time and travel the country to see Dave Matthews shows.

For the friends I can't drive to, social media helps me maintain bonds. I love Instagram stories. Karyn has a unique perspective on the world, so when I see what she posts, it's as though we're having a conversation. A couple of years ago, she discovered that the people across the courtyard were making a porno, and she decided to livestream it. She didn't show anything untoward, capturing her own reactions instead. Karyn was deeply concerned that the girl was doing the film to pay for grad school, and stressed that her dogs might be traumatized by seeing the action unfold; it was just like being there with her.

In so many ways, social media is . . . social. It brings us further into each other's lives, and can deepen bonds and provide a connection to the rest of the world, but it exists outside of what I think of as traditional friendship. It doesn't follow the same rules, and the results can be distressing.

Not long ago, an author I adore tweeted me to say she was in my town for a writing conference. We'd never met in person, but we'd interacted online and had a mutual respect. I dropped everything to join her for lunch. Despite it being our first time in the same room, we had a terrific time, with no weird breaks in the conversation or awkward questions. Her online "persona" is exactly who she is in person. True and lasting friendships can be forged online. That lunch was proof. The issues with social media friendships often stem from someone's real behavior not aligning with the portrait they've painted of themselves.

A few years back, I had a meal with a woman I thought I knew from all that she'd posted online. The gal I thought I was meeting was vulnerable and anxious, self-deprecating and hilarious. Reading her posts, I wanted to hug her and feed her soup; she was the best. In person, she yelled at the waitress and talked about all the celebrities who wanted to buy the rights to her work. Her cocky self-assurance was diametrically opposed to the person she claimed to be online, and she was, in reality, the worst. Mind you, I'm fine with jerks. I love jerks! Just tell me you're an asshole and then I won't be surprised. Be authentic. No one wants to eat tacos with a real-life Keyser Söze.

So there are online relationships that turn out to be solid, fulfilling connections, and others that crumble like a house of cards. And still, there are others that are both fascinating and confounding. For years,

I was Facebook friends with Harvey, a guy I knew in high school. I accepted his friend request because I used to accept every request; I didn't want to hurt anyone's feelings. I'd try to community build on Facebook, back in the heyday, by asking open-ended questions, such as "We're putting a Fourth of July playlist together; what songs should we include?" While most people would offer suggestions, a few would rant about patriotic songs and tell me the whole idea was stupid. After breaking up one too many fights in my comments feed, and tired of feeling my stomach clench every time I perused that which was supposed to be enjoyable, I purged 4,850 "friends" from my personal Facebook page, opting to keep only those people I knew. Dunbar's number theory says that 150 is the maximum number of social relationships a person can maintain with any level of stability.[177] As for close friends, that number drops to five. Turns out, I was right on the money.

Harvey had only a handful of Facebook friends, which seemed a shame because he'd been nice thirty years ago. His Facebook feed was filled with Bible quotes. That wasn't my thing, but I figured his relationship with his Lord was his business.

After a few years, I noticed a pattern. Each November 1, Harvey would freak out over the Starbucks holiday cup design. I could set my clock by his post over the red cups not being religious enough for his liking, as though he couldn't enjoy his mocha if the Virgin Mary weren't depicted crowning.

I understand why people are bothered on all sides about the cups. Christians are aggravated by Starbucks trying to take away the reason for the season. But those who don't believe, who practice a different religion, who struggle with their faith, who dislike the annual reminder of the very thing that causes them distress, I can see their point too.

Harvey and I attended the same fundamental Baptist church in Indiana. In that house of worship, religion wasn't a comfort, it was something to fear, a barrier to ever measuring up. Ours was a vengeful God, one who couldn't wait to smite the nonbelievers the second the

Rapture came. Spring of our freshman year, I went home with Joanna for Easter and attended her Lutheran church service. Everything about it was lovely and caring. Her God was mellow and laid-back; he was the kind of dude who wore sandals and was happy to lend you five dollars, and don't worry, he'd take care of the wine. There was no guilt, there were no recriminations; it was weird. I kept asking her, "When do we talk about sinners burning forever in the lake of fire?" Different Gods work for different people, it turns out.

Each holiday season, I'd root for Harvey to be too busy having fun to panic about the cups. Yet there he'd be, banging out his angry missive by November 2, all Keyboard Cat, just slapping the keys as he registered displeasure. "They're trying to take the Christ out of Christmas!" he'd cry, never once thinking it might not be Starbucks's job to put it in, or considering all the thought and the hundreds of thousands of dollars it had taken them to find the least offensive design.

Now, I don't know what makes Harvey the arbiter of the correct amount of Jesus the coffee chain should offer, but I didn't unfriend him, and not because I'm noble. I stuck around because I wanted to watch Carl, another one of our classmates, bait him. Carl is a super metal atheist who also went to our church. Every year, after Harvey's post, Carl would log a video response of himself sipping from the not-religious-enough red cup, saying things like, "I'm drinking a gingerbread latte out of Satan's own chalice!" In high school, everyone thought Carl was strange, myself included. Now I realize he just had a dark sense of humor. I bet he loved *The Kids in the Hall*. I was my own version of a basic bitch back then; I wasn't funny yet and didn't appreciate those who were.

Eventually, I realized Harvey's issue wasn't the cups, it was his being lonely and disconnected, and those posts sparked much-desired interaction. He didn't mind dissension in the comments section, because he'd get that ping of dopamine every time someone registered a reaction. In his other posts, almost no one responded to him.

Things turned more complicated when Facebook's algorithm decided I needed insight on every aspect of Harvey's life due to our shared friends from high school and college. I saw the dozens of comments he posted daily, most of them on foreign Christian dating groups where he'd tell scantily clad eastern European catfishers and call girls that they had beautiful eyes. His isolation was palpable, and I felt like I was witnessing a slow-motion car crash.

The more I watched, the more it seemed that the entirety of his interactions existed online. He'd perpetually write about where he was headed to see a basketball game after another bad day at work, hoping someone would join him for a beer. I would feel secondhand anxiety each time I'd see him post.

In 2017, the *American Journal of Preventive Medicine* studied participants who spent the most time accessing social media sites, meaning fifty or more visits per week. Those users perceived three times the isolation and social anxiety than those who visited nine times or less.[178] Harvey's usage had to be in the hundreds.

When something would go wrong in his life, he'd lay out the problem in detail and then say he was going to turn it over to God. I had to stop myself from jumping in with unsolicited advice. While I believe in the power of prayer, I also place my faith in the power of *doing something about it*. I hadn't spoken with Harvey in decades and, for all I knew, offering suggestions may have been the worst thing for him. Even with Fletch, whom I know better than anyone, I still ask if he wants me to problem-solve or if he needs me to commiserate when there's an issue.

When Harvey posted about feeling alone and desperate, those on his timeline sent him notes like, "You got this, buddy!" I'd studied enough about suicidal ideation when I wrote my YA novel that I knew how to spot a warning sign. I hadn't seen him in thirty years, but I felt obligated to respond to someone who was clearly drowning. I reached out, begging him to get counseling and try a course of antidepressants.

I made him talk to me, and I derided everyone in his friend group who hadn't done the same. Around the same time, others in his actual life started to step up. I rooted for him to pull it together.

He eventually did . . . sort of.

Instead of seeking medical intervention, or pursuing self-reflection, he finally spoke with his minister and got involved in a new cause—fighting the plague of homosexuality. Hate was to be his bulwark against his unhappiness. That was my tipping point.

I unfriended.

A while back, our comedy class group faced a crisis from which we could not recover. Connor had returned to Colorado for some time with his family and sent us all a video of him salsa dancing with an elderly Colombian aunt.

After we complimented his impressive moves, Connor texted something to the group about how all of his Colombian relatives could dance. The text chain took a turn, discussing stereotypes, and Andre took offense to Connor's quickness to assign a trait to an entire country of individuals, and then a lot of the group jumped on Andre for overreacting.

I missed all of this in real time because I am over thirty and keep my phone in my purse.

When I saw the wall o' texts the next morning, I had a sinking feeling. Something important had gone down and half the group was now missing from the text chain, so I attempted to understand each point of view as I read.

As Andre's in a minority group of a minority group, he has faced the kind of discrimination I can't even imagine. I wanted to cut him some slack. I believed he was right to point out the soft tyranny of relying on stereotypes.

Instead of embracing his point, the rest of the group—each proud to be inclusive and woke—took offense not to his ideas but his attitude.

Andre came out of the gate so hard and fast in his passion against all forms of racism that he took everyone by surprise.

People assumed he was just being funny. It was a comedy class text thread. One can understand the assumption.

The response from all the millennials was that in taking offense to Connor talking about his Colombian family's love of dance, Andre was conflating race with culture.

Then Heidi, who had not been paying attention, jumped in when Andre made a comparison to generalizations about Jews. She was offended by the example, and the situation completely devolved.

Andre felt alone, misunderstood, fighting the good fight.

Connor was busy having family fun with aunties who could bust a move. Those actively participating in the conversation were mad at Andre for accusing them of insensitivity, and everyone lost it.

If we'd all been talking face to face, the entire thing would never have happened, but over text, it ended up being the death knell for our group text and for our tight group.

Here's the thing—no one was at fault. Andre was right for not allowing us to default to accepting stereotypes, even one that was seemingly flattering. He was just making the group aware of his perspective on the comment. Yet Connor never had bad intentions. And Heidi was justified in defending what she assumed was an attack on her belief system.

But once something breaks, it's near impossible to glue it back into its original form, and that was the end of us all being one cohesive group.

We never regrouped, but I've remained friends with everyone. We stay connected through social media, and every now and then there will be an Instagram of a few of us together, but given the chance, I choose to hang with them in person.

My class and my classmates were exactly what I needed when I was at a point in my career and in my life when I wasn't sure what was next. They provided the ballast that kept me tethered and focused. They helped me understand that even though I was an older dog, my days of learning new tricks weren't over. Those friendships gave me direction, purpose, and support.

While I wasn't sure where I was headed next, Second City showed me my future would be better if it included laughter, levity, and mirth.

Ultimately, what I learned from my time with the group is that in not attempting to understand each other, in allowing misunderstandings to fester, and in not having the ability to laugh at ourselves, we are doomed.

And that's the thing—toxic friendships aren't just unhealthy mentally, they can affect your body, too. Higher blood pressure, higher blood sugar, lower immunity, depression, and anxiety are all physical manifestations of being in a harmful relationship.[179] While it's sad, a friendship can devolve from a satisfying relationship to one that induces stress. I know when I find myself dodging calls or dreading spending time with a person, it is time to reassess the relationship. I just ask myself if I'm still fulfilled by our connection.

Sometimes we need a break.

Even Joanna and I lost touch for a while after college. We were in very different stages of our lives. Prior to social media, it was especially hard to keep up. I was working on my career, and she had two toddlers; our lives didn't mesh. While we amicably drifted apart, we eventually drifted back together—thanks to my finding her on Facebook—stronger than ever for having had the chance to miss each other.

I worry that the way we connect now is both bringing us together and driving us apart. Dear friends are throwing away their long-standing, deeply satisfying relationships in the current political climate, tired of seeing opposing posts, each too swept up in the movement to remember that there's someone they love on the other side.

I've seen far too many people in my timeline say, "I could never be friends with someone who believed *X*," without ever bothering to find out *why* they believe *X*. Within reason, our dogma doesn't need to keep us apart. Rhetoric won't bring us a casserole after our knee surgery. Philosophy won't cheer us on as we make the case for a promotion. A viewpoint won't take us out to get sloppy drunk when we've been dumped.

In the past decade and a half, my close friends have kept me sane. Even though we don't agree on everything, my love and respect for them overrides my need to be right. That I can relax enough to trust these people is the product of years of hard work and therapy. They're my family now.

Thanks to Joanna, I know what it's like to have a fiercely protective, entirely supportive, unconditionally loving maternal figure in my life. With Gina, I understand what it's like to have a sister. All of us are in an ever-escalating arms race for who can be the most considerate.

I'd venture that while I've made honest friends online, and had meaningful interactions, there's no replicating on social media that off-line bond. My Facebook friends are never going to be my core team; we just can't achieve the same closeness without a period of off-line interaction.

With my chosen family, I'd never allow anything as trivial as a difference of opinion to build a wall between our friendships.

PART V

ESTEEM NEEDS: JOY, CREATIVITY, HAPPINESS, DESIRE FOR FAME AND GLORY

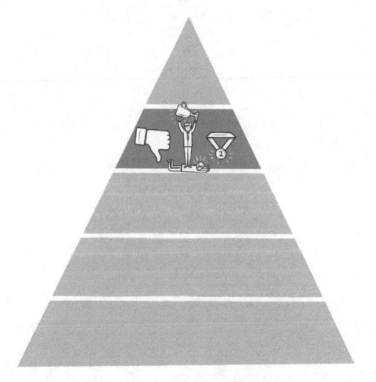

Lee's mother's recipe for happiness is simple. She says everyone needs someone to love and something to do.

Her thought neatly coincides with Maslow's penultimate layer on the hierarchy of his theory of human motivation, that of esteem needs.

Accomplishments, both professional and creative, feed into this level, as do yearnings for joy, happiness, and glory, which are manifested through team activities, hobbies, and other forms of shared participation. In other words, that which brings us together—and tears us apart—in the name of esteem.

Spoiler alert? It's gonna get messy.

The Lobby for a Hobby

One of the best things we can do to get out of our heads, to stop living in so much fear and panic, to lose ourselves in the zen of a singular focus, is to find a project or activity. But increasingly, the hobbies that we're most interested in lead down complicated paths that contain more than pure joy and love of the game. One person might pour their energies into rock climbing. Another might improve their golf game. Maybe it's knitting, or pottery, or a comedy class, or karaoke, or scouring the globe, seeking out the elusive Inverted Jenny stamp. Maybe it's tracing the family tree.

No, it's *definitely* tracing the family tree.

Genealogy has become the second-most popular hobby in the US after gardening. There's some speculation that Alex Haley's *Roots* is the inciting incident that sparked the trend, launching genealogy on a trajectory to become a billion-dollar industry.[180] The online sources that amateurs use to chart lineage have grown over the last decades, and now, many of them have the ability to examine old public records and analyze biological samples to find shared DNA, creating as complete a historical picture as possible. Ancestry sites are now the second-most-visited category of websites . . . after pornography.

Gina took one of the Ancestry DNA tests and found a new first cousin in Texas—she's a white woman, traced through an uncle who, it turns out, was even more of a rolling stone than the family suspected. When Gina first contacted the cousin, she wasn't entirely sure how to spring the news on her.

"So I emailed her and said, 'Surprise! You're half-black!' My rationale is, don't ask a question if you're not prepared for the answer," Gina said.

"What if that wasn't her question? What if she just wanted to know if she was German at all, to rationalize wearing slutty lederhosen next Halloween? So, how did she react?" I asked.

"She didn't. She seems to have disappeared from the site."

"Well . . . that is some bullshit," I said. "I would love to find out you're my cousin. Then you could take me to your next reunion and I could get one of those matching shirts, too. Anyway, the sites say right up front that you might encounter some life-altering information. How could your cousin not expect a curveball? Do you think she just did Ancestry to see if she was related to George Washington?"

"Maybe. But nobody wants to find out they're related to *Leroy* Washington."

Then we laughed until pants wetting became less of a possibility and more of an eventuality. But I stopped myself and asked if it was okay for me to find that funny, to which Gina replied, "You'd better."

I honestly find myself questioning when it's appropriate to be in on the joke, and when it's appropriate to not be included, thanks to my hobby of pursuing a comedy education.

The more time I spend with the younger generation, the more aware I become that we all need to be vigilant about accidentally committing microaggressions. I don't want to be ignorant, and when I am, I want it called out. We all make mistakes, we all act insensitively at times, but the important thing is to be willing to listen to criticism and learn from it.

In comedy class, the sweetest, most woke, most progressive and socially aware millennial got her words tangled once, and instead of referring to persons of color, she said "coloreds" so sincerely that it didn't occur to her what had accidentally come out of her mouth. I was sitting between Gina and Andre, and as soon as it happened, they both roared with laughter. It was infectious—but was it "mine" to find funny?

I leaned over and whispered to Andre, "Wait, was I allowed to laugh there?"

"Girl, if it's funny, yes. And that shit was hysterical," he replied, wiping tears out of the corners of his eyes. "Colored," he sputtered again.

My millennial friend had no idea what she'd accidentally said, so she continued with her point, reveling in the fact that her audience was so damn *live* that night.

The rules when I was young were much different, and not for the better. No one I knew felt uncomfortable when John Hughes used Long Duk Dong as a comedic stereotype in *Sixteen Candles*. The proof of how far I've come happened while watching the full, rich, complete portrait of Asian culture in *Crazy Rich Asians*. Because women like me are consistently represented in media, it hadn't previously occurred to me how much representation matters to those who aren't.

While I hate that my inclination now is to worry over whether I'm allowed to laugh, I also recognize that the first step of counteracting privilege is to identify it.

Also, jokes from the traditionally nonoppressed that embrace racial stereotypes are lazy; do better.

Anyway, as it turned out, Gina's cousin just needed a minute to process and talk the development over with her mother. Dealing with the family myths that had been constructed turned out to be much harder than her shifting racial identity. The new cousins are in the midst of building a relationship.

Eventually, I took the DNA test, too. I discovered that everything my parents told me about my ancestry was a complete fabrication. Apparently, I am not the first person to pen fiction in our family.

Someone, at some point, concocted a story about my very British paternal lineage. When I finally went to London in 2014, it felt like home, like I belonged there. The blue of my blood had called me back.

One DNA test later, not so much.

Turned out, the rumor that my father was adopted—something no one was permitted to discuss in my house—was true. I finally understood why I loved Saint Paddy's Day so much in college. And why I had such an easy time learning French.

I'm not even 1 percent English. Gina is 17 percent British, and Lee is a full 50 percent. It was a total shock. But I am not about to purge the dozens of Union Jack–emblazoned items in my house. I'm still an Anglophile, even if I'm not Anglo-Saxon proper. I *identify* as English.

The second shock that I received was even more sinister. After I conducted the document search, I discovered that my great-grandfather materialized out of nowhere, and that he was in all the same places as Jack the Ripper, at the same time.

I decided to let that search go fallow.

Again, don't ask questions when you don't want the answers.

After our DNA maps connected us, a handful of people I'd never heard of were in contact on Ancestry, all first and second cousins on my paternal side, but none of us could determine our grandparentage. Adoption was a terrible scandal eighty-plus years ago, a social black mark, so I'm not surprised the information was kept under wraps.

One pushy new cousin emailed me daily, demanding I call her. She believed, for some unknown reason, that I had information I wasn't sharing. There was no doubt that she was truly related to me, because she'd already made it to my last nerve. I never did reply. I'm content with my ad hoc family.

While DNA tests like Ancestry and 23andMe can be a fun way to create connections (provided your new cousins aren't bossy), the results can also tear a family apart. Every year around Mother's and Father's Days, the services are heavily promoted. I wonder how often an offspring's gift turns a celebration into an episode of *The Maury Povich Show*.

"You are not the father . . . ?"

These same DNA searches have become a crucial piece of the puzzle to solving cold cases. In theory, this is an outstanding idea. For example, after decades of searching for any connection to a string of gruesome rapes and murders in the '70s and '80s, investigators caught a lucky break because a relative to the alleged Golden State Killer had uploaded a sample to GEDmatch, allowing investigator Paul Holes to create a genetic road map that eventually led him to Joseph James DeAngelo.[181]

The problem occurs when those who submitted the DNA aren't aware of the terms of service, or the extent to which their genetic material might be used and how that might impact their extended family.

The truth is that submitting DNA to ancestry sites may violate another relative's privacy.

In *Maryland v. King*, the Supreme Court ruled that swabbing a suspect for DNA without consent does not constitute a violation of the unreasonable search and seizure clause, because it does not capture and store any biologically relevant or identifying information—like skin and hair color. However, those same identifying genetic traits can be revealed when matched against any ancestry site.[182] Law enforcement is constitutionally obligated to obtain a search warrant before rifling through your home, but no such statute exists when it comes to rifling through your DNA helix.

So, in trying to figure out if we tan nicely due to a Greek great-yaya, we may be inadvertently opening the door for law enforcement to skirt around a relative's Fourth Amendment rights.

Again, that's going to make for an awkward Thanksgiving.

While the theoretical impacts of social anxiety as it relates to privacy are still being studied, it's possible we'd lessen our anxiety if we simply defaulted to America's number-one favorite online pastime and spent our free time browsing pornography.

The good news is that many of us are doing just that. According to CNN, 18.4 million viewers watched the *Game of Thrones* finale, with an average of 44.2 million viewers per episode when you add in those who view on demand. (Please, try to tell me that show isn't softcore.)

Prior to the last episode, *InsideHook* explained it best: "No matter who wins the Iron Throne, it's clear that *Game of Thrones* has conquered not just the kingdom of television, but the continent of American culture in a way few other cultural touchstones can in these divided times. It's a show that's watched by Republicans and Democrats; discussed in nerdy fan forums and *The New Yorker*; watched in dive bars and corporate boardrooms. Maybe the only thing that unites us in 2019 is a TV show about fictional warring kingdoms, evil ice elves and winged lizards."[183]

George R. R. Martin based this wildly popular series on his research of historic events like the Wars of the Roses, a conflict that involved the house of York and the house of Lancaster, to whom I am now related in name only, goddamn it. I'm a fan of Martin's books, but when I watched the first couple of episodes, every time Fletch walked in, he laughed at me for watching what he assumed were Ren faire skin flicks, and I was embarrassed.

In retrospect, I should have shamed *him* for mocking America's most beloved hobby.

Regardless, the show was a spectacle, providing a way for those with little else in common to connect. That's a blessing. Ultimately, we're desperate to form bonds around the water cooler, but we're perpetually fed information that fragments us. So when something—anything—happens to bring us together, whether a raccoon climbs the side of the UBS Tower or a giraffe is about to give birth on a live feed or Chilean miners are rescued after sixty-nine days trapped underground and we all have something to root for together? It's magic.

As for *Game of Thrones*, television being what it is today, I can always go back and binge the show later.

Ten years ago, "binge" would have involved fifteen slices of pizza and self-loathing. No longer!

My assumption was that the uptick in quality programming, in choice, and in streaming, has made us happier—a customizable pastime that we all can enjoy. But part of me doubted the golden age, and I needed to know, Were we happier when we had only three channels? We all have the opportunity to consume solely the shows and news broadcasts that align with our views. Everything is so specialized now that we're given the ability to actively shield ourselves from anything that might challenge our set thoughts. What if we're less likely to consider opposing viewpoints because we can simply choose to isolate ourselves from them?

In the book *The Paradox of Choice*, author and Swarthmore psychology professor Barry Schwartz made the point that infinite choice is paralyzing and exhausting, leading us to consistently second-guess ourselves and maintain unreasonably high expectations.[184] Schwartz's research was inspired by a 2000 study that observed the buying habits of shoppers in an upscale grocery store. When shown a display of two dozen varieties of gourmet jam, shoppers demonstrated more interest in that display than they did the next day when only six varieties were highlighted. However, shoppers *bought* more when they didn't have to decide between so many. It's basically the entire ethos of Trader Joe's.

Schwartz wrote, "Each new option subtracts a little from the feeling of well-being, until the marginal benefits of added choice level off. What's more, psychologists and business academics alike have largely ignored another outcome of choice: More of it requires increased time and effort and can lead to anxiety, regret, excessively high expectations, and self-blame if the choices don't work out."[185]

I guess this explains that when given the selection of hundreds of shows via cable, Apple TV, Hulu, Netflix, and Amazon Prime, my husband can lose half an hour (and me, my patience) simply scrolling through the guide.

Given all the alternatives, and after a bit of yelling on my part, we unfailingly default to murder documentaries. I don't mind the result, but I wouldn't say the process is one that's increased my joy. So the very act of sitting down to watch TV at the end of a busy day—absent a massively popular sanctioned porno like *GOT*—has, arguably, become a source of some anxiety.

Fletch and I are not alone. Who do you know that *didn't* watch *Making a Murderer*? Did anyone *not* listen to *Serial* or *Dirty John* or *S-Town*? Raise your hand if you can name more mass murderers than Supreme Court justices. And though I'd immediately think that surrounding ourselves with so much murder and crime would be a clear correlation to increased anxiety, again, I had to wonder.

(It *is* exhausting to be me, thanks for asking.)

A few years ago, comedians Georgia Hardstark and Karen Kilgariff met at a party where they discovered a mutual fascination with true crime. Until they happened upon each other, people would scatter when either of them tried to discuss the grisly details of the homicides that kept them awake at night.

As an outlet to relieve their existential angst, they started a tiny podcast called *My Favorite Murder*, where the women would each share the semiresearched details of a case with the other, told along with personal stories, expecting nothing more than a moment to discuss what scared and fascinated them with a kindred spirit each week.

Since their podcast's inception in January 2016, the duo now boasts twenty million listeners per month and recently sold out the 7,100-seat Microsoft Theater on the LA stop of their last tour.[186] I didn't know I was a "murderino" (a term created by their fan base) until I found them. I'm halfway through my second round of listening to almost three hundred episodes and minisodes, which is nothing in comparison to the *real* fans, who go to their live shows, participate in their fan cult, create murderino-inspired artwork, and get tattoos of their catchphrase (Stay Sexy and Don't Get Murdered).

But *why* are we obsessed with true crime, and is it really helping us to indulge in that fascination? Jooyoung Lee, associate professor of sociology at the University of Toronto, sees it as pure primal fascination. "Bingeing true crime is not that much different from people watching a 24-hour news cycle covering a killing spree or a terrorist attack. I think human beings, in general, are just drawn to extreme cases of violence. And when I say drawn to them, I don't mean that they watch something and hope to emulate it; there's just this fascination."[187]

New York Times writer Amanda Hess explained her own obsession: "Like any woman I am surrounded by images of dead girls all the time, it's this kind of self-fulfilling prophecy where because we're told to be afraid of this I think we want to watch these shows to somehow work through that."[188]

Maybe as we dissect each story, we figure out how we would avoid the same fate in the future, almost as though tuning into an instruction manual, as a way to lessen our fears.

The ways we've transformed as a society since my childhood encompass many shifts that were rooted in fear and anxiety—again, two emotions that are intrinsically linked for me.

There must be a part of us that quietly enjoys being afraid. If we didn't somehow embrace fear, there'd be no reason for us to actively pursue that which scares us.

But this fascination seems linked to the lower levels of Maslow's Hierarchy that deal with safety and survival. To my mind, it's easier to worry about the simpler goal of just staying alive than trying to pursue the loftier, more introspective, and mentally challenging goals of self-actualization. And yet, over decades and centuries, it's also clear that our society has become safer, that we are living longer, healthier lives. So it's incredibly telling to observe that we've shifted part of that fascination with survival to a form of entertainment—we increasingly get our survival fix in the form of easily consumable podcasts, television shows, and documentaries.

In shifting the concern with survival to a place that serves as a warning and a connection point, it's possible we're claiming that the reason we stay stuck in the quest of achieving self-actualization is because of fear instead of any of these more elusive goals.

There is an established neural connection between fear and anger. When it relates to podcasts about crimes, or documentaries about wrongfully accused people, that anger is constructive. It's usually got a clear space to land, and helps us connect to a human experience that exists outside our perspective. What's more concerning is the clear surge in anger online—in feeds and rants and general callouts. I've established that I'm not a huge fan of delving into emotions, but since I've gotten into the habit of questioning all my assumptions, it's worth a closer look at anger.

Anger, it seems, isn't inherently bad—physiologically, anger reduces cortisol, which then releases a shot of norepinephrine, nature's own painkiller. Anger can spring forth wells of motivation, spurring us on to create change. Anger's got some good qualities! Harry Mills explained that "anger creates a sense of power and control in a situation where prior to anger these positive, motivating feelings did not exist. The feelings of control and righteousness that come from anger can motivate you to challenge and change difficult interpersonal and social injustices. [. . .] Anger can provide you with a rest from feelings of vulnerability, and a way of venting tensions and frustrations."[189]

Like John Lydon said, anger is an energy.

And then there's Dr. Martin Luther King Jr., who put it simply: "The supreme task is to organize and unite people so that their anger becomes a transforming force."

Take my husband, for example. His life is one long honey-do list, which is largely ignored until something makes him angry. He's literally walked by the new plastic stopper he ordered for the master bath for seventeen months, never once stopping to install it. But the day the dying tree spat those weird pods on his freshly washed car? Gone after ten minutes with a chainsaw.

The downside of anger is that when it's expressed on social media, it can so often go awry. Oliver Burkeman wrote, "The algorithms of the attention economy relentlessly expose us to enraging stories and opinions, for the straightforward reason that anger spreads more virally than other emotions—so you're more likely to click, like, share and stay glued to Twitter or Facebook when you're furious. Tabloid newspapers and Fox News figured this out years ago; but online, the diet of outrage can be customised precisely to include whatever drives you, personally, up the wall. It's not so much that social media platforms are full of bigoted trolls and idiots with harebrained opinions, but rather that, however many there really are, the platforms are designed to ensure you can't avoid the ones who infuriate you the most."[190]

He added that the only constructive way to rid ourselves of anger is taking concrete action—and tweets generally don't count, saying, "Anger can be the start of something. But then you need the something."

What truly should scare us, and what absolutely tears us asunder, is when that anger goes unchecked, particularly when coupled with isolation, loneliness, disconnection, or the desire for fame and notoriety. To me, this phenomenon, which is occurring with increasing frequency, represents the most significant change between my childhood and present day.

Was I ever afraid as a kid in school? Sure, plenty of times. I feared showering in the group bay after eighth grade gym class. I feared forgetting my locker combination. I feared missing the bus. I feared dropping my tray in the lunchroom and having everyone clap. *The horror!*

I had a particular fear of word problems. I could never concentrate on the math because I was too wrapped up in the narrative. As always, I was too nosy for ciphering. I wanted to know someone else's story and figure out why there were two different people on two different trains, coming from two different cities, traveling at two different rates of speed. Were they lovers? Were they friends? Were they dirty hipsters trying to travel ironically? Don't leave me hanging!

But I can honestly say that I never feared someone would shoot up my civics class, even though many of my classmates brought guns to school during deer hunting season.

Something has changed, and I'd love to know how the hell we change it back.

To start to decode the solution, we must begin by keeping up with the Kardashians.

Remember My Name

Gina and I started a podcast because, one day over brunch, she tried to explain the fracas between Rob Kardashian and Blac Chyna, a concept that included a lot of words I'd heard before, but never strung together in the same sentence. Our back-and-forth made people at the next table laugh, and that seemed reason enough to bring it to broadcast.

Eventually, we recorded an episode on the Kardashians, which required me to watch the show. Despite my love of reality TV, the Kardashians were the Rubicon I'd never crossed.

The Kardashians, for the purposes of this argument, exist as an entity, an emblem, rather than a group of individuals. Looking at the individuals becomes too complicated. For instance, Kim Kardashian has been quietly studying for the bar exam, as she's become an advocate for criminal justice reform.

In an interview with *Vogue*, she explained, "I just felt like I wanted to be able to fight for people who have paid their dues to society. I just felt like the system could be so different, and I wanted to fight to fix it, and if I *knew* more, I could *do* more."[191]

While her motivation is admirable, it won't close the Pandora's box that's been opened.

To prep for our podcast, I watched an entire season of *Keeping Up with the Kardashians* during my workouts and found it largely inoffensive, once I got past the first two minutes of Kim smacking her gum so hard that I almost threw my iPhone at the wall. I'd played Kim's game on my iPad, and wasted way too much money buying new hairstyles for my avatar—so much that Fletch temporarily changed my iTunes password because he thought we'd been hacked. That was my only Kardashian experience before the binge.

I'm all for wealth, but something's changed in this country regarding our perceptions of the super-rich. In fact, 61 percent of Americans between ages eighteen and twenty-four (Generation Z) have a positive reaction to the word "socialism" and only 58 percent reacted positively to "capitalism."[192]

Recently, Howard Schultz, former CEO of Starbucks, came out against the term "billionaire," instead preferring to be called "a person of means," as though he's now ashamed of what he's built.[193] I worked on a project with someone who could—if she chose—literally swim around Scrooge McDuck–style in her swimming pool full of gold coins, but she's far too busy creating scholarships and opportunities for the forgotten and disadvantaged. She made every dime of her wealth herself, and I have mad respect for her. I don't begrudge her any luxuries; instead, she's a role model.

So, as it appears that Kim may be attempting to shift toward using her influence to do good, I'm all for lining her pockets. Girl, I will buy new hair in your game any day.

As for said game, while it's well designed, the Kardashians might as well be animated penguins in it. They're one dimensional and irrelevant, save for having put their name on it (and taking my money, ten dollars at a time). Clearly the game's designers worked with a behavioral therapist to come up with a million little opportunities for a dopamine dump. It's like live-action paper dolls. There are no elements of skill, no clock running out, so there's zero stress. The only point of the game is to consume, which appears to be the point of the TV show, too.

Ten years ago, I stayed at a New York hotel full of The CW cast members, in town for their advertiser up-fronts. Every star of every show was there for a big network presentation to the ad buyers. There were a dozen paparazzi in front of the hotel. Every time I exited my publisher-arranged Town Car, the photographers would gather . . . and then sigh with disappointment when they saw my Capri-pant-clad sturdy calf and arch-support sandal emerge.

I, on the other hand, was thrilled to see them each time I stepped out of the car. I love questioning people with inside information, so I took the opportunity to grill a photographer on Paris Hilton and the Kardashians. I couldn't understand why any of them were famous. As far as I could tell, they didn't do anything, they didn't produce anything, they didn't have any discernable skill. The photographer shrugged and replied, "They're famous because they pose." Before I could ask what that meant, he elbowed me in the throat to get a shot of AnnaLynne McCord, who'd just exited her own Town Car.

As no one explained how posing could make anyone who wasn't a professional model famous, I figured it had to be the show. Mind you, I live for garbage TV. Every real housewife is my favorite real housewife. I'm a Bravo devotee because the housewives consistently bring con-flict, drama, and humor. I can see parts of myself in them. Watching *KUWTK* years later, I couldn't identify with them. The girls walked around slow talking with vocal fry, their dead doll eyes perfectly framed in fake lashes and smoky shadow, discussing nothing except what event they might go to and how hard it was to be them. They sat slumped at tables, listlessly chewing salads. It seemed like a sad existence. Why would I want to keep up with *that*? No one was funny or quick, no one had ideas, and they weren't sharing interesting opinions.

In a lot of ways, I found them to be like women in the Victorian age, maybe Jane Austen characters . . . with Brazilian butt lifts. The show was like beautifully shot Prozac. LA looked almost pastoral. I found the girls mostly inoffensive, but they seemed like empty vessels, existing only to shill.

Also, I couldn't believe them as a tight family, when they all looked so awkward with each other. They seemed more like coworkers who'd just met. When poor Kendall had to go to a courtroom and testify against her stalker alone—the other sisters at home sprawled on their fainting couches, wearing designer sweats, holding plastic tubs of greens—I really started to question the unit. Their salads could wait.

I determined that in the Kardashian family, the fish were rotting from the head down.

Matriarch Kris Jenner has proven herself to be the ultimate marketer, turning every one of her children into millionaires and, in Kylie Jenner's case, a billionaire. Per *Forbes*, Kylie is the world's youngest self-made billionaire, beating out Mark Zuckerberg, who didn't hit the three-comma club until twenty-three.[194]

I delved into Ian Halperin's book *Kardashian Dynasty: The Controversial Rise of America's Royal Family* to find out more. The book focused mostly on Kris Jenner, as he asserted she's the lynchpin. Halperin made the point that Jenner is diabolical, the ultimate pageant mom, times a million. What disturbed me most was Halperin's allegation that Kim's sex tape with Ray J wasn't "leaked." Rather, Jenner partnered with Vivid Entertainment, the company that distributed the tape, as the family had been advised that a sex tape was a sure ticket to fame and fortune.

Halperin went undercover at Vivid, interviewing CEO Stephen Hirsh, posing as someone looking to distribute a sex tape for a famous client, where he received multiple corroborations that Jenner masterminded the deal.[195] When questioned about the veracity of this accusation, a family spokesperson denied all allegations.

In 2018, Ellen DeGeneres accused Kris of routinely lying to advance the family, saying, "I know you're lying about everything, so whatever I ask you, I just automatically think you're lying to me."[196] DeGeneres was referencing a pattern of mistruths regarding previous milestones on the show, including pregnancies, divorces, et cetera. Jenner always directed those asking questions to watch the show and find out.

The more I considered the family, the more my wheels turned.

While this may sound like a stretch, my theory is that there's a dotted line between the rise of the Kardashians and the escalation of mass shootings in this country.

Listen, I'm not about to tell you that Lee Harvey Oswald was a patsy or that Senator Ted Cruz is the Zodiac Killer. I'm just saying that there has been some shift in our society that has led to these types of mass shootings, and I think that looking at our fascination with the Kardashians could help identify it.

Stay with me, I promise it's less insane than it sounds.

It's true that I'm best known for writing silly stories about getting drunk in a pool, but I've conducted a huge amount of research on mass shootings. Like everyone, I'm desperate for a solution. The "it can't happen here" mentality is long gone; in fact, one of last year's shootings happened at Fletch's old junior high school. I believe we can't solve a problem until we fully understand its origin story, and that's become my mission.

The Kardashians/Jenners themselves are the tipping point, but I do think they are emblematic of our fundamental shift.

So here goes.

Gun sales spiked when Barack Obama took office because people thought that they were going to lose their Second Amendment rights. *Forbes* reported that the gun industry grew 158 percent from 2008 to 2016, with the economic impact of the firearms and ammunition industries growing from $19.1 billion to $49.3 billion.[197] This timeline also coincides with the Kardashians gaining popularity, as the show started in 2007. (Interesting point, sales have dropped under Trump, as have the Kardashians' ratings.)

In 2010, the *Independent* reported on a poll that found that more than half the teens they interviewed didn't want a career, they just sought fame.[198] The *Huffington Post* reported that researchers found the more time children spend consuming media, the more likely they are to value fame.[199]

The United States leads the world in mass shootings. Criminologist Adam Lankford wrote about the phenomenon in his book *The Myth of Martyrdom: What Really Drives Suicide Bombers, Rampage Shooters, and Other Self-Destructive Killers* and determined that the factors influencing the rise have to do with "the dark side of American Exceptionalism," cultural difference, access to mental health, availability of firearms, and the valorization of fame.[200] While guns are a significant portion of the equation, he argues, they aren't the only piece.

He sees a huge gap between what Americans expect for themselves versus what they're achieving. Couple the adulation of fame with the extent and ease of gun ownership, and throw in badly managed mental illnesses, and boom, it's the perfect storm, as we see far too often.

University of Michigan researchers found that college students post-2000 have 40 percent lower empathy levels than those before them, attributing the decline to multiple factors, including less outdoor group play, more screen time, the self-esteem movement, and economic inequality, among other factors.[201]

While the lack of empathy, a narcissistic personality, and the overarching desire for fame might be entertaining traits to chronicle and watch on a reality show, it's a recipe for disaster in real life. Lankford asserts that the line between fame and infamy has blurred in recent years, citing a study that analyzed *People* magazine from 1974 to 1998 and found that the cover stories morphed from uplifting human interest to stories of people who were caught lying, cheating, or stealing.[202]

In those decades and beyond, the message is clear: bad behavior sells magazines.

Bad behavior puts people in the public eye.

Instead of lauding the hard work, innovation, sacrifice, and achievement that used to bring fame, instead of wanting to emulate those difficult yet rewarding processes, society has begun to laud fame itself—at any cost.

In a joint study between the US Secret Service and the US Department of Education, they found that in 81 percent of active shooter incidents, at least one person knew of the attacker's plans, and in 59 percent, more than one person knew.[203]

LEAD is a Lake County, Illinois, based organization that created an anonymous text-communication system for teens soliciting immediate help for themselves or someone they know. Not only can users discuss their problems on Text-a-Tip, they can also report their concerns. During an emergency, proper authorities, including police and first responders, are notified. When I met with the organizers, the system had just successfully stopped a potential school shooting in McHenry County.

As much as we assume it is, the internet isn't being surveilled by law enforcement, so these self-reporting agencies are key. Trolling the internet for potential offenders is a violation of First Amendment rights. And although shootings happen far too often, they're statistically infrequent enough that no algorithm can help predict them.

The best strategy for prevention is to encourage people with potential information to express concern, and texting a tip to authorities is a sterling example.

Esquire interviewed a former prisoner called Trunk, who received that nickname because he'd been found with a trunk full of guns on his way to conduct a school shooting. *Esquire* wanted to find out if he had any ideas about how to stop mass shootings.

Trunk's refrain was that isolation, pain, and desperation were the biggest motivators. Trunk said, "I'd be lying in bed wondering what I was doing wrong. Why didn't anybody like me? Why was everybody against me? I could have thought, *Well, I'm a loser.* But I didn't want to think that. So I started thinking *they* were losers. I started thinking that they didn't like me because they were afraid of me—because I had power and they didn't. Because I was special. And that's when it all really got started: when I began thinking I was special."[204]

We're witnessing what has historically been manifested in suicidal ideation now being turned outward, directed at others, and morphing into homicidal ideation. Instead of "I'm unhappy, so I'm going to end it," we're seeing the aftereffects of "I'm unhappy, so I'm ending it for everyone because it's *their* fault."

According to the *Esquire* article, "Columbine combined the school shooting with a purposeful act of theater. Columbine was meant to be *spectacular*, and it has beckoned mass shooters ever since as an example, a template, and a challenge. They study it, and they try to top it in terms of either body count or showmanship."

If the media would stop glorifying these shooters—stop saying their names, stop showing their photos, stop broadcasting their self-serving statements—they could discourage potential shooters from seeking that attention, preventing copycat attacks.

The FBI reports that gunmen study previous high-profile attacks.[205] Per Rhitu Chatterjee, an NPR mental health correspondent, "[Potential shooters] can go online and read up about the lives and actions of those who felt like them and who acted on their violent, dissatisfied thinking, and now they have somebody to identify with, and there's a sense of belonging and purpose that comes with that identification, and they feel justified in how they think and what they want to act on."[206]

The #NoNotoriety campaign is aiming to stem the amount of public information released about these catastrophes, even though some journalists disagree: they advance the counterargument that the perpetrators of such violence are only held accountable through the release of public information.[207]

And while I respect that view, I also disagree. That argument totally discounts the fact that shooters can and should be held responsible through the legal system.

What makes the whole situation murkier is that the media—in some perverse ways—benefits from releasing the details about horrific events. They sell more papers. Attract more eyeballs on screens. People click through more, adding subscriptions. I would never accuse most journalists of willfully encouraging that type of violence, but we should all be questioning the purpose of releasing public details—names and photos—and how that impacts our world.

Threat assessment professionals have conducted research, and their surveys show that college-aged students exhibit more narcissistic traits than ever before. The research cites the contributing factors as the attention they generate from online self-promotion on social networks and the empty praise they receive that causes them to feel entitled. Without an established relationship to accomplishment-based confidence, kids have a harder time developing a positive self-image.[208]

In planning attacks, potential shooters hope to make a bigger splash than the last one, because, in our culture, infamy and fame have become one and the same.

So I don't think it's ridiculous to say that when people witness fourteen seasons of young, rich, vapid people having every one of their wishes fulfilled, a life of unimaginable luxury and worldwide adulation, none of it predicated by skill and all of it stemming from a leaked sex tape, their wheels start to turn.

Fame is worth whatever bad behavior it takes to get there, and the Kardashians are the cover girls for this movement.

Dotted freaking line.

As reality shows grow this fame myth—that your worth is directly related to your number of followers and the amount of attention you get, whether it's because you dump a bucket of ice water over your head or eat a Tide Pod—and then reinforce it with the bizarre and escalating bad behavior that's exhibited on screen, your obsession becomes entrenched. The feeling kids have that they are meant for fame, and their disappointment in their reality, leads to rash and sometimes violent behaviors.

After the Parkland shooting, Kim Kardashian tweeted an impassioned plea:

> *We owe it to our children and our teachers to keep them safe while at school. Prayers won't do this: action will. Congress, please do your job and protect Americans from senseless gun violence.*[209]

Arming teachers is one proposed answer. An educator in my comedy class said she works with a bunch of sixty-year-olds who can't figure out how to open a Google document or enlarge a YouTube screen, so I'm not too optimistic about it.

There's one school that has proactively considered arming their classrooms. At Oakland University in Michigan, teachers and students have been armed with . . . hockey pucks. "According to the university's police chief, the program stemmed from an idea raised during an active shooter training session, in which 'one attendee asked what staff and students could bring to prepare themselves for a fight.' The chief recalled once being struck in the head with a puck and said it 'caused a fair amount of damage to me.'"[210]

I had to double-check that the article hadn't been published in the *Onion* or on April Fools' Day.

I haven't any solutions here, save for "probably not hockey pucks." But I do confidently believe that we're never going to find answers if we can't have rational discussions without shouting, virtue signaling, or a links-based Twitter war.

We need to fully explore the reasons behind the violence and create a workable solution to each of the problems. Now, I'm not a constitutional scholar, nor do I play one on Facebook. I don't know the Founding Fathers' intent on the Second Amendment. I can't speak to the balance between children's safety and the Bill of Rights, but I am willing to listen to all sides of the conversation, without judgment, without being tied to a preconceived notion of what's right. Damn it, we're America. We put a man on the moon! We invented the cyclotron atom smasher and the internet and the chocolate chip cookie. When we rally together, we've been proven unstoppable.

Within the past few years, Kim Kardashian has become a creative council member of Everytown for Gun Safety. She's decried a since-revoked regulation that required 75,000 citizens with registered mental illnesses be included in a national background-check database. She's getting her hands dirty, taking a stand. She's talking to people, and more importantly, she's listening. That inspires hope.

What would be ironic is if it's Kim Kardashian who, through her experience and influence and her newfound study of law, not only takes ownership of a culture she helped create, but also figures out a common-sense way to bring us back from it.

I'd watch that show.

FUNNY GIRL

You've been hiding Dave Chappelle from me," I announced when I arrived at Gina's house.

"I did what now?" Gina replied. She took my hideous down coat and stashed it in her entry closet while I removed my snowy boots.

"I feel like Dave Chappelle is a secret you have been keeping from me. You have been *hoarding* him. You have been bogarting the Chappelle."

Gina snorted. "Um, yeah, he's world-famous and has been for decades. No one's been keeping him a secret."

Lee met my eye and gave me a subtle nod. *He* knew Gina had been hiding things from me. She was like that.

"Well, no one told me he's the smartest, most fearless man in comedy. Honestly, I thought he just did stoner humor." I'd spent the holidays bingeing his *Equanimity* and *The Bird Revelation* Netflix comedy specials, completely disarmed by his intelligence and honesty.

"I could have told you that, but sometimes you're hesitant to adapt."

"That ends here. I am Team Chappelle from now on."

Gina shrugged and poured me a glass of sauvignon blanc. "I'm sure he'll be excited to hear it."

I settled into my spot on the couch opposite hers. "Years ago, I was doing a bookstore event somewhere in Ohio, and right before I got there, Dave Chappelle had been shopping in the store. Some of my readers had run into him and they were super excited. And I was all, 'He can't be that fantastic if he's hanging out in Ohio.'"

"Except he is. He walked away from something like $50 million because he wasn't happy. He went home to Ohio because it wasn't worth it to him to sell his soul."

"That's brave and it only makes me realize how off I've been about him."

"How does it feel to be wrong?"

I took a sip of my wine. "Better than I expected."

In the few months since I'd joined my stand-up class, I'd become a different person. I was suddenly accustomed to being wrong, having everything I'd previously valued and appreciated completely disrupted.

I signed up for the class because I figured comedy training might help add some flavor to our podcast—which was basically just an excuse for Gina and me to get together and drink wine. My intention was to do what I always did, involve myself tangentially in something vaguely uncomfortable, observe, remain uncommitted, and then report back with a lot of mockery and very little self-reflection.

Hell, I'd built an entire career on the "it's you, not me" philosophy.

What I didn't anticipate was how quickly and profoundly my worldview could change, that I'd have so much of my thinking not only challenged but found wanting.

I'd never have guessed I'd fall in love with so many of my class-mates. *Mock* them? *These* people? Over my dead body. That year, as fall turned to winter, I became a mother bear, ready to protect my cubs with all I had.

I felt lucky to be in their orbit.

As for Gina? Our class let me see her in a new light, one where she was vulnerable and uncertain, instead of tough and impenetrable.

Until Second City, I never understood the importance of consider-ing the world from another perspective. Now, that's all I do.

Comedy has changed over my lifetime. Stand-up started to come into its own in the 1970s with the advent of the comedy club. In New York, Catch a Rising Star opened in 1972, and in the same year on the west coast, the Comedy Store, owned by Pauly Shore's parents, opened. The Comedy Store added two more locations in the next few years.[211] The medium, which had once been hackneyed, with tired setups followed by obvious punch lines, had become revitalized, cool, and edgy. Voices like George Carlin and Richard Pryor delivered sets that were both sociopolitical and fast paced, their observations biting and incisive. Late night shows started featuring talented young performers like Jay Leno and Jerry Seinfeld.

Living alone for the first time in the early 1990s, I kept my TV tuned to Comedy Central twenty-four seven. I started to seek out stand-up. I discovered Denis Leary, whose *No Cure for Cancer* performance on Showtime is one of the biggest reasons Fletch and I bonded. For everyone who loved Jon Stewart on *The Daily Show*, I'm so sorry you never saw him perform sets about George H. W. Bush in his padded-shouldered blazer and Girbaud jeans. (Don't even start me on his brilliance in writing for the ill-fated *George* magazine.)

Comedy is an ever-changing medium, more in tune with cultural shifts than almost anything else. And because it's expected to morph and grow with the times, on college campuses, comics are now told to keep it PC, as clean as possible. Edge is out, and I'm not sure that's for the best.

The *Atlantic* covered the National Association for Campus Activities conference, where all the collegiate activity directors go to a huge stand-up showcase. There are more than 350 universities attending with the intention of booking acts.

In theory, this massive comedy showcase sounds awesome, but the campuses are all looking for comedy that's risk-free. "It became clear that to get work, a comic had to be at once funny—genuinely funny—and also deeply respectful of a particular set of beliefs. These beliefs included, but were in no way limited to, the following: women, as a group, should never be made to feel uncomfortable; people whose sexual orientation falls beyond the spectrum of heterosexuality must be reassured of their special value; racial injustice is best addressed in tones of bitter anguish or inspirational calls to action; Muslims are friendly helpers whom we should cherish; and belonging to any potentially 'marginalized' community involves a crippling hypersensitivity that must always be respected."[212]

Straight white males remained the only acceptable target.

George Carlin built his career on college campus performances, but I can't imagine if he were alive today that he'd be booked by any of them. I've made it clear that, over the years, and particularly in recent years as I've forged real friendships with younger friends, I've learned a lot about being attentive to other opinions and perspectives. I think that there is good work to be done around cultural sensitivity and mutual respect—it's a current that runs through every thought I have about anxiety. And yet, when the *Atlantic* article pointed out that Generation Z expects and demands that their whims and affectations be catered to, and thus, they can't take it when someone challenges their thought processes, I get mad. They are only interested in and tolerant of being supported and championed. Every single joke must be inclusive.

Talents like Chris Rock and Jerry Seinfeld won't go near college campuses now. Rock refuses to perform because kids are "raised on a culture of 'We're not going to keep score in the game because we don't want anybody to lose.' Or just ignoring race to a fault. You can't say 'the black kid over there.' No, it's 'the guy with the red shoes.' You can't even be offensive on your way to being inoffensive."[213]

At Thanksgiving, Gina and I have a favorite tradition, playing card games after dinner. Generally, the sharps around the table include me, Fletch, Lee, Tracey, and Daddy G, Gina's dad, who, even in his nineties has better things to do than hang around with us for too long. Every year, we play Cards Against Humanity, and every year, Fletch hits the bourbon the hardest, yet manages to school all of us. It's annoying.

So we were excited about the new expansion pack last year, assuming this development might give us the upper hand over Fletch. Not so. Instead, every card was some version of a dick joke. Gone were the outrageous, edgy missives that made us howl in previous years.

Fletch, the champion, even decried it. "This is just gross."

In some weird way, it felt like a (group of men's?) bizarre sanitization of that which existed entirely to provoke.

It is absolutely possible to be funny without offense. Jim Gaffigan presents onstage as such a good guy, able to be hilarious while staying family friendly, which is near impossible. The key is his whip-smart ability as an observer, paired with his level of unmatched sincerity. One year on a book tour, I somehow hit each city right after him, and our publishers contracted the same services. Every single Town Car driver sang his praises. According to them, he'd sit up front and ask the drivers all about their lives. He was engaged and interested and left new fans in his wake.

Gaffigan quit his lovable TV Land sitcom, which was a fictionalized version of his life, after he realized it was taking time away from his family; that makes me respect him even more.

In an episode of the show titled "The List," he visited alternative and underground comedy clubs, which were full of Generation Z audiences, and when he performed a joke, someone told him, "We feel that punch lines are too confrontational."

It was a moment of hyperbole, but so very close to the truth that it stung a bit. The whole point of comedy, of art itself, is to confront. I like being challenged; I adore a quest for facts. So I'm always open to criticism. In terms of censorship, I believe anyone has the right to say whatever they'd like, but with the understanding that if their interactions cause them or others anxiety, dismay, or negative consequences, they should learn from that moment.

I'm bothered that creative outlets have come under scrutiny lately, to the point of becoming didactic. Didacticism, per Carolyn Burdett, is "a means of self-improvement or a spur to good works," instead of just creating art for art's sake.[214]

The *Irish Times* ran an opinion piece from John Power, who examined this recent phenomenon. Power argued that art (specifically referring to Oscar-nominated films) is exactly where we *should* be free to explore offensive or contentious ideas, as doing so in that realm will cause no harm and spark needed discussions. Instead, we're seeing a massive cultural shift away from this practice. He wrote, "Embedded in these critiques is a curiously old-fashioned and indeed puritanical idea: that art exists only, or at least primarily, for our moral betterment. Forget the local priest or university philosopher professor—the instructions for a good life should be laid out in easy-to-follow steps in your favourite Netflix series or romance novel. To this mindset, it seems, entertaining or engaging the audience is an afterthought at best."[215]

What I've learned about comedy is that it often comes at a cost. So much of comedy stems from pain. When that important hurtful element's removed, it loses something. There's no feeling behind it. Sure, I'll laugh at a generic joke about Costco, but I won't remember it. A snappy one-liner won't stay with me like Sam Kinison screaming about how he hopes the ex-love of his life slides under a gas truck and dies tasting her own blood. He's been gone for more than twenty-five years, yet I can still hear him scream this joke.

By playing to what's most politically correct, I worry we'll never be challenged by the brilliant insights from the next generation's George Carlin and Lenny Bruce, that we'll lose what's genuine and uncomfortable and forces us into introspection. As Chappelle said in his *The Bird Revelation* special, "Motherfuckers, you have a responsibility to speak recklessly, otherwise my kids might not know what reckless talk sounds like, the joys of being wrong."

In a Vox interview, comedian Chris Gethard addressed the new comedy culture: "What comedians often forget is that while we are allowed to offend, audiences are also allowed to get offended. This idea that comedians often [have], which is, like, 'You're being too PC. Why does everybody get offended?' It's, like, because you said something offensive! And that's fine. And your impulse that comedians have to be able to be truth tellers—I agree with it. But this idea of, 'We get to be able to say whatever we want,' while I do think it's true, it's very much a double standard to say, 'But you don't get to react the way you want.'"[216]

If a comic went onstage at a college campus and accidentally said something offensive, there would be hell to pay. Instead of just not laughing, students would call the comic's agent, the student activities director, and every college where the comic was supposed to appear next, a total scorched-earth policy. One imagines social media assassination would be part of this strategy. The mentality that if a comic doesn't conform to a specific ideal, they should not exist is terrifying. Comic Nimesh Patel lived this reality when his mic was cut off after twenty minutes of stand-up at Columbia University. But ironically, some of the Columbia students came to a later performance to apologize.

A few years ago, I read an article saying that the mortality rate for comedians is higher than those serving in the military. How heartbreaking is that? When we think of comedy, we think funny, light, and uplifting, never considering those for whom the burden was too much, like Robin Williams, Richard Jeni, Drake Sather, or Charles Rocket.

The power to hold an entire audience in thrall is intoxicating. Applause is the most addictive drug imaginable. The feedback from likes on social media can replicate this feeling. Every like is an audience member clapping. In my career as an author, I've been onstage in front of thousands of people at book events, but what sticks with me, what fortifies me, are the few times a handful of random hipsters laughed at my open mic performances in small, tired dive bars.

Comedy is an outlet that can build bridges. For example, Saudi Arabia just had a rare comedy festival a few years ago. Up until recently, the country didn't even have an awareness of comedy as an art form. I love that progression. They had women and men attending the club. No women performed, but the festival hoped to add female comics in the future. They definitely avoided topics like sex and religion and politics, but they're trying. A-plus for the effort. As much as I loved my time learning comedy at Second City, and as alive as I've felt in those dive bars, that's not a lifestyle I can pursue. Not only is the learning period often years long, but it's even more often unpaid. I can't start over with nothing in my fifties. I can't help it, I like *things*, not because they impress people, but because they make me happy.

Neither the travel nor the hours of a comedy career would gel with my lifestyle, either. If there were an opportunity to perform during the daytime, I'd take it.

But being a daytime comic is a lot like being a daytime sex worker: sad, exhausting, and ultimately, a poor life choice.

PART VI

SELF-ACTUALIZATION NEEDS: THINKING, LEARNING, DECISION-MAKING, VALUES, BELIEFS, FULFILLMENT

Maslow amended his needs hierarchy late in life, adding an extra layer to an already complicated pyramid. Like when you think the spin class is about to go into cool down, but the instructor has you dial up the resistance and sprint for one last impossible hill.

He decided, like a real ass, that self-actualization could only be possible by transcending the self. And doing that required the act of helping others on their own path to self-actualization.

He wrote, "Transcendence refers to the very highest and most inclusive or holistic levels of human consciousness, behaving and relating, as ends rather than means, to oneself, to significant others, to human beings in general, to other species, to nature, and to the cosmos."[217]

I suspect *someone* discovered edibles late in life.

Now What?

The plane was going down.

I gripped the armrest, tied myself in knots over what would happen next.

It wasn't exactly that I was in danger. My flight was routine. What stressed me out so much was what would happen once we landed.

I always rent a car in LA from Sixt because they stock convertibles. Driving with the top down is a way to keep myself calm between meetings. And I'm not yet confident enough in my talent as a screenwriter to roll up to a movie studio in a battered Kia. I know my limitations.

The problem is, because Sixt's business is more specialty cars, their shuttle service from the rental lot comes about as often as the blood moon. The wait for the shuttle is never less than half an hour of crowds and diesel fumes and being jostled and trying to keep my toes safe from all the roll-aboards.

Uber also takes forever at LAX, so I started hailing cabs to the rental place, even though it's just two unwalkable miles from the airport. The cab drivers, unfortunately, are always very angry about losing their place in line over a short fare. They bitch the whole way and then I get mad and then I replay the incident repeatedly in my head until I lose the entire afternoon to slow-simmering anger.

That day, I decided on a different strategy. Sure, I caught a cab, and yes, the guy was pissed. But I decided to change my reaction to him. He complained the whole way to the rental place, hissing about me into his cell phone.

I could have recorded his medallion number and reported him. I could have filmed him. I could have shamed him on social media, overcompensating for what wasn't actually a huge slight in the scheme of things. But none of that felt right.

Instead, I put myself in his place, knowing that a short trip kept him from a more lucrative downtown fare. Rideshare services are killing the taxi industry, and he was probably stressed over the factors he couldn't control. Hell, that's pretty close to why I was in LA, looking for a backup plan to balance all the changes in the book industry from the past few years.

I decided to try something new—kindness.

When we pulled up at Sixt, he was still fuming. I paid the fare and then said, "I understand this short trip kept you from getting a longer ride, and I'd like to compensate you for it because I appreciate your time." I handed him a twenty-dollar tip and thanked him again. He stood there, stunned and sheepish, quiet for the first time since I'd set foot in his vehicle.

As I was headed to my first meeting, I felt unburdened, not carrying the twenty-dollar bill I'd had—sure—but also not carrying the unpleasant exchange with me all afternoon. I had better things to do.

I've thought a lot about what self-actualization means to me over the course of writing this book.

Truth?

I haven't figured it out yet, and even if I had, it would probably transcend the page—some real Dalai Lama shit. But if I had somehow achieved the final goal of self-actualization, planting my stake in it, determining that to be a landing spot seems like the surest way to lose all that I've learned.

I wanted to uncover the facts about what makes us all anxious. I wanted to look at where we've been as a nation over the past fifty years and where it seems like we're headed. For all the backbiting and infighting, for all the damage, chaos, and carnage, for all that's gone off the rails, we aren't without hope or progress.

And in looking at our progress, I've seen some terrible behaviors, but also an amazing amount of good.

When we don't have to worry if our kid will ever get polio? Score.

When we can FaceTime our nana in Florida every morning at ten o'clock to see her sweet mug and tell her she's loved, without paying twenty-five cents per minute? Score.

When we run across a snake on our patio and can use our phone to access the info that not only don't poisonous snakes exist in our part of Illinois but our snakes are beneficial, and this knowledge allows us to name him Hissy and keeps us from setting our whole damn yard on fire? Score.

In the past few months, I've been so tied up with project deadlines that I've abandoned Facebook almost entirely. Turns out, I don't miss it. It's no longer something I feel compelled to check multiple times a day, and it doesn't feel like an obligation I'm shunning. Not constantly measuring myself against others has lowered my anxiety level.

While I've covered the downside of social media and the ways our increasingly plugged-in world can tear us apart, there's still plenty of upside. Instagram pets and people who make cakes make me happy. Keep what brings you joy, such as liking every single Brussels griffon dog on Instagram, or perusing shots of beautifully plated food even though you're happy to be eating cold Chinese food from the carton.

When I believed Twitter was largely an angry cesspool and had planned to delete my profile, Chrissy Teigen started following me.

So you can see my dilemma.

My point is, social media is a tool; use it to build what *you* want and take that from it. Try to surround yourself with kind, diverse perspectives. Listen and share openly.

If you're mired in anxiety, seek facts that bolster you, and if that fails, consider introspection. Ask yourself if your tension is as much over the state of politics as, say, having overextended yourself, or having made unfair comparisons.

What's possible is that you just need some fun. While taking a couple of hours to see an Adam Sandler movie won't change the world, it might change your mindset.

If you're worried about the inequity of your privilege, use it to lift someone else up.

If you're angry, channel that energy into change. Can you stop China from pumping so many carbon emissions into the atmosphere? Directly? By yourself? Today? No. But you can make a point to buy American products. You can adopt a small portion of highway and orchestrate the cleanup efforts. You can start a recycling program in your office. You can begin to chip away; you can control what *you* do.

More important, you can share your experience with others, knowing that a face-to-face, personal connection is the surest way to change hearts, minds, and habits.

Not long ago, I saw a name trending on Twitter that caused my heart to sink. In 95 percent of Twitter mentions, the person has died or said something racist. Only 5 percent of the time is anyone featured because of something awesome, like footage of Keanu Reeves giving up his subway seat to a woman or Steve Harvey crowning the wrong Miss Universe.

So when I ran across Prince William's name, I gasped.

He doesn't host award shows *or* use public transportation.

I've been invested in the monarchy ever since I set my alarm for three o'clock in the morning to watch Lady Di marry Prince Charles. My interest waned quite a bit after her passing, but then Prince Harry became superhot, so . . .

When the story came out about Queen Elizabeth insisting on chauffeuring Saudi Arabian Crown Prince Abdullah during a visit to

Balmoral as (what I interpreted as) a diplomatic way to express her displeasure about Saudi women's rights, I was intrigued.

Then Kate Middleton showed up with her bouncy hair and nautical striped shirts and I hopped back on the royals train forever.

Per the trending column, Prince William was rumored to have cheated on Kate.

It seemed impossible—not after how his father's infidelity tore up the family!

Lost and confused, I turned to the one place I assumed I could find clarity: Go Fug Yourself. This is a popular site run by Heather Cocks and Jessica Morgan, two friends who began critiquing celebrity red carpet looks more than a decade ago. Their tagline is Because Fugly is the New Pretty. They're renowned for being positive. The Fug Girls are diligent about keeping their critique to the clothes and the styling, never engaging in personal attacks or body shaming. They feature male and female celebs, along with commensurate amounts of praise and criticism.

The Fug Girls are admirably obsessed with the royals; they fictionalized Kate and Will's romance in the novel *The Royal We*, one of my all-time favorite books. I sought their counsel and guidance immediately in my crisis; I needed them to tell me that Mom and Dad were going to be okay.

Unfortunately, the Girls were unavailable for commentary, as they were busy fending off attacks from actress Olivia Munn's almost one million Twitter followers. Munn had published a scathing—and unfounded, I believe—essay, accusing the Fug Girls of body shaming earlier that day. She equated their questioning the cut of her pantsuit with rape culture.

While Munn raised valid societal points, none of them applied to the Fug Girls. They're not an attack site. They don't drag women for their sizes, shapes, or appearances, especially when they're off the red carpet and out living their daily lives. The Fug wheelhouse is critiquing styling and the fashions that celebrities are paid to wear.

There are an awful lot of problematic places on the internet, perpetrating the kind of talk that sets women back decades. But Go Fug Yourself isn't one of them. It's possible I'd be more sympathetic to Munn's misguided sentiment, had she not penned the following in her memoir: "I will fix America's obesity problems by taking all motorized transport away from fat people. In turn, I will build an infrastructure of Fat Tunnels, where all the fat people can walk. This will create jobs and subsequent weight loss."[218]

While the Girls faced an initial onslaught of negativity, I was glad to see more and more coverage defending them as the week continued. Support for the Girls rolled in from everywhere from *Slate* to comments on *USA Today*. I happened upon a piece in the *Huffington Post* that seemed fair and balanced. Then I made the fatal flaw of reading the article comments. As always, a comment by someone named Kevin drew me in.

We need to talk about Kevin.

In this instance, Kevin was firmly Team Munn, pontificating at length about how she was right, and how those evil shrews (the c-word wasn't used, but I'm pretty sure it was implied) were both wrong and jealous of Munn, having never created anything themselves. I was aggravated that he'd based his judgment on nothing but a hot take from a celebrity, without evaluating the other side of the story, which was clearly stated in the article. Violating my own rules, I responded to him, listing facts regarding their accomplishments.

The next morning, I received an email notification that Kevin had responded to my comment on the site. I hesitated before I clicked the link to the response.

Could I expect Kevin to have reconsidered his opinion? To apologize after verifying the facts of the Girls' accomplishments, having scanned the site to discover it's a positive, uplifting place?

To have searched his own soul and found that he'd been too quick to defend on the off chance that Olivia Munn had been trolling for some supportive *strange* in the *HuffPo* comments section?

Or could I expect Kevin to respond like a *Kevin* and then I'd spend a day being angry?

I deleted the link, closed my computer, and went outside to work in my rose garden.

And you know what?

I had a great day.

But please do @ me if you know some hot gossip about those royals. #PrincessDiForLife

ACKNOWLEDGMENTS

For my longtime readers, thank you for coming down this new road with me. I hope you weren't too thrown by endnotes containing facts and not just snarky asides. You're the reason I do this, and I'm so grateful to each of you.

To the team at Little A, all my respect and admiration for the work you've done, especially to my editor Laura Van der Veer, who pushed me far outside my comfort zone with the perfect blend of patience and irreverence. This wouldn't—and couldn't—have been the same book without you.

I'd like to add massive appreciation to sales, marketing, production, and publicity—it doesn't happen without you. For Philip Pascuzzo, a big hooray for creating a cover that made me squeal. Extra thanks extended to my editing team and my fact-checker. Pretty sure I owe you guys a round, at a minimum. (I'll understand if you prefer to drink them without me.) And I can't express how happy I am to be on the Amazon team. Keep your eye on that Bezos fellow; I feel like he's going places.

Many, many thanks to the Folio dream team of Steve Troha and Erin Niumata, who have been instrumental in helping create my second act. Your guidance has been critical in determining the shape of what's to come, and I'm so proud of what we've built.

To my first family at Second City, your commitment to rigorous honesty and unvarnished feedback taught me the value of embracing the third thought, especially Dale Chapman and the screenwriters' lab crew. You're the funniest, most talented people on the planet, and I'm so excited for the rest of the world to see you shine.

To my girls, surely you're tired of me telling you how great you are after sixteen books. Just know that there are matching caftans in our future.

And for Fletch, I wouldn't want to quarantine with anyone but you.

NOTES

1   "Children: Reducing Mortality," World Health Organization, September 19, 2019, www.who.int/news-room/fact-sheets/detail/children-reducing-mortality.

2   John Gramlich, "5 Facts about Crime in the U.S.," Pew Research Center, October 17, 2019, www.pewresearch.org/fact-tank/2019/10/17/facts-about-crime-in-the-u-s.

3   Rob Verger, "Uber Can Actually Help Prevent Drunk Driving Accidents—in Some Cities," *Popular Science*, October 5, 2017, www.popsci.com/uber-drunk-driving.

4   The fact-checker would like me to provide a source for these numbers. My reference is my father opening the phone bill and losing his shit while touting these numbers one Saturday a month for my entire childhood. It's possible he was using hyperbole, much like the time he claimed to have swilled margaritas with Jack Kerouac until dawn and then raced his Jaguar the length of the Mass Turnpike.

5   Lea Winerman, "By the Numbers: Antidepressant Use on the Rise," *American Psychological Association* 48, no. 10 (November 2017): 120, www.apa.org/monitor/2017/11/numbers.

6   Julie Ray, "Americans' Stress, Worry and Anger Intensified in 2018," Gallup News, April 25, 2019, https://news.gallup.com/poll/249098/americans-stress-worry-anger-intensified-2018.aspx.

7   Peter Wilson, "Venezuela Food Shortages Cause Some to Hunt Dogs, Cats, Pigeons," *USA Today*, May 18, 2016, www.usatoday.com/story/news/world/2016/05/18/venezuela-food-shortages-cause-some-hunt-dogs-cats-pigeons/84547888.

8   Oliver Smith, "Have Plane Seats Really Shrunk—and Which Is the Worst Airline on Earth for Legroom?," *Telegraph*, October 2, 2019, www.telegraph.co.uk/travel/comment/plane-seats-legroom-shrunk-worst-airline.

9   Queviv, "Was Air Travel in the 1970s Really as Groovy (and Boozy) as We Remember?," *USA Today*, February 14, 2016, www.usatoday.com/story/travel/roadwarriorvoices/2016/02/14/was-air-travel-in-the-1970s-really-as-groovy-and-boozy-as-we-remember/83199262.

10   Olga Khazan, "The Selling of the Avocado," *Atlantic*, January 31, 2015, www.theatlantic.com/health/archive/2015/01/the-selling-of-the-avocado/385047.

11   Krystal D'Costa, "How Marketing Changed the Way We See Avocados," *Scientific American*, May 5, 2017, https://blogs.scientificamerican.com/anthropology-in-practice/how-marketing-changed-the-way-we-see-avocados.

12   Sophie Egan, "The Defining Dozen: 12 Ways the American Diet Has Changed in the Last 30 Years," *Bon Appétit*, July 11, 2016, www.bonappetit.com/entertaining-style/trends-news/article/american-diet-changed-30-years.

13   The fact-checker would like me to verify that doughy-armed Italian women have appeared on jars of Prego. I can't verify this, but I can say it *feels* true.

14   Get some wine in her and she will go on and on about this.

15   Louise Petty, "Changes in Eating Habits over the Years: Comparing Diets Now & Then," High Speed Training, June 5, 2017, www.highspeedtraining.co.uk/hub/changes-in-eating-habits/.

16   Clea Guy-Allen, "The Top 10 Hungriest Countries in the World," Global Citizen, March 10, 2014, www.globalcitizen.org/en/content/the-worlds-10-hungriest-countries.

17   Miguel Andrade, "How Instagram Is Transforming Professional Cooking," *Wired*, June 6, 2015, www.wired.com/2015/06/instagram-transforming-professional-cooking.

18   Sarah Lee, "Picture Perfect? How Instagram Changed the Food We Eat," BBC News, December 29, 2017, www.bbc.com/news/uk-england-london-42012732.

19   Alexandra Talty, "New Study Finds Millennials Spend 44 Percent of Food Dollars on Eating Out," *Forbes*, October 17, 2016, www.forbes.com/sites/alexandratalty/2016/10/17/millennials-spend-44-percent-of-food-dollars-on-eating-out-says-food-institute.

20   Victoria Pope, "The Joy of Food," *National Geographic*, accessed April 1, 2019, www.nationalgeographic.com/foodfeatures/joy-of-food.

21   Roxane Gay, "Episode 589: Tell Me I'm Fat," June 17, 2016, in *This American Life*, podcast, audio, www.thisamericanlife.org/589/tell-me-im-fat.

22   Lecia Bushak, "History of Body Image in America: How the 'Ideal' Female and Male Body Has Changed over Time," Medical Daily, November 6, 2015, www.medicaldaily.com/history-body-image-america-how-ideal-female-and-male-body-has-changed-over-360492.

23   "American Women and World War II," Khan Academy, accessed April 2019, www.khanacademy.org/humanities/us-history/rise-to-world-power/us-wwii/a/american-women-and-world-war-ii.

24   Maria Hart, "See How Much the 'Perfect' Female Body Has Changed in 100 Years (It's Crazy!)," Greatist, January 15, 2015, https://greatist.com/grow/100-years-womens-body-image.

25   David Wigg, "Twiggy Goes to War on Obesity," *Daily Mail*, October 17, 2014, www.dailymail.co.uk/femail/article-2795365/twiggy-goes-war-obesity-superskinny-model-claims-ate-like-horse-says-bulging-waistlines-national-tragedy.html.

26   Susanna McBee, "The End of the Rainbow May Be Tragic: Scandal of the Diet Pills," *Life*, January 26, 1968, reproduced in *Diet Pill (Amphetamines) Traffic, Abuse and Regulation, Hearings, Before the Subcommittee to Investigate Juvenile Delinquency, Senate Committee on the Judiciary, Pursuant to S. Res. 32, Section 12*, 92nd Cong., 1st Session, February 7, 1972: 245–51.

27   "Obesity and Overweight," World Health Organization, February 16, 2018, www.who.int/news-room/fact-sheets/detail/obesity-and-overweight.

28   Michael Hobbes, "Everything You Know about Obesity Is Wrong," *Huffington Post*, September 19, 2018, https://highline.huffingtonpost. com/articles/en/everything-you-know-about-obesity-is-wrong.

29   Personal opinion, not fact.

30   World Health Organization, "Obesity and Overweight."

31   Corinne Gretler and Naomi Kresge, "Big Food Blamed for Ills Far beyond Flab in Sweeping Report," Bloomberg, January 27, 2019, www.bloomberg.com/news/articles/2019-01-27/big-food-gets- blamed-for-ills-far-beyond-flab-in-sweeping-report.

32   "Client Profile: National Rifle Association," Open Secrets, accessed April 2019, www.opensecrets.org/federal-lobbying/clients/summary?c ycle=2018&id=d000000082.

33   "Client Profile: Everytown for Gun Safety," Open Secrets, accessed April 2019, www.opensecrets.org/federal-lobbying/clients/summary?c ycle=2018&id=D000067401.

34   Michael Hobbes, "What to Do If Your Doctor Fat Shames You," *Huffington Post*, September 25, 2018, www.huffpost.com/entry/ what-to-do-about-fat-shaming-doctors_n_5ba9604ee4b0181540df d54d.

35   "Can You Be Overweight and Still Be Fit?," *Harvard Men's Health Watch*, July 2018, www.health.harvard.edu/staying-healthy/can-you- be-overweight-and-still-be-fit.

36   Susruthi Rajanala, Mayra B. C. Maymone, and Neelam A. Vashi, "Selfies—Living in the Era of Filtered Photographs," *JAMA Facial Plastic*

Surgery 20, no. 6 (November/December 2018): 443–4, https://jamanetwork.com/journals/jamafacialplasticsurgery/article-abstract/2688763.

37   Carly Mallenbaum, "Barbie in 2018 and Beyond: How the Doll Is Getting More 'Inclusive,'" *USA Today*, April 25, 2018, www.usatoday.com/story/life/entertainthis/2018/04/25/tiny-shoulders-rethinking-barbie-hulu-documentary-curvy-doll/540663002.

38   "The Rise of Social Media Influencers," *CBS News Sunday Morning*, May 6, 2018, www.cbsnews.com/news/the-rise-of-social-media-influencers.

39   Morgan Smith, "Chicago's Instagram Influencers on Staying Authentic While #Sponsored," *Chicago Tribune*, July 20, 2018, www.chicagotribune.com/lifestyles/style/sc-fashion-0730-influencers-uncovered-20180711-story.html.

40   Erin Peralta, "Generation X: The Small But Financially Powerful Generation," *Centro* (blog), September 17, 2015, www.centro.net/blog/generation-x-the-small-but-mighty-generation.

41   T. L. Stanley, "Payless Opened a Fake Luxury Store, 'Palessi,' to See How Much People Would Pay for $20 Shoes," *Adweek*, November 28, 2018, www.adweek.com/brand-marketing/payless-opened-a-fake-luxury-store-palessi-to-see-how-much-people-would-pay-for-20-shoes.

42   Peter Gasca, "Why This Holiday's Most Brilliant Retail Promotion Will Fail," *Inc.*, November 30, 2018, www.inc.com/peter-gasca/why-this-holidays-most-brilliant-retail-promotion-will-fail.html.

43   Kelly Tyko, "Payless ShoeSource Closing all 2,100 U.S. Stores, Starting Liquidation Sales Sunday," *USA Today*, February 15, 2019, www.

usatoday.com/story/money/2019/02/15/payless-shoesource-all-u-s-stores-liquidating-and-closing/2885949002.

44   Victoria LeBlanc, ed., "How What You're Wearing Can Affect Your Anxiety," CalmClinic, October 28, 2018, www.calmclinic.com/anxiety/clothing-matters.

45   Alexa Tanney, "Social Comparison Theory: How Our Social Media Habits Make Us Unhappy," Elite Daily, June 18, 2015, www.elitedaily.com/life/media-affects-self-worth/1055695.

46   Eric Wilson, "Now You Know: The Evolution of Donna Karan's Seven Easy Pieces," *InStyle*, July 1, 2015, www.instyle.com/news/history-donna-karan-seven-easy-pieces.

47   Chuck Palahniuk, *Fight Club* (New York: W. W. Norton, 1996), 44.

48   Marissa Hermanson, "An Inside Look at Home Decor through the Decades," *Domino*, October 1, 2018, www.domino.com/content/home-decor-by-decade.

49   Mark Roth, "The Historic Roots of the Middle Class," *Pittsburgh Post-Gazette*, November 20, 2011, www.post-gazette.com/local/region/2011/11/20/The-historic-roots-of-the-middle-class/stories/201111200308.

50   Dinah Eng, "Crate & Barrel's 50 Year 'Fun Run,'" *Fortune*, January 13, 2012, http://archive.fortune.com/2012/01/12/smallbusiness/crate_barrel_carole_gordon_segal.fortune/index.htm.

51   Matt Valley, "The Crate and Barrel Story," *National Real Estate Investor*, June 1, 2001, www.nreionline.com/mag/crate-and-barrel-story.

52   Leslie Mann, "The 'Cocooning' Trend Draws Reinforcement," *Chicago Tribune*, October 21, 2001, www.chicagotribune.com/news/ct-xpm-2001-10-21-0110210261-story.html.

53   Mike Snider, "Cocooning: It's Back and Thanks to Tech, It's Bigger," *USA Today*, February 17, 2013, www.usatoday.com/story/tech/personal/2013/02/15/internet-tv-super-cocoons/1880473.

54   Lorena Blas, "Sold! HGTV Flips over Big Ratings Growth," *USA Today*, July 27, 2016, www.usatoday.com/story/life/tv/2016/07/27/hgtv-big-ratings-growth/87401088.

55   Anne Helen Petersen, " 'Fixer Upper' Is over, but Waco's Transformation Is Just Beginning," BuzzFeed News, April 20, 2019, www.buzzfeednews.com/article/annehelenpetersen/waco-texas-magnolia-fixer-upper-antioch-chip-joanna-gaines.

56   I brought home a handful of pope-embellished Bic lighters from Rome, largely due to the clerk's insistence that they'd been blessed.

57   Cindy Fox-Griffey, "Your Place to Call Home: Keeping Up with the Joneses Usually Not the Smart Move," *St. Louis Post-Dispatch*, October 12, 2016, www.stltoday.com/suburban-journals/stcharles/your-place-to-call-home-keeping-up-with-the-joneses/article_1550702c-a1f7-5af3-9a66-9d9a5a1dd80e.html.

58   Randi Stevenson, "Meet the Chicagoans Renovating, Restoring and Living in the City's Historic Mansions," *Chicago Tribune*, March 13, 2019, www.chicagotribune.com/classified/realestate/ct-re-chicago-historic-mansion-renovation-20190324-story.html.

59   Jung Hyun Choi, Jun Zhu, and Laurie Goodman, "The State of Millennial Homeownership," *Urban Wire* (blog), July 11, 2018, www.urban.org/urban-wire/state-millennial-homeownership.

60   N'dea Yancey-Bragg, "Drink Hot Tea at Your Own Risk: New Study Is Latest to Show Link to Esophageal Cancer," *USA Today,* March 20, 2019, www.usatoday.com/story/news/health/2019/03/20/hot-tea-linked-cancer-international-journal-study/3229339002.

61   Adrienne Crezo, "9 Ways People Used Radium before We Understood the Risks," *Mental Floss*, October 9, 2012, http://mentalfloss.com/article/12732/9-ways-people-used-radium-we-understood-risks.

62   "Heroin History: 1900s," Narconon, accessed May 2019, www.narconon.org/drug-information/heroin-history-1900s.html.

63   Cecil Adams, "Is It True Coca-Cola Once Contained Cocaine?," The Straight Dope, June 14, 1985, www.straightdope.com/columns/read/384/is-it-true-coca-cola-once-contained-cocaine.

64   Christian Amondson, "10 Dangerous Drugs Once Marketed as Medicine," Best Medical Degrees, April 8, 2013, www.bestmedical-degrees.com/10-dangerous-drugs-once-marketed-as-medicine.

65   Maurice Chammah, "The Many Lives of a Death Drug," *Texas Monthly*, June 9, 2014, www.texasmonthly.com/politics/the-many-lives-of-a-death-drug.

66   Kate Thayer, "Wilmette Mom Investigated for Letting 8-Year-Old Walk Dog around the Block. For Something like This to Happen to Me, There's Something Really Wrong,'" *Chicago Tribune*, August 23, 2018,

www.chicagotribune.com/lifestyles/ct-life-leaving-kids-alone-moms-shamed-20180820-story.html.

67   "United States Cancer Statistics: Data Visualizations," Centers for Disease Control and Prevention, accessed May 2019, https://gis.cdc.gov/Cancer/USCS/DataViz.html.

68   David Mikkelson, "Mutilated Boy," Snopes, last modified July 12, 2011, www.snopes.com/fact-check/mutilated-boy.

69   Erin Blakemore, "The Latchkey Generation: How Bad Was It?," JSTOR Daily, November 9, 2015, https://daily.jstor.org/latchkey-generation-bad.

70   History.com, "Child Labor," A&E Television Networks, October 27, 2009, www.history.com/topics/industrial-revolution/child-labor.

71   Christopher Ingraham, "There's Never Been a Safer Time to Be a Kid in America," *Washington Post*, April 14, 2015, www.washingtonpost.com/news/wonk/wp/2015/04/14/theres-never-been-a-safer-time-to-be-a-kid-in-america.

72   Cory L. Armstrong, *Media Disparity: A Gender Battleground* (New York: Lexington Books, 2013), 21.

73   Krissy Brady, "This Is Why You Get More Anxious after Something Good Happens," *Huffington Post*, April 9, 2019, www.huffpost.com/entry/anxiety-good-things_l_5ca78fc1e4b047edf959e2fe.

74   Srinivas Rao, "How Our Use of Social Media Fuels Envy, Comparison, Anxiety, and Depression," Medium, October 17, 2018, https://medium.

com/the-mission/how-our-use-of-social-media-fuels-envy-comparison-anxiety-and-depression-538e4c87b963.

75 Laura Turner, "How Twitter Fuels Anxiety," *Atlantic*, July 19, 2017, www.theatlantic.com/technology/archive/2017/07/how-twitter-fuels-anxiety/534021.

76 Sophie Bethune, "Money Stress Weighs on Americans' Health," *American Psychological Association* 46, no. 4 (April 2015): 38, www.apa.org/monitor/2015/04/money-stress.

77 Brett Whysel, "3 Vicious Cycles: Links among Financial, Physical and Mental Health," *Forbes*, June 27, 2018, www.forbes.com/sites/brettwhysel/2018/06/27/3-vicious-cycles/#2b178b2b540d.

78 "The Link between Physical and Financial Health," Marcus by Goldman Sachs, accessed May 2019, www.marcus.com/us/en/resources/personal-finance/physical-and-financial-health.

79 "Suicide Rising Across the US," Centers for Disease Control and Prevention, last reviewed June 7, 2018, www.cdc.gov/vitalsigns/suicide/index.html.

80 Dyvonne Body and Financial Security Program, "The Burden of Debt on Mental and Physical Health," The Aspen Institute, August 2, 2018, www.aspeninstitute.org/blog-posts/hidden-costs-of-consumer-debt.

81 Angela Stringfellow, "What Is a Side Hustle? Definition of Side Hustle, Examples, Benefits of Side Hustles, and More," *Wonolo* (blog), July 10, 2019, www.wonolo.com/blog/what-is-a-side-hustle.

82   SWNS, "Half of Millennials Have a 'Side Hustle,'" *New York Post*, November 14, 2017, https://nypost.com/2017/11/14/half-of-millennials-have-a-side-hustle.

83   Valerie Bauerlein, "As Houston Begins Cleanup, Residents Face Up to Losses," *Wall Street Journal*, last modified August 31, 2017, www.wsj.com/articles/evacuees-crowd-into-shelters-as-harvey-hits-louisiana-1504190720.

84   Kimberly Amadeo, "Hurricane Harvey Facts, Damage and Costs," The Balance, last modified June 25, 2019, www.thebalance.com/hurricane-harvey-facts-damage-costs-4150087.

85   "Geophysicist: Weight of Harvey Rains Caused Houston to Sink," NBC DFW, September 7, 2017, www.nbcdfw.com/weather/stories/Geophysicist-Weight-of-Harvey-Rains-Caused-Houston-to-Sink-443057633.html.

86   Richard Wiles, "It's 50 Years since Climate Change Was First Seen. Now Time Is Running Out," *Guardian*, March 15, 2018, www.theguardian.com/commentisfree/2018/mar/15/50-years-climate-change-denial.

87   Bob Silberg, "Why a Half-Degree Temperature Rise Is a Big Deal," NASA Global Climate Change, June 29, 2016, https://climate.nasa.gov/news/2458/why-a-half-degree-temperature-rise-is-a-big-deal.

88   Kert Davies, "Top Ten Documents Every Reporter Covering ExxonMobil Should Know," Climate Investigations Center, May 23, 2016, https://climateinvestigations.org/top-ten-documents-every-reporter-covering-exxon-should-know.

89   Greg Myre, "Gas Lines Evoke Memories of Oil Crises in the 1970s," NPR, November 10, 2012, www.npr.org/sections/picture-show/2012/11/10/164792293/gas-lines-evoke-memories-oil-crises-in-the-1970s.

90   Niall McCarthy, "Oil and Gas Giants Spend Millions Lobbying to Block Climate Change Policies," *Forbes*, March 25, 2019, www.forbes.com/sites/niallmccarthy/2019/03/25/oil-and-gas-giants-spend-millions-lobbying-to-block-climate-change-policies-infographic.

91   "Oil & Gas: Money to Congress," Open Secrets, www.opensecrets.org/industries/summary.php?ind=E01.

92   Craig Miller, "Scientists Say 25 Years Left to Fight Climate Change," Public Radio International, September 13, 2018, www.pri.org/stories/2018-09-13/scientists-say-25-years-left-fight-climate-change

93   Tess Riley, "Just 100 Companies Responsible for 71% of Global Emissions, Study Says," *Guardian*, July 10, 2017, www.theguardian.com/sustainable-business/2017/jul/10/100-fossil-fuel-companies-investors-responsible-71-global-emissions-cdp-study-climate-change.

94   Since this chapter was written, Amazon's Jeff Bezos has committed $10 billion toward fighting climate change. And *that* is how billionaires can lead the cause for climate change!

95   Stephen Moore, "Follow the (Climate Change) Money," The Heritage Foundation, December 18, 2018, www.heritage.org/environment/commentary/follow-the-climate-change-money.

96   Jason Daley, "The Rich Get Richer under Climate Change, 50 Years of Data Shows," *Smithsonian*, April 23, 2019, www.smithsonianmag.

com/smart-news/climate-change-has-worsened-income-inequality-over-last-50-years-180972021.

97   Brendan Cole, "Luxury Brands Prefer to Burn Millions of Dollars' Worth of Clothes to Letting 'Wrong' Shoppers Buy Them at Discount," *Newsweek*, July 19, 2018, www.newsweek.com/luxury-brands-prefer-burn-millions-dollars-worth-clothes-over-letting-wrong-1032088.

98   Lauren Phipps, "Unraveling Fast Fashion Headlines," GreenBiz, August 1, 2018, www.greenbiz.com/article/unraveling-fast-fashion-headlines.

99   Elewisa Young, "Fashion Waste Is Rubbish: How Do We Solve the Issue?," WTVOX, December 20, 2018, https://wtvox.com/fashion/fashion-waste.

100   "Putting the Brakes on Fast Fashion," UN Environment Programme, November 12, 2018, www.unenvironment.org/news-and-stories/story/putting-brakes-fast-fashion.

101   Which simply isn't true. I've learned plenty. For example, my footnotes now contain facts, and not just asides such as "I was all, whatever."

102   Nathalie Remy, Eveline Speelman, and Steven Swartz, "Style That's Sustainable: A New Fast-Fashion Formula," McKinsey & Company, October 2016, www.mckinsey.com/business-functions/sustainability/our-insights/style-thats-sustainable-a-new-fast-fashion-formula.

103   Okay, yes, Nasty Gal has since shit the bed and Amoruso filed for bankruptcy, but the fact remains that she had a Netflix show about her life and I do not.

104   Andrew Revkin, "Most Americans Now Worry about Climate Change—And Want to Fix It," *National Geographic*, January 23, 2019, www.nationalgeographic.com/environment/2019/01/climate-change-awareness-polls-show-rising-concern-for-global-warming.

105   "Youssef Zaghba: Overview," Counter Extremism Project, accessed May 2019, www.counterextremism.com/extremists/youssef-zaghba.

106   Stephanie Kirchgaessner and Lorenzo Tondo, "Why Has Italy Been Spared Mass Terror Attacks in Recent Years?," *Guardian*, June 23, 2017, www.theguardian.com/world/2017/jun/23/why-has-italy-been-spared-mass-terror-attacks-in-recent-years.

107   Benji Hart, "Giving Black Children 'the Talk' Won't Save Them from Police Brutality," *Huffington Post*, May 3, 2017, www.huffpost.com/entry/its-time-to-rethink-the-talk-teaching-black-kids_b_590a133ee4b084f59b49fef0.

108   Justin McCarthy, "Most Americans Still See Crime up over Last Year," Gallup, November 21, 2014, https://news.gallup.com/poll/179546/americans-crime-last-year.aspx.

109   Justin Wolfers, "Perceptions Haven't Caught up to Decline in Crime," *New York Times*, September 16, 2014, www.nytimes.com/2014/09/17/upshot/perceptions-havent-caught-up-to-decline-in-crime.html.

110   Neil Howe, "What's behind the Decline in Crime?," *Forbes*, May 28, 2015, www.forbes.com/sites/neilhowe/2015/05/28/whats-behind-the-decline-in-crime.

111   Bambi Majumdar, "Police Technology Linked to Lower Crime Rates," *MultiBriefs*, January 24, 2018, http://exclusive.multibriefs.com/con-

tent/technology-linked-to-lower-crime-rates/law-enforcement-de-fense-security.

112   Logan Strother, Charles Menifield, and Geiguen Shin, "We Gathered Data on Every Confirmed, Line-of-Duty Police Killing of a Civilian in 2014 and 2015. Here's What We Found," *Washington Post*, August 29, 2018, www.washingtonpost.com/news/monkey-cage/wp/2018/08/29/we-gathered-data-on-every-confirmed-line-of-duty-police-killing-of-a-civilian-in-2014-and-2015-heres-what-we-found.

113   Frederic Lemieux, "Why Is It So Hard to Improve American Policing?," The Conversation, July 8, 2016, https://theconversation.com/why-is-it-so-hard-to-improve-american-policing-62259.

114   "Crime Falls as New York Abandons Stop-and-Frisk," Equal Justice Initiative, January 19, 2018, https://eji.org/news/new-york-crime-falls-as-police-end-stop-and-frisk.

115   Kyle Smith, "We Were Wrong about Stop-and-Frisk," *National Review*, January 1, 2018, www.nationalreview.com/2018/01/new-york-city-stop-and-frisk-crime-decline-conservatives-wrong.

116   Nusrat Choudhury, "New Data Reveals Milwaukee Police Stops Are about Race and Ethnicity," ACLU, February 23, 2018, www.aclu.org/blog/criminal-law-reform/reforming-police-practices/new-data-reveals-milwaukee-police-stops-are.

117   Angelica Sanchez, "Chief Ed Flynn Talks Tenure, Retirement from MPD: 'I Need to De-Stress a Bit,'" Fox6 News, February 8, 2018, https://fox6now.com/2018/02/08/chief-ed-flynn-talks-tenure-retirement-from-milwaukee-police-department.

118   Ashley Luthern, "Chief Flynn's Viral Moment Revisited," *Milwaukee Journal Sentinel*, February 8, 2018, www.jsonline.com/story/news/crime/2018/02/08/remember-viral-video-milwaukee-police-chief-edward-flynn-heres-story-behind/313514002.

119   Joy Powers and Lauren Sigfusson, "Stop-and-Frisk Settlement Requires Significant Milwaukee Police Department Reforms," WUWM, August 20, 2018, www.wuwm.com/post/stop-and-frisk-settlement-requires-significant-milwaukee-police-department-reforms.

120   Val Van Brocklin, "Alaska's Police, Troopers Do Best as Guardians, Not Warriors," *Anchorage Daily News*, June 24, 2015, www.adn.com/commentary/article/police-troopers-do-best-guardians-not-warriors/2015/06/25.

121   Wesley Lowery, "Should Police Officers Be Required to Provide Medical Aid to People They've Shot?," *Washington Post*, September 21, 2016, www.washingtonpost.com/news/post-nation/wp/2016/09/20/should-police-officers-be-required-to-provide-medical-aid-to-people-theyve-shot.

122   Elizabeth Van Brocklin, "Philly Police Are Saving Lives by Taking Shooting Victims to the Hospital without Waiting for Paramedics," *Slate*, November 14, 2018, https://slate.com/news-and-politics/2018/11/philadelphia-police-scoop-and-run-ambulance.html.

123   Andrew Fan, "The Most Dangerous Neighborhood, the Most Inexperienced Cops," The Marshall Project, September 20, 2016, www.themarshallproject.org/2016/09/20/the-most-dangerous-neighborhood-the-most-inexperienced-cops.

124   Jennifer Vogel, "Three Case Studies: When Police Untrained in De-Escalation Shoot Unarmed People," APM Reports, May 5, 2017, www.apmreports.org/story/2017/05/05/case-study-police-kill-unarmed.

125   Joshua Correll et al., "The Police Officer's Dilemma: Using Ethnicity to Disambiguate Potentially Threatening Individuals," *Journal of Personality and Social Psychology* 83, no. 6 (December 2002): 1314-1329, http://psych.colorado.edu/~jclab/publications.html.

126   Zachary P. Neal, "A Sign of the Times? Weak and Strong Polarization in the U.S. Congress, 1973–2016," *Social Networks* 60 (September 24, 2018): 103–12, https://doi.org/10.1016/j.socnet.2018.07.007.

127   Plato, *The Republic* (Cambridge, Massachusetts: Harvard University Press), 1935–37.

128   That's right, bitches. I quoted Plato. I think. Who's best known for writing about getting drunk in a pool now?

129   Tayari Jones, "There's Nothing Virtuous about Finding Common Ground," *Time*, October 25, 2018, http://time.com/5434381/tayari-jones-moral-middle-myth.

130   David Broockman and Joshua Kalla, "Durably Reducing Transphobia: A Field Experiment on Door-to-Door Canvassing," *Science* 352, no. 6282 (April 8, 2016): 220–24, https://science.sciencemag.org/content/352/6282/220.

131   Sharon Jayson and Kaiser Health News, "What Makes People Join Hate Groups?," *US News and World Report*, August 23, 2017, www.usnews.com/news/national-news/articles/2017-08-23/what-makes-people-join-hate-groups-studies-say-childhood-torment-social-isolation.

132   Ryan Lenz, "Life after Hate: Staffed by Former Racists, an 'Exit' Program Aimed at Disillusioned White Supremacist Radicals in the U.S. Is Picking Up Steam," *Intelligence Report*, February 17, 2016, www.splcenter.org/fighting-hate/intelligence-report/2016/life-after-hate.

133   Thomas P. O'Neill, "Frenemies: A Love Story," *New York Times*, October 5, 2012, https://campaignstops.blogs.nytimes.com/2012/10/05/frenemies-a-love-story/.

134   Monika Bauerlein and Clara Jeffery, "How Facebook Screwed Us All," *Mother Jones*, March/April 2019, www.motherjones.com/politics/2019/02/how-facebook-screwed-us-all.

135   Evan Osnos, "Can Mark Zuckerberg Fix Facebook before It Breaks Democracy?," *New Yorker*, September 17, 2018, www.newyorker.com/magazine/2018/09/17/can-mark-zuckerberg-fix-facebook-before-it-breaks-democracy.

136   Holly B. Shakya and Nicholas A. Christakis, "A New, More Rigorous Study Confirms: The More You Use Facebook, the Worse You Feel," *Harvard Business Review*, April 10, 2017, https://hbr.org/2017/04/a-new-more-rigorous-study-confirms-the-more-you-use-facebook-the-worse-you-feel.

137   Osnos, "Fix Facebook."

138   wikiHow staff, "How to Stop a Goose Attack," wikiHow, last modified November 19, 2019, www.wikihow.com/Stop-a-Goose-Attack.

139   Christopher Mellon, "Friend, Foe or Unknown Force Flying Overhead? Congress Should Find Out," *Hill*, May 19, 2019, https://the-

hill.com/opinion/national-security/444422-friend-foe-or-unknown-force-flying-overhead-congress-should-find.

140   Jessica Grose and Hanna Rosin, "The Shortening Leash," *Slate*, August 6, 2014, www.slate.com/articles/life/family/2014/08/slate_childhood_survey_results_kids_today_have_a_lot_less_freedom_than_their.html.

141   Grace Cook, "How Millennial Culture Is Driving the Luxury Kidswear Market," Business of Fashion, October 14, 2017, www.businessoffashion.com/articles/intelligence/how-kiddie-street-style-stars-are-driving-the-childrenswear-market.

142   Angela Velasquez, "Thanks to Social Media, Children's Wear May Never Be the Same Again," *Rivet*, May 11, 2018, https://sourcingjournal.com/denim/denim-trends/thanks-to-social-media-childrens-wear-may-never-be-the-same-again-105844.

143   Amy Ellis Nutt, "Why Kids and Teens May Face Far More Anxiety These Days," *Washington Post*, May 10, 2018, www.washingtonpost.com/news/to-your-health/wp/2018/05/10/why-kids-and-teens-may-face-far-more-anxiety-these-days.

144   Hanady Kader, "How Violence in Video Games and Media Harm Child Development," *On the Pulse* (blog), July 18, 2016, https://pulse.seattlechildrens.org/how-violence-in-video-games-and-media-harm-child-development.

145   "Pedophiles Are Hunting Children as Young as 5 on Instagram as Grooming Triples on Social Media," RT, March 1, 2019, www.rt.com/uk/452752-grooming-instagram-increase-pedophiles.

146   Meghan Holohan, "'Pause Before You Post': How to Share Your Kids' Photos Safely Online," Today, April 3, 2018, www.today.com/parents/ kids-privacy-educates-parents-sharing-photos-online-t126349.

147   Darcia F. Narvaez, "Research on Spanking: It's Bad for All Kids," Psychology Today, September 8, 2013, www.psychologytoday.com/us/ blog/moral-landscapes/201309/research-spanking-it-s-bad-all-kids.

148   Kim Simon, "The Top 7 Reasons Why You're Mom-Shaming," Scary Mommy, August 26, 2013, www.scarymommy.com/mom-shaming.

149   Anna North, "'You're Doing It Wrong': The Century-Old Roots of Mom-Shaming," Vox, April 23, 2019, www.vox.com/2019/4/23/ 18508136/pregnancy-mothers-moms-babies-advice-quinlan-john- son.

150   Sara Stewart, "Meet NYC's Supersized Families," New York Post, March 3, 2011, https://nypost.com/2011/03/03/meet-nycs-super- sized-families.

151   Tina Fey, "Confessions of a Juggler," New Yorker, February 7, 2011, www.newyorker.com/magazine/2011/02/14/confessions-of-a-juggler.

152   Wednesday Martin, Primates of Park Avenue (New York: Simon & Schuster, 2015), 49.

153   Mark Lino, "The Cost of Raising a Child," USDA, March 8, 2017, www.usda.gov/media/blog/2017/01/13/cost-raising-child.

154   Cheryl Wetzstein, "Education Level Inversely Related to Childbear- ing," Washington Times, May 9, 2011, www.washingtontimes.com/ news/2011/may/9/education-level-inversely-related-to-childbearing.

155   Jamie Doward and Gaby Bissett, "High-Fliers Have More Babies, According to Study," *Guardian*, October 25, 2014, www.theguardian.com/lifeandstyle/2014/oct/25/women-wealth-childcare-family-babies-study.

156   Rachel Leingang, "Arizona State University Gets Dissed in College Bribery Scandal Court Documents," azcentral, March 12, 2019, www.azcentral.com/story/news/local/arizona-education/2019/03/12/asu-mentioned-university-bribery-scandal-court-documents-lori-loughlin/3141574002.

157   Carla K. Johnson, "U.S. Birth Rate Falls to 32-Year Low," PBS, May 15, 2019, www.pbs.org/newshour/nation/u-s-birth-rate-falls-to-32-year-low.

158   Steven Mintz, "How Parent-Child Relations Have Changed," *Psychology Today*, April 7, 2015, www.psychologytoday.com/us/blog/the-prime-life/201504/how-parent-child-relations-have-changed.

159   George F. Will, "Shaming and Judgmental Culture Drives Fear-Based Parenting," *Denver Post*, September 23, 2018, www.denverpost.com/2018/09/23/fear-based-parenting-shame-judgement.

160   Anne Godlasky, "Kim Brooks Left Her Small Son in the Car. Then All Hell Broke Loose," *USA Today*, August 22, 2018, www.usatoday.com/story/life/books/2018/08/22/kim-brooks-small-animals-parenting-fear-anxiety/958892002.

161   Nicole Pelletiere, "Utah's 'Free-Range Parenting' Law Is Now Officially in Effect," *Good Morning America*, May 8, 2018, www.goodmorningamerica.com/family/story/utahs-free-range-parenting-law-now-officially-effect-55021088.

162   Adam Piore, "Post-9/11 Baby Boom in City of New York Startles the Census," *New York Sun*, September 30, 2004, www.nysun.com/newyork/post-9-11-baby-boom-in-city-of-new-york-startles.

163   "The Influencer Marketing Industry Global Ad Spend: A $5–$10 Billion Market by 2020," Mediakix, last modified March 6, 2018, http://mediakix.com/2018/03/influencer-marketing-industry-ad-spend-chart/#gs.d7lkqt.

164   Sarah Pulliam Bailey, "How the Mom Internet Became a Spotless, Sponsored Void," *Washington Post*, January 26, 2018, www.washingtonpost.com/outlook/how-the-mom-internet-became-a-spotless-sponsored-void/2018/01/26/072b46ac-01d6-11e8-bb03-722769454f82_story.html.

165   Christie Tate, "My Daughter Asked Me to Stop Writing about Motherhood. Here's Why I Can't Do That," *Washington Post*, January 3, 2019, www.washingtonpost.com/lifestyle/2019/01/03/my-daughter-asked-me-stop-writing-about-motherhood-heres-why-i-cant-do-that.

166   Tanith Carey, "Oh Great Another Baby Picture! How 'Over-Sharenting' Invaded Social Media," *Telegraph*, October 25, 2015, www.telegraph.co.uk/women/mother-tongue/11941105/Over-sharenting-baby-photos-on-social-media-has-ruined-it.html.

167   Taylor Lorenz, "The Controversy over Parents Who Eat Lunch with Their Children at School," *Atlantic*, December 1, 2018, www.theatlantic.com/education/archive/2018/12/should-parents-eat-lunch-their-children-school/577117.

168   Holly H. Schiffrin et al., "Helping or Hovering? The Effects of Helicopter Parenting on College Students' Well-Being," *Journal of*

Child and Family Studies 23, no. 3 (April 2014): 548–57, https://doi.org/10.1007/s10826-013-9716-3.

169   Gretchen Livingston and D'Vera Cohn, "Childlessness Up among All Women; Down among Women with Advanced Degrees," Pew Research Center, June 25, 2010, www.pewsocialtrends.org/2010/06/25/childlessness-up-among-all-women-down-among-women-with-advanced-degrees.

170   "In Japan, First Graders Travel Solo to School on the Train," *CBS This Morning*, December 15, 2015, www.cbsnews.com/news/japanese-young-children-solo-commute-subway-school.

171   Helena Lee, "The Babies Who Nap in Sub-Zero Temperatures," BBC News, February 22, 2013, www.bbc.com/news/magazine-21537988.

172   Laura Blue, "Italian Kids Who Drink with Meals Are Less Likely to Grow Up as Binge-Drinkers," *Time*, August 19, 2010, http://healthland.time.com/2010/08/19/italian-kids-who-drink-with-meals-are-less-likely-to-grow-up-as-binge-drinkers.

173   Ryan E. Adams et al., "The Presence of a Best Friend Buffers the Effects of Negative Experiences," *Developmental Psychology* 47, no. 6 (November 2011): 1786–91, https://doi.org/10.1037/a0025401.

174   "The Importance of Teen Friendship," Newport Academy, July 2, 2018, www.newportacademy.com/resources/empowering-teens/teen-friendships.

175   Arie Shirom et al., "Work-Based Predictors of Mortality: A 20-Year Follow-Up of Healthy Employees," *Health Psychology* 30, no. 3 (May

2011): 268–75, https://www.apa.org/pubs/journals/releases/hea-30-3-268.pdf.

176   Stephanie Pappas, "7 Ways Friendships Are Great for Your Health," Live Science, January 8, 2016, www.livescience.com/53315-how-friendships-are-good-for-your-health.html.

177   David Nield, "Humans Can Really Only Maintain Five Close Friends, According to This Equation," ScienceAlert, May 5, 2016, www.sciencealert.com/the-latest-data-suggests-you-can-only-keep-five-close-friends.

178   Sherry Amatenstein, "Not So Social Media: How Social Media Increases Loneliness," Psycom, www.psycom.net/mental-health-wellbeing/mental-health-wellbeing-mental-health-wellbeing-how-social-media-increases-loneliness.

179   Susan Heitler, "8 Signs of a Toxic Friendship," *Psychology Today*, March 25, 2016, www.psychologytoday.com/us/blog/resolution-not-conflict/201603/8-signs-toxic-friendship.

180   Gregory Rodriguez, "How Genealogy Became Almost as Popular as Porn," *Time*, May 30, 2014, http://time.com/133811/how-genealogy-became-almost-as-popular-as-porn.

181   Justin Jouvenal, "To Find Alleged Golden State Killer, Investigators First Found His Great-Great-Great-Grandparents," *Washington Post*, April 30, 2018, www.washingtonpost.com/local/public-safety/to-find-alleged-golden-state-killer-investigators-first-found-his-great-great-great-grandparents/2018/04/30/3c865fe7-dfcc-4a0e-b6b2-0bec548d501f_story.html.

182   Brian Resnick, "How Your Third Cousin's Ancestry DNA Test Could Jeopardize Your Privacy," Vox, October 15, 2018, www.vox.com/science-and-health/2018/10/12/17957268/science-ancestry-dna-privacy.

183   Lincoln Michel, "Game of Thrones: The Last Bipartisan Television Show," InsideHook, April 12, 2019, www.insidehook.com/article/television/game-of-thrones-the-last-bipartisan-television-show.

184   Barry Schwartz, "The Pursuit of Happiness," May 2, 2012, in *TED Radio Hour*, audio, www.npr.org/2012/05/04/151879693/does-having-options-make-us-happier.

185   Barry Schwartz, "More Isn't Always Better," *Harvard Business Review*, June 2006, https://hbr.org/2006/06/more-isnt-always-better.

186   Michael O'Connell, "'My Favorite Murder' Duo on Growing a Podcast Empire, New Book and Co-Therapy," *Hollywood Reporter*, May 28, 2019, www.hollywoodreporter.com/news/killing-it-my-favorite-murder-duo-discuss-growing-empire-new-book-1213592.

187   Laura Hensley, "Why Are We Obsessed with True Crime and What Is It Doing to Our Minds?," Global News, January 26, 2019, https://globalnews.ca/news/4888508/how-does-true-crime-affect-you.

188   Maia Efrem, "*After After Party* Dissects the Dark Reason We Are So Enthralled by All Things True Crime," Refinery29, August 31, 2018, www.refinery29.com/en-us/2018/08/208798/true-crime-obsession-after-after-party.

189   Harry Mills, "Motivational Effects of Anger," Gulf Bend Center, accessed May 2019, www.gulfbend.org/poc/view_doc.php?type= doc&id=5808&cn=116.

190   Oliver Burkeman, "The Age of Rage: Are We Really Living in Angrier Times?," *Guardian*, May 11, 2019, www.theguardian.com/lifeand-style/2019/may/11/all-fired-up-are-we-really-living-angrier-times.

191   Abigail Hess, "Kim Kardashian West Plans to Become a Lawyer without Going to Law School—Here's How," CNBC, April 17, 2019, www.cnbc.com/2019/04/17/how-kim-kardashian-can-become-a-lawyer-without-getting-a-law-degree.html.

192   Felix Salmon, "Gen Z Prefers 'Socialism' to 'Capitalism,'" Axios, January 27, 2019, www.axios.com/socialism-capitalism-poll-generation-z-preference-1ffb8800-0ce5-4368-8a6f-dc3b82662347.html.

193   Arwa Mahdawi, "Don't Call Howard Schultz a Billionaire. He's a 'Person of Means,'" *Guardian*, February 6, 2019, www.theguardian.com/commentisfree/2019/feb/06/dont-call-howard-schultz-billionaire-wealth-washing.

194   Natalie Robehmed, "At 21, Kylie Jenner Becomes the Youngest Self-Made Billionaire Ever," *Forbes*, March 5, 2019, www.forbes.com/sites/natalierobehmed/2019/03/05/at-21-kylie-jenner-becomes-the-youngest-self-made-billionaire-ever.

195   Mitchell Sunderland, "The Best-Kept Secrets of the Kardashians' Rise to Fame," *Vice*, August 28, 2017, www.vice.com/en_asia/article/kzzkew/the-best-kept-secrets-of-the-kardashians-rise-to-fame.

196   Stephanie Eckardt, "Kris Jenner Dishes on a Whole Bunch of Recent Kardashian Drama, Then Freely Admits Most of What She Says Is Lies," *W*, May 4, 2018, www.wmagazine.com/story/kris-jenner-kardashian-lies-ellen-degeneres.

197   Frank Miniter, "The Gun Industry Says It Has Grown 158% Since Obama Took Office," *Forbes*, April 12, 2016, www.forbes.com/sites/frankminiter/2016/04/12/the-gun-industry-says-it-has-grown-158-since-obama-took-office.

198   Alison Kershaw, "Fame the Career Choice for Half of 16-Year-Olds," *Independent*, February 17, 2010, www.independent.co.uk/news/education/education-news/fame-the-career-choice-for-half-of-16-year-olds-1902338.html.

199   Catherine Pearson, "Social Media May Make Kids More Likely to Value Fame: Survey," *Huffington Post*, April 18, 2013, www.huffpost.com/entry/social-media-kids_n_3111259.

200   Scott Timberg, "Mass Shootings and the Dark Side of American Exceptionalism: 'They Happen Because There's a Large Gap between What People Are Aspiring to and What They Can Realistically Achieve,'" Salon, August 27, 2015, www.salon.com/2015/08/27/mass_shootings_and_the_dark_side_of_american_exceptionalism_they_happen_because_theres_a_large_gap_between_what_people_are_aspiring_to_and_what_they_can_realistically_achieve.

201   Maia Szalavitz, "Shocker: Empathy Dropped 40% in College Students since 2000," *Psychology Today*, May 28, 2010, www.psychologytoday.com/us/blog/born-love/201005/shocker-empathy-dropped-40-in-college-students-2000.

202   Stephanie Pappas, "Why America Is Prone to Mass Shootings," Live Science, August 26, 2015, www.livescience.com/51991-why-america-is-prone-to-mass-shootings.html.

203   Jaclyn Cosgrove, "Before a School Shooting, Something Usually Happens—The Shooter Tells Someone," *Los Angeles Times*, February 16, 2018, www.latimes.com/nation/la-na-florida-shooting-research-20180216-story.html.

204   Tom Junod, "Why Mass Shootings Keep Happening," *Esquire*, October 2, 2017, www.esquire.com/news-politics/a30024/mass-shooters-1014.

205   US Department of Justice, *A Study of Pre-Attack Behaviors of Active Shooters in the United States Between 2000 and 2013*, June 2018, www.fbi.gov/file-repository/pre-attack-behaviors-of-active-shooters-in-us-2000-2013.pdf/view.

206   Rhitu Chatterjee, "Researchers Who Study Mass Shootings Say Perpetrators Often Idolize and Copy Others," March 15, 2019, in *All Things Considered*, podcast, audio, www.npr.org/2019/03/15/703912094/researchers-who-study-mass-shootings-say-perpetrators-often-idolize-and-copy-oth.

207   Chandra Johnson, "How the Media Can Help Stop Mass Shootings," *Deseret News*, December 3, 2015, www.deseretnews.com/article/865642823/The-media7s-role-in-stopping-the-contagion-effect-of-rampage-shootings.html.

208   Lisa Firestone, "Is Social Media to Blame for the Rise in Narcissism?," PsychAlive, accessed May 1, 2019, www.psychalive.org/is-social-media-to-blame-for-the-rise-in-narcissism.

209   Heather Gardner, "Maybe Don't Roll Your Eyes at Kim Kardashian's Gun Control Stance," Yahoo!, February 16, 2018, www.yahoo.com/lifestyle/maybe-dont-roll-eyes-kim-kardashians-gun-control-stance-200033650.html.

210   Daniel Payne, "Michigan University Gives Professors Hockey Pucks to Fight Off Shooters," The College Fix, November 28, 2018, www.thecollegefix.com/michigan-university-gives-professors-hockey-pucks-to-fight-off-shooters.

211   Patrick Bromley, "History of Stand-Up Comedy in the 1970s," LiveAbout, February 22, 2019, www.liveabout.com/history-of-stand-up-comedy-in-the-1970s-801532.

212   Caitlin Flanagan, "That's Not Funny!," *Atlantic*, September 2015, www.theatlantic.com/magazine/archive/2015/09/thats-not-funny/399335.

213   Clarence Page, "College Kids Can't Take a Joke," *Chicago Tribune*, February 4, 2015, www.chicagotribune.com/politics/ct-college-students-prudes-comics-perspec-0204-20150203-column.html.

214   Carolyn Burdett, "Aestheticism and Decadence," British Library, March 15, 2014, www.bl.uk/romantics-and-victorians/articles/aestheticism-and-decadence.

215 John Power, "Art Should Not Have to Bow Down to Political Correctness," *Irish Times*, February 2, 2018, www.irishtimes.com/opinion/art-should-not-have-to-bow-down-to-political-correctness-1.3376733.

216 Emily Todd VanDerWerff, "Comedian Chris Gethard on Offensive Humor: Tell the Jokes but Don't Police the Response," Vox, November 30, 2018, www.vox.com/i-think-youre-interesting/2018/11/30/18119237/chris-gethard-lose-well-interview-jokes.

217 "The 5 Levels of Maslow's Hierarchy of Needs and How They Affect Your Life," Oxford Royale Academy, October 2, 2017, www.oxford-royale.co.uk/articles/5-levels-maslows-hierarchy-needs-affect-life.html.

218 Olivia Munn, *Suck It, Wonder Woman! The Misadventures of a Hollywood Geek* (New York: St. Martin's Press, 2010), 85.

ABOUT THE AUTHOR

Photo © 2016 Jolene Siana

Jen Lancaster is the *New York Times* bestselling author of the novels *Here I Go Again* and *The Gatekeepers*; the nonfiction works *Bitter Is the New Black*, *The Tao of Martha*, *Such a Pretty Fat*, and *Bright Lights, Big Ass*; and the memoirs *Stories I'd Tell in Bars*, *Jeneration X*, *My Fair Lazy*, *Pretty in Plaid*, and *I Regret Nothing*, which was named an Amazon Best Book of the Year. Regularly a finalist in the Goodreads Choice Awards, Jen has sold well over a million books documenting her attempts to shape up, grow up, and have it all—sometimes with disastrous results. She's also been seen on the *Today* show, as well as *CBS This Morning*, Fox News, NPR's *All Things Considered*, and *The Joy Behar Show*, among others. She lives in the Chicago suburbs with her husband and her many ill-behaved pets. Visit her website at www.jenlancaster.com.